Corporations and Partnerships in Canada

Corporations and Partnerships in Canada

Third Edition

Mark Gillen

This book was originally published as a monograph in the International Encyclopaedia of Laws/Corporations and Partnerships.

Founding Editor: Roger Blanpain
General Editor: Frank Hendrickx
Volume Editor: Koen Geens

Wolters Kluwer

Published by:
Kluwer Law International B.V.
PO Box 316
2400 AH Alphen aan den Rijn
The Netherlands
E-mail: international-sales@wolterskluwer.com
Website: lrus.wolterskluwer.com

Sold and distributed in North, Central and South America by:
Wolters Kluwer Legal & Regulatory U.S.
7201 McKinney Circle
Frederick, MD 21704
United States of America
Email: customer.service@wolterskluwer.com

Sold and distributed in all other countries by:
Air Business Subscriptions
Rockwood House
Haywards Heath
West Sussex
RH16 3DH
United Kingdom
Email: international-customerservice@wolterskluwer.com

Printed on acid-free paper

ISBN 978-94-035-0162-8

e-Book: ISBN 978-94-035-0163-5
web-PDF: ISBN 978-90-411-9065-9

Printed in the United Kingdom.

The Author

Mark Gillen (born 1957) is a Professor of Law at the University of Victoria, Canada. He received a B. Com. (University of Toronto) in 1981, an MBA (York University, Toronto) in 1983, an LLB (Osgoode Hall Law School, Toronto) in 1985 and an LLM (University of Toronto) in 1987. He is the author of *Securities Regulation in Canada*, 3rd ed. (Carswell, 2007); co-author (with Donovan Waters and Lionel Smith) of *Waters' Law of Trusts in Canada*, 3rd ed. (Carswell, 2005) and the 4th ed. (Carswell, 2012); co-author (with Robert Yalden, Janis Sarra, Paul Paton, Ron Davis and Mary Condon) of *Business Organizations: Principles, Policies and Practice* (Emond Montgomery, 2007); co-author and co-editor of (with Faye Woodman) of *The Law of Trusts: A Contextual Approach*, 3rd ed. (Emond Montgomery, 2015). He teaches Business Associations, Securities Regulation, Trusts, Taxation, and Competition Law at the Faculty of Law, University of Victoria.

The Original Contributors

Several persons contributed to the original version of this Canadian segment of the *International Encyclopaedia of Laws* on Corporations and Partnerships when it was first prepared in 1992. Professor Mark Gillen of the Faculty of Law, University of Victoria, assembled the team of contributors and did the initial editing of the manuscript. He also wrote the 'Introduction' and Part I, Chapter I, §5 on 'Mergers and Takeovers' and §6 on 'Holding Corporations and Subsidiaries'. Professor Jean Turgeon of the Faculty of Law, University of Laval, Quebec wrote Part I, Chapter 1, §1 on the formation of companies and §2 on 'Capital and Shares'. Professor Jeff MacIntosh of the Faculty of Law, University of Toronto, wrote Part I, Chapter 1, §3, subpart I on 'Shareholder Control Mechanisms (Rights and Remedies)' and §4 on 'Liquidation of the Corporation'. Ann McLean of the British Columbia bar and the Alberta bar wrote Part I, Chapter 1, §3, subpart II on 'Directors, Officers and the Management of the Corporation', subpart III on the 'Auditor' and subpart IV on 'Worker Participation'. Professor Lisa Philipps of Osgoode Hall Law School, York University, Toronto, wrote Part I, Chapter 1, §7 on 'The Taxation of Corporations and Shareholders' and the note on the taxation of closely held corporations. Professor Brian Cheffins of the Faculty of Law, University of British Columbia, now of the Faculty of Law, University of Cambridge, wrote Part I, Chapter 2, on 'The Closely Held Corporation' and Professor Mary Anne Waldron of the Faculty of Law, University of Victoria, wrote Part II on 'Partnerships'. This Canadian segment of the Encyclopaedia was updated in 2008 prior to this update in 2013. Updating for all sections in 2008 and in 2013 was done by Mark Gillen of the Faculty of Law, University of Victoria.

The Author

Table of Contents

Table of Contents

Table of Contents

List of Abbreviations

Alberta

ABCA	Alberta *Business Corporations Act*, R.S.A. 2000, c. B-9, as amended.
APA	Alberta *Partnership Act*, R.S.A. 2000, c. P-3, as amended.
ASA	Alberta *Securities Act*, R.S.A. 2000, c. S-4, as amended.

British Columbia

BCBCA	British Columbia *Business Corporations Act*, S.B.C. 2002, c. 57, as amended.
BCPA	British Columbia *Partnership Act*, R.S.B.C. 1996, c. 348, as amended.
BCSA	British Columbia *Securities Act*, R.S.B.C. 1996, c. 418, as amended.

Canada (Federal)

CBCA	*Canada Business Corporations Act*, R.S.C. 1985, c. C-44, as amended.
ITA	*Income Tax Act*, R.S.C. 1985, c. 1 (5th Supp.), as amended.

Manitoba

MCA	Manitoba *The Corporations Act*, R.S.M. 1987, c. C225, as amended.
MPA	Manitoba *The Partnership Act*, R.S.M. 1987, c. P30, as amended.
MSA	Manitoba, *The Securities Act*, R.S.M. 1987, c. S50, as amended.

List of Abbreviations

New Brunswick

NBBCA	New Brunswick *Business Corporations Act*, S.N.B. 1981, c. B-9.1, as amended.
NBLPA	New Brunswick *Limited Partnerships Act*, S.N.B. 1984, c. L-9.1, as amended.
NBPA	New Brunswick *Partnership Act*, R.S.N.B. 1973, c. P-4, as amended.
NBSA	New Brunswick *Securities Act*, S.N.B. 2004, c. S-5.5, as amended.

Newfoundland and Labrador

NCA	Newfoundland *Corporations Act*, R.S.N.L. 1990, c. C-36, as amended.
NLPA	Newfoundland *Limited Partnerships Act*, R.S.N.L. 1990, c. L-17, as amended.
NPA	Newfoundland *Partnership Act*, R.S.N.L. 1990, c. P-3, as amended.
NSA	Newfoundland *Securities Act*, R.S.N.L. 1990, c. S-13, as amended.

Nova Scotia

NSCA	Nova Scotia *Companies Act*, R.S.N.S. 1989, c. 81, as amended.
NSPA	Nova Scotia *Partnership Act*, R.S.N.S. 1989, c. 334, as amended.
NSLPA	Nova Scotia *Limited Partnerships Act*, R.S.N.S. 1989, c. 259, as amended.
NSSA	Nova Scotia *Securities Act*, R.S.N.S. 1989, c. 418, as amended.

Northwest Territories

NWTBCA	Northwest Territories *Business Corporations Act*, S.N.W.T. 1996, c. 19, as amended.
NWTPA	Northwest Territories *Partnership Act*, R.S.N.W.T. 1988, c. P-1, as amended.
NWTSA	Northwest Territories *Securities Act*, R.S.N.W.T. 1988, c. S-5, as amended.

Nunavut

NVBCA	Nunavut *Business Corporations Act*, S.N.W.T. 1996, c. 19, as amended, as enacted for Nunavut, pursuant to the *Nunavut Act*, S.C. 1993, c. 28.
NVPA	Nunavut *Partnership Act*, R.S.N.W.T. 1988, c. P-1, as amended, as enacted for Nunavut, pursuant to the *Nunavut Act*, S.C. 1993, c. 28.
NVSA	Nunavut *Securities Act*, R.S.N.W.T. 1988, c. S-5, as amended, as enacted for Nunavut, pursuant to the *Nunavut Act*, S.C. 1993, c. 28.

Ontario

OBCA	Ontario *Business Corporations Act*, R.S.O. 1990, c. B.16, as amended.
OPA	Ontario *Partnerships Act*, R.S.O. 1990, c. P.5, as amended.
OLPA	Ontario *Limited Partnerships Act*, R.S.O. 1990, c. L.16, as amended.
OSA	Ontario *Securities Act*, R.S.O. 1990, c. S.5, as amended.

Prince Edward Island

PEICA	Prince Edward Island *Companies Act*, R.S.P.E.I. 1988, c. C-14, as amended.
PEILP	Prince Edward Island *Limited Partnerships Act*, R.S.P.E.I. 1988, c. L-13, as amended.

List of Abbreviations

PEIPA	Prince Edward Island *Partnership Act*, R.S.P.E.I. 1988, c. P-1, as amended.
PEISA	Prince Edward Island *Securities Act*, R.S.P.E.I. 1988, c. S-3.1, as amended.

Quebec

QBCA	Quebec *Business Corporations Act*, Consolidated Statutes of Quebec, c. S-31.1.
QSA	Quebec *Securities Act*, R.S.Q., c. V-1.1, as amended.

Saskatchewan

SBCA	Saskatchewan *Business Corporations Act*, R.S.S. 1978, c. B-10, as amended.
SPA	Saskatchewan *Partnership Act*, R.S.S. 1978, c. P-3, as amended.
SSA	Saskatchewan *The Securities Act*, S.S. 1988, c. S-42.2, as amended.

Yukon

YBC	Yukon *Business Corporations Act*, R.S.Y. 2002, c. 20, as amended.
YPA	Yukon *Partnership and Business Names Act*, R.S.Y. 2002, c. 166, as amended.
YSA	Yukon *Securities Act*, R.S.Y. 2002, c. 201, as amended.

Preface and Disclaimer

This segment of the Canadian law of corporations and partnerships has been prepared so as to comply with the organization of contents for the Corporations and Partnerships edition of the *International Encyclopaedia of Laws* so that comparisons can be made with other jurisdictions. Consequently, the organization of the topics may be less than ideal for the purposes of facilitating an understanding of the law as it applies in Canada. This segment on Canada has also been prepared to meet restrictions with respect to length. The brevity of the discussion often hides a wealth of other important information about corporations and partnerships in Canada.

Canada has fourteen jurisdictions each of which has a general incorporation statute. Several of the fourteen jurisdictions have separate incorporation statutes for corporations engaging in specific types of business. Thirteen of the fourteen jurisdictions have their own laws with respect to partnerships. Thirteen of the fourteen jurisdictions also have securities acts that regulate the distribution of securities, takeovers, and insider trading. One of the ten provinces is a civil law jurisdiction while the remaining nine provinces and three territories are common law jurisdictions. Needless to say, this creates a level of complexity that cannot be reduced to a mere 200 pages. Consequently, *this information is not intended as legal advice. While every effort has been made to ensure the accuracy of the information provided, the information should not be relied on.* It is strongly recommended that Canadian legal counsel, in the appropriate jurisdiction within Canada, be retained to deal with matters relating to corporations and partnerships in Canada.

Since several jurisdictions in Canada have followed the modifications made by the *Canada Business Corporations Act* enacted in the mid-1970s, the summary of the Canadian law of corporations contained herein focuses primarily on the *Canada Business Corporations Act* making reference to the corporation acts of other jurisdictions only where there are significant differences.

General Introduction

Chapter 1. The General Background of the Country

§1. Geography

1. Canada is the second largest country in the world with an area of nearly 10 million square kilometres (approximately 9,984,670 square kilometres).[1,2] The country is bounded on the north by the Arctic ocean, on the south by the US, on the east by the Atlantic Ocean and on the west by the Pacific Ocean. From Cape Columbia on Elsemere Island in the north to Middle Island on Lake Erie in the south the country stretches a distance of 4,634 kilometres (2,896 miles). From Cape Spear Newfoundland in the east to the Yukon-Alaska border in the west the country stretches a distance of 5,514 kilometres (3,446 miles).

2. The country has a wide variety of topographical features. For instance, to the north there is a large area of arctic tundra. To the west there are numerous ranges of rugged mountains. In the central provinces, there are vast grassy plains. Much of the provinces of Manitoba, Ontario, and Quebec consist of glacial peneplain with rolling terrain covered with forests interspersed with numerous lakes. The St. Lawrence Seaway gives access to ports on the Great Lakes over 1,600 kilometres (a 1,000 miles) inland. The Great lakes are the remains of large glacial lakes that receded and left very arable land along the shores of the Great Lakes in the province of Ontario and along the St. Lawrence River in the province of Quebec. Along the east coast there are rugged shorelines beyond which lie forested interiors. With its vast land mass and the variety of geographic features Canada has extensive natural resources. Forestry, mining, oil and gas, and agriculture rank among Canada's major industries.[3]

1. For a general background on Canada *see* the *Canada Yearbook 2012* (Ottawa: Statistics Canada, 2012) http://www.statcan.gc.ca/pub/11-402-x/11-402-x2012000-eng.htm. The book provides data on a wide range of topics including demographics, health, education, culture and leisure, ethnic diversity and immigration, labour, economic accounts, income, pensions, spending and wealth, languages, families, households and housing, government, communications, transportation, agriculture, and business.
2. *See Canada Yearbook 2012* (Ottawa: Statistics Canada, 2012) at 210.
3. *Canada Yearbook 2012* (Ottawa: Statistics Canada, 2012) Table 9.4 at 128–129.

§2. CULTURAL COMPOSITION

3. Canada's two main founding cultures were the French, the predominant population in Lower Canada (modern day Quebec), and the English, the predominant population in Upper Canada (modern day Ontario), New Brunswick and Nova Scotia. These two cultural groups remain the dominant cultural groups in the country. Approximately 21.8% of the population considers French their native tongue.[4] The French speaking population resides primarily in the province of Quebec with smaller French speaking communities scattered throughout the country.[5] Approximately 57.2% of the population considers English their mother tongue.[6] The English-speaking population resides throughout the country including the province of Quebec.[7] English and French are the official languages of the country.[8]

4. Other cultures with substantial populations in the country include German, Italian, Chinese, Ukrainian, Dutch, Polish, and East Indian.[9] Also, about 4.0% of the population claims Aboriginal origins.[10]

§3. POLITICAL SYSTEM

I. The Constitutional Division of Powers

5. Canada has a federal system of government consisting of ten provincial governments and a federal government. There is a division of powers between the two

---

4. This is based on 2006 census data. *Canada Yearbook 2012* (Ottawa: Statistics Canada, 2012) at 322.
5. Of the 6,817,655 persons who claimed French to be their mother tongue, 5,877,660 (approximately 86%) resided in the province of Quebec. The French speaking population residing outside of the province of Quebec is located primarily in Ontario (488,815) and New Brunswick (232,975). *See Canada Yearbook 2012, supra* n. 1, Table 22.1 at 332–333.
6. This is based on 2006 census data. Table 22.1 in *Canada Yearbook 2012, supra* n. 1 at 332–333 lists 17,882,775 persons out of a total of 31,241,030 who gave English as a single response when asked what language they considered to be their mother tongue.
7. Of those who gave English as a single response when asked what language they considered to be their mother tongue 575,555 resided in the province of Quebec. This represents 7.7% of the population of Quebec. *See Canada Yearbook 2012,* Table 22.1, *supra* n. 1 at 332–333.
8. *See* the *Official Languages Act*, R.S.C. 1985, c. 31 (4th Supp.).
9. Based on 2006 census data the percentages of persons reporting origins other than British, Scottish, Irish, or French were: German (10.1%), Italian (4.6%), Chinese (4.3%), North American Indian (4.0%), Ukrainian (4.1%), Dutch (3.3%), Polish (3.1%), and East Indian (3.1.%). *See Canada Yearbook 2012* (Ottawa: Statistics Canada, 2012) Table 13.6 at 190.
10. The calculation is based on census data for 2006. A total of 1,253,615 people identified themselves as North American Indian. The total population of Canada, according to the 2006 census, was 31,241,030. *See Canada Yearbook 2012, supra* n. 1, Table 13.6 at 190. The 2016 Statistics Canada census for 10 May 2016 showed a total for Canada of 35,151,728 (*see* www.statscan.gc.ca).

levels of government set out in sections 91 and 92 of the *Constitution Act*.[11] The powers given to the two levels of government under sections 91–95 of the *Constitution Act* are exclusive powers of the level of government to which they are given. Generally, the federal government may not legislate with respect to the powers assigned to the provinces under section 92 and a province may not legislate with respect to the powers assigned to the federal government under section 91.[12] Thus federal legislation that in its 'pith and substance' deals with a matter that comes within provincial powers is *ultra vires* the federal government and, therefore, invalid. Similarly, provincial legislation that in its 'pith and substance' deals with a matter that comes within the powers of the federal government is *ultra vires* the provincial government and, therefore, invalid.[13]

Either of the two levels of government may, however, enact legislation that in its 'pith and substance' deals with a matter that is within one or more of its powers but which has an ancillary aspect relating to the powers of the other level of government or which incidentally affects matters that fall within the jurisdiction of the other level of government.[14] There can, therefore, be overlapping provincial and federal legislation. Where there is valid overlapping federal and provincial legislation the federal legislation is paramount to the extent it conflicts with provincial legislation.[15]

6. At least conceptually, except for protections with respect to denominational schools, any legislation that could be conceived of would fall within the powers of either the provinces or the federal government. The *Canadian Charter of Rights and Freedoms* (the '*Charter*' adopted in 1982),[16] however, constrains the powers of both levels of government. Legislation that infringes on the rights set out in the *Charter* may be declared invalid.[17]

II. Provinces

7. There are ten provinces in Canada that from west to east are: British Columbia, Alberta, Saskatchewan, Manitoba, Ontario, Quebec, New Brunswick, Prince Edward Island, Nova Scotia, and Newfoundland and Labrador.[18] Each province has a legislature

---

11. Formerly referred to as the *British North America Act*, 1867, 30–31 Victoria, c. 3 (UK) it was renamed the *Constitution Act*, 1867, by the *Constitution Act*, 1982, which was enacted as Schedule B to the *Canada Act* 1982, (UK) 1982, c. 11.
12. *See* P.W. Hogg, *Constitutional Law of Canada*, 5th ed., (Toronto: Carswell, 2007 Supplemented) s. 15.9(b).
13. *See* generally Hogg, *ibid.*, ss 5.1–5.8, 15.1–15.9.
14. *Ibid.*, s. 15.9(c). It is also possible to have similar legislation at both the provincial and federal levels. The legislation may, in one aspect, fit within a provincial head of power while, in another aspect, fit within a federal head of power. *See* Hogg, *ibid.*, s. 15.5(c).
15. *Ibid.*, ss 16.1–16.6.
16. Part I of the *Constitution Act*, 1982, enacted as Schedule B to the *Canada Act* 1982, (UK) 1982, c. 11.
17. *Constitution Act*, 1982, *supra* n. 11, s. 52(1). *See* the discussion in P.W. Hogg, *Constitutional Law of Canada*, 5th ed., (Toronto: Carswell, 2007 Supplemented) ss 37.2 (a)–37.2(c).
18. The reference to 'Newfoundland and Labrador' is not a reference to two separate provinces. It is the name of one province and is the eastern-most province in Canada.

the members of which are elected by the public. The provincial legislatures, as noted above, have their own exclusive powers subject to the *Charter*.[19]

III. Territories

8. There are territories in the north that from west to east are: the Yukon Territories, the Northwest Territories, and Nunavut. The territories are within federal jurisdiction but pass local ordinances pursuant to a delegation of authority from the federal government. In many respects the legislation of the territories resembles that of the provinces.[20]

IV. Municipal Governments

9. Municipal governments in Canada have wide ranging powers to govern their respective municipalities pursuant to powers delegated to the municipalities by provincial and territorial governments. There are also evolving forms of aboriginal governments. Some of these aboriginal governments have taken the form of delegated authority. Other developing forms of aboriginal government may take the form of a third level of government on a par with the federal and provincial governments.

V. The Judicial Power

10. Courts in Canada interpret and apply the constitution, the *Charter*, legislation, and the common law (and in Quebec the *Civil Code*). Perhaps the most significant power of the courts is the power to interpret and apply the *Constitution Act*[21] and the *Canadian Charter of Rights and Freedoms*.[22] The courts can strike down legislation that is in violation of the *Charter*, the division of powers under the *Constitution Act* or under other provisions of the *Constitution Act*.[23] The courts interpret and apply legislation. They also interpret, apply, and develop court made law (the 'common law') where it is not overruled by or inconsistent with valid provincial or federal legislation.

11. Unlike the distribution of legislative powers that set up a federal system, the court structure is unitary in character. Except for the Federal Court of Canada, which deals with certain prescribed federal matters, the superior courts of the provinces

19. *See supra* §3 I.
20. P.W. Hogg, *Constitutional Law of Canada*, 5th ed., (Toronto: Carswell, 2007 Supplemented) ss 2.5(b) and 14.1(d). *See* the *Northwest Territories Act*, R.S.C. 1985, c. N-27; the *Yukon Act*, S.C. 2002, c. 7; and the *Nunavut Act*, S.C. 1993, c. 28.
21. *See supra* n. 11.
22. *See supra* n. 16.
23. *See supra* §3 I.

have a broad jurisdiction to determine federal as well as provincial issues.[24] The court structure in Canada varies somewhat from province to province. Generally, there are courts of first instance in which trials are held with examinations of witnesses before a judge alone or before a judge and jury. There are also provincial courts of appeal that hear appeals from Courts of First Instance primarily on questions of law without a repetition of the trial process. Appeals from these provincial courts of appeal can also be made to Canada's highest court, the Supreme Court of Canada.[25]

VI. Political Parties

12. There are currently three main federal political parties: the Liberal Party, the Conservative Party, and the New Democratic Party. Representation in the House of Commons as of December 2016 was as follows:[26]

Liberal Party	182
Conservative Party	97
New Democratic Party	44
Bloc Quebecois	10
Green	1
Independent	1

13. The Liberal Party, the Conservative Party, and the New Democratic Party are typically also the dominant political parties in the provinces. There are, however, exceptions such as the Parti Québécois and Coalition Avenir in the province of Quebec, the Wildrose Party in Alberta, the Saskatchewan Party in Saskatchewan, and the Yukon Party in the Yukon Territories.

24. Thus, Canada does not have the dual federal and state court system of the United States. *See* generally P.W. Hogg, *Constitutional Law* of *Canada*, 5th ed., (Toronto: Carswell, 2007 Supplemented) at s. 7.2. The Federal Court of Canada has jurisdiction over matters such as claims involving the federal Crown, revenue, copyright, trademarks, patents, admiralty, tax, citizenship, claims with respect to inter-provincial undertakings, and aeronautics, and the power to review decisions of federal agencies and officials.

25. For a discussion of the court structure in Canada *see* Hogg, *ibid.*, at ss 7.1–7.3.

26. *See* http://www.parl.gc.ca/partliamentarians/en/party/standings.

§4. Population and Employment Statistics

I. Population Statistics

14. In 2013 the population of Canada was just over 35,000,000.[27] Given the large land mass of the country, the population density of the country is roughly three and a half persons per square kilometre. The majority of the population (68%) lives in urban areas.[28] Due to climatic and economic factors the urban areas are located primarily toward the south. Roughly 30% of the population lives in the country's three largest cities of Toronto, Montreal, and Vancouver.[29] Other major cities include Ottawa, Calgary, Edmonton, Winnipeg, Quebec City, Hamilton, Kitchener, London, Halifax, St. Catherines, and Victoria.[30]

II. Employment Statistics

15. The Canadian labour force is a highly skilled labour force.[31,32] A significant trend has been the growth in employment in service-producing industries. In the early 1970s goods-producing industries accounted for approximately 37% of employment.[33] By 1989 goods-producing industries accounted for only 29% of employment.[34] From

27. According to a Statistics Canada estimate in April 2013 the population of Canada was 35,141,542. As of 2011 roughly 29.7 million of this population was in the provinces of Ontario (13,373,000), Quebec (7,980,000), British Columbia (4,573,000) and Alberta (3,779,000). *See Canada Yeabook 2012* (Ottawa: Statistics Canada, 2007) Table 24.2 at 358.
28. *See Canada Yearbook 2007* (Ottawa: Statistics Canada, 2007), at 221.
29. Populations for the Census Metropolitan Areas of Toronto, Montreal, and Vancouver, according to 2006 census data, were: Toronto (5,838,838), Montreal (3,908,723), Vancouver (2,419,733). *See Canada Yearbook 2012, supra* n. 1, Table 24.3 at 360.
30. According to the *Canada Yearbook 2012, supra* n. 1, Table 24.3 at 360 the populations for the Census Metropolitan Areas of these cities were: Ottawa-Gatineau (1,258,914), Calgary (1,265,119), Edmonton (1,196,342), Winnipeg (762,759), Quebec City (761,745), Hamilton (750,213), Kitchener (498,533), London (496,941), Halifax (408,198), St. Catherines-Niagara (405,256), and Victoria (360,876). *See Canada Yearbook 2012, supra* n. 1, Table 24.3 at 360.
31. For a general overview on employment statistics in Canada *see* the *Canada Yearbook 2012, supra* n. 1 (the chapter on Labour – http://www.statcan.gc.ca/pub/11-402-x/2012000/chap/lab-tra/lab-tra-eng.htm). For more detailed employment statistics *see The Labour Force*, monthly (Ottawa: Statistics Canada) http://www23.statcan.gc.ca/imdb/p2SV.pl?Function=getSurvey&SDDS=3701&Item_Id=103716&lang=en.
32. Roughly 80.5% of the working-age population had completed high school. Those with university degrees accounted for 21.5% of the population while 6.8% of the population had graduate degrees. *See the Canada Yearbook 2012, supra* n. 1, Table 10.1 at 140–141. PISA scores (the OECD Programme for International Student Assessment that measures the skills of students toward the end of the period of compulsory education) for Canada were the third highest among OECD countries. *See Canada Yearbook 2012* (Ottawa: Statistics Canada, 2012), Chart 10.4 at 139.
33. *See* the *Canada Yearbook 1992* (Ottawa: Statistics Canada, 1991), at 144.
34. *Ibid.*

1970 to 1979, 79% of employment growth was in service-producing industries.[35] By 2006 the service-producing industries accounted for 76% of jobs in Canada and by 2011 it accounted for 78% of jobs in Canada.[36]

16. The participation rate (percentage of the population in the labour force) was approximately 63% in 1979.[37] The participation rate had grown to approximately 67% by 1989.[38] The participation rate for men was 78.5% in 1979 and 76.7% in 1989.[39] The participation rate for women was 49% in 1979 and 57.9% in 1989.[40] In 2011 the overall participation rate was 66.8% with the participation rate for males at 71.5% and for females at 62.3%.[41]

17. Federal and provincial legislation sets minimum standards for working conditions, wages, and termination procedures. Federal and provincial industrial relations legislation provides a framework for the certification of unions and the process of collective bargaining. There is also federal and provincial legislation dealing with occupational health and safety. Occupational health and safety legislation regulates such matters as fire safety, sanitation, ventilation, lighting, heating, materials handling, protective equipment, and protection from dangerous machinery, noise, and radiation. Regulations also deal with the handling of toxic substances and safety in hazardous industries such as mining, construction, logging, and demolition. Enforcement is effected through inspections and the imposition of penalties for failure to comply with the regulations or the directions given by inspectors.[42]

18. The proportion of unionized employees has fallen in Canada over the last several years. In 1989, the proportion of unionized employees was 38% but by 2004 the proportion of unionized employees had fallen to 31% and in 2011 was about 29.7%.[43] The number of work days lost per worker annually was 8.5% in 2001, 9.1% in 2002, 9.2% in 2003, 9.2% in 2004, 9.6% in 2005, 9.7% in 2006, and 9.1% in 2010.[44] The number of work days lost per worker annually due to illness or disability was

---

35. *Ibid.*
36. *See Canada Yearbook 2007* (Ottawa: Statistics Canada, 2007) Table 21.7 at 336–337 and for 2011 *see Canada Yearbook 2012* (Ottawa: Statistics Canada, 2012) Table 21.7 at 316–317.
37. *See* the *Canada Yearbook 1992* (Ottawa: Statistics Canada, 1991) Table 6.1 at 154.
38. *Ibid.*
39. *Ibid.*
40. *Ibid.* As of 1989, 55.9% of the labour force were men and 44.1% of the labour force were women. Also, as of 1989, 19% of the labour force was between the ages of 15 and 24, 70.8% was between the ages of 25 and 54 and 10.2% was over the age of 55. *See* the *Canada Yearbook 1992* (Ottawa: Statistics Canada, 2007) Table 6.2 at 155.
41. *See Canada Yearbook 2012* (Ottawa: Statistics Canada, 2012) Table 21.1 at 308.
42. For a brief discussion of the legislation *see* the *Canada Yearbook 1992* (Ottawa: Statistics Canada, 1991) at 148–151. For a more extensive discussion of labour laws in Canada *See*, for example, Donald G. Carter, G. England & G. Trudeau, *Labour Law in Canada*, 5th ed., (The Hague: Kluwer, 2002); and G. England, *Employment Law in Canada*, 4th ed., (Markham, Ont.: LexisNexis Canada, 2005 looseleaf).
43. *See* R. Morissette, G.Schellenberg & A Johnson, '*Diverging Trends in Unionization*' in *Perspectives on Labour and Income* (Ottawa: Statistics Canada, April 2005). For the 2011 data *see* 'Unionization 2011' (Statistics Canada, 2011), catalogue no. 75-001-X at p. 3.
44. *See Canada Yearbook 2007* (Ottawa: Statistics Canada, 2007) Table 21.17 at 347 and for 2010 *see Canada Yearbook 2012* (Ottawa: Statistics Canada, 2007) Table 21.15 at 324.

7.0% in 2001, 7.4% in 2002, 7.5% in 2003, 7.5% in 2004, 7.8% in 2005, 7.6% in 2006, and 7.4% in 2010.[45]

§5. Corporation and Partnership Statistics

19. Data on the number of incorporations in Canada are not readily available. A collection of such data was done for 1988. In that year, there were 137,835 incorporations done under federal or provincial legislation in Canada. Of these incorporations, the largest number of incorporations was done under Ontario legislation (55,657). This was followed by Quebec at 24,521, British Columbia at 19,494, and Alberta at 14,890. Incorporations under the federal legislation in 1988 were 11,962. Incorporations under legislation in the remaining provinces were substantially less with Manitoba at 2,450, Saskatchewan at 2,416, Nova Scotia at 2,190, New Brunswick at 2,012, Newfoundland at 1,811, and Prince Edward Island at 432.[46] The percentages of the total number of incorporations in each jurisdiction in 1988 were as follows:[47]

Federal	8.7%
Ontario	40.4%
Quebec	17.8%
British Columbia	14.1%
Alberta	10.8%
Manitoba	1.8%
Saskatchewan	1.8%
Nova Scotia	1.6%
New Brunswick	1.4%
Newfoundland	1.3%
Prince Edward Island	0.3%

These percentages have fluctuated considerably over the years and the fluctuations may, in part, be due to a degree of corporate forum shopping in response to substantial changes that have occurred in corporate legislation throughout the country over the past forty years.[48]

45. *See Canada Yearbook 2007* (Ottawa: Statistics Canada, 2007) Table 21.17 at 347 for data to 2006 and *See Canada Yearbook 2012* (Ottawa: Statistics Canada, 2007) Table 21.16 at 324 for 2010.
46. These figures were collected and reported in R.J. Daniels, '*Should Provinces Compete? The Case for a Competitive Law Market*' (1991) 36 McGill L.J. 130, at 158, Table 2.
47. *Ibid.*
48. *See* the discussion in Daniels, *supra* n. 46.

More recent data for 2007 were available from the federal Corporations Canada and from the Registrar in British Columbia. In British Columbia, there were 30,549 incorporations between 1 April 2006 and 31 March 2007. Federal incorporations under the *Canada Business Corporations Act* (CBCA) during the 2007 calendar year were 22,531.

20. Although general partnerships do not have the benefit of limited liability, a substantial number of general partnerships are still registered. For instance, in the year ending 31 March 1986, 30,925 new general partnerships were registered in the province of Ontario compared with 43,262 new share corporations incorporated in the province during the same period.[49] In 2003–2004 there were 98,400 registrations of new sole proprietorships and general partnerships under the Ontario *Business Names Act* while the number of corporation business name registrations under that Act in the same period were just 22,100.[50] General partnerships are often used by professionals who are often not permitted to incorporate. There can also be tax advantages to operating in partnership form. The formalities with respect to the creation and dissolution of partnerships are simpler and the partnership form provides a greater degree of flexibility than the corporate form.

§6. Social and Cultural Values

21. The social and cultural values of Canada might briefly be described as fundamentally a combination of Judeo-Christian and liberal values.[51] It has been suggested that before the Second World War Canada's social values were characterized by elitism[52] and that liberal values such as 'achievement, individualism and self-reliance were paramount'. It has also been suggested that with respect to state involvement the view was that 'the state should only intervene to protect those unable to protect themselves against the economic vicissitudes of the capitalist system'.[53]

22. The elitist and liberal values described above gave way to a degree of egalitarianism and collectivism. This is evidenced, in part, by the introduction of

49. *See* J.S. Ziegel, R.J. Daniels, D.L. Johnston & J.G. Macintosh, *Cases and Materials on Partnerships and Canadian Business Corporations*, 2nd ed., (Toronto: Carswell, 1989) at 3.
50. *See* Harris et al., *Cases, Materials and Notes on Partnerships and Canadian Business Corporations*, 4th ed., (Toronto: Carswell, 2004) at 1.
51. This summary of social and cultural values in Canada is drawn primarily from B. Blishen, '*Continuity and Change in Canadian Values*' in A. Cairns & C. Williams, eds, *The Politics of Gender, Ethnicity and Language in Canada* (Toronto: University of Toronto Press, 1986) 1. *See also* R. Breton, '*Multiculturalism and Canadian Nation-Building*' in A. Cairns & C. Williams, eds, *The Politics of Gender, Ethnicity and Language in Canada* (Toronto: University of Toronto Press, 1982) 27, E. Waddell, '*State, Language and Society*' in A. Cairns & C. Williams, eds, *The Politics of Gender, Ethnicity and Language in Canada* (Toronto: University of Toronto Press, 1982) 67, A. Cairns & C. Williams, '*Constitutionalism, Citizenship and Society in Canada: An Overview*' in A. Cairns & C. Williams, eds, *Constitutionalism, Citizenship and Society in Canada* (Toronto: University of Toronto Press, 1985) 1.
52. *See* Blishen, *supra* n. 51, at 3–7.
53. *See* Blishen, *supra* n. 51, at 10.

several social programmes since the Second World War.[54] The move toward more egalitarian principles might also be said to have been evident in the official policy of multiculturalism adopted by the federal government since the early 1970s[55] and in human rights legislation throughout the country that attempts to reduce discriminatory practices with respect to such matters as employment, housing, and the provision of goods and services.[56] Financial restraint in the 1990s and in recent years, however, led to some cutbacks in the extent of social programmes.

23. While there is evidence of developing egalitarianism and collectivism, there is also evidence of an expansion of individualistic values. Individualistic values are reflected in the *Canadian Charter of Rights and Freedoms*[57] (the *Charter*) adopted in 1982. The *Charter* provides such rights as: freedom of conscience and religion;[58] freedom of thought, belief, opinion, and expression;[59] the right to move to and take up residence in any province and to pursue the gaining of a livelihood in any province.[60] Other rights set out in the *Charter* include the right to life, liberty, and security of the person; and the right not to be deprived thereof except in accordance with the principles of fundamental justice;[61] to be secure against unreasonable search and seizure;[62] not to be arbitrarily detained or imprisoned;[63] and to equal protection and equal benefit of the law without discrimination based on race, national, or ethnic origin, colour, religion, sex, age, or mental or physical disability.[64]

24. Canada's social and cultural values might also be characterized in part as involving a tension between national and regional values. This tension was particularly evident in constitutional debates from 1990 through 1992 leading up to a referendum on the constitution in October 1992. Perhaps the most pronounced regional tension involves the province of Quebec and demands by many Quebec residents for either a special status for Quebec within a federal union or a sovereign Quebec. The regional tension with respect to the province of Quebec is rooted in the values of the predominantly Francophone population of Quebec which are based on a linguistic, religious, and

---

54. *See,* for example, the *Old Age Assistance Act*, S.C. 1951, c. 55; the *Unemployment Insurance Act*, S.C. 1940, c. 44; the *Canada Pension Plan*, S.C. 1964–65, c. 51; the *Disabled Persons Act*, S.C. 1953–54, c. 55 and the *Blind Persons Act*, S.C. 1951, c. 38. *See also* the discussion in Blishen, *supra* n. 51, at 10–12.
55. The development and implementation of the policy of multiculturalism in Canada is reviewed in, for example, R. Breton, *supra* n. 51.
56. *See,* for example, *Canadian Human Rights Act*, R.S.C. 1985, c. H-6; *Human Rights Act*, S.B.C. 1984, c. 22 [now R.S.B.C. 1996, c. 210]; *Individual's Rights Protection Act*, R.S.A. 1980, c. I-2 [now the *Human Rights, Citizenship and Multiculturalism Act*, R.S.A. 2000, c. H-14]; *Saskatchewan Human Rights Code*, S.S. 1979, c. S-24.1; *Human Rights Code*, R.S.O. 1990, c. H. 19.
57. Part I of the *Constitution Act, 1982*, enacted as Schedule B to the *Canada Act 1982, (UK)* 1982, c. 11.
58. Section 2(a).
59. Section 2(b).
60. Section 6.
61. Section 7.
62. Section 8.
63. Section 9.
64. Section 15.

legal culture distinct from the predominantly Anglophone and British derived linguistic, religious, and legal culture in the rest of the country.[65]

25. There are continuing pressures to address distributive inequities and sources of systemic discrimination with respect to women and minority groups.[66] In the latter half of the twentieth century Aboriginal peoples in Canada became more active in pursuing land claims and asserting rights to self-government and these activities are continuing.[67] In 2015 the Truth and Reconciliation Commission of Canada released a report dealing with concerns over the history of residential schools in Canada that operated for over 100 years until as recently as the late 1990s and that had, over the years, separated an estimated minimum of 150,000 Aboriginal children from their families. The Truth and Reconciliation Commission of Canada set out ninety-four 'calls to action' with a view to a reconciliation in the form of coming to terms with events of the past in a manner intended to overcome conflict and establish a respectful and healthy relationship going forward. These increasing pressures are indicative of a shift in the political influence of these groups perhaps due in part to changing social values which are more receptive to their concerns.

---

65. For a discussion of the issue with respect to Quebec *See*, for example, Waddell, *supra* n. 51.
66. *See* Blishen, *supra* n. 51, at 18–24. For an overview of the increasing influence of women in Canada in the 1970s and 1980s *see* S. Burt, '*Women's Issues and the Women's Movement in Canada Since 1970*' in A. Cairns & C. Williams, eds, *The Politics of Gender, Ethnicity and Language in Canada* (Toronto: University of Toronto Press) 111. For more recent discussions of these continuing pressures *see* F. Faraday, M. Denike & M.K. Stephenson (eds), *Making Equality Rights Real: Securing Substantive Equality under the Charter* (Toronto: Irwin Law, 2006).
67. For an overview of the concept of aboriginal self-government and its potential impact *see* R. Gibbins & J.R. Pouting, '*An Assessment of the Probable Impact of Aboriginal Self-Government in Canada,*' in A. Cairns & C. Williams, eds, *The Politics of Gender, Ethnicity and Language in Canada* (Toronto: University of Toronto Press, 1982) 171. For an overview of Aboriginal title in Canada and developments concerning Aboriginal title in Canada since the 1970s *see* C. Godlewska & J. Webber, '*The Calder Decision, Aboriginal Title, Treaties and the Nisga'a*' in H. Foster, H. Raven & J. Webber (eds), *Let Right be Done* (Vancouver: UBC Press, 2007) 1 at 9–25.

Chapter 2. Introduction to Corporations and Partnerships

§1. General Partnerships and Limited Partnerships

26. In Canada there are three types of partnerships: general partnerships, limited partnerships, and limited liability partnerships. Whether the partnership is a general partnership, limited partnership, or a limited liability partnership the partnership is not considered a separate legal entity. In a general partnership, the general partners are personally liable for all the debts of the partnership business. This is so whether the general partner is an active, working partner or a 'dormant' or 'sleeping' partner not active in the business and not apparent to a third party as a partner.[68]

27. A limited partnership is created by the filing of a certificate containing specified information about the limited partnership. A limited partnership has one or more limited partners and one or more general partners. The general partner(s) is (are) personally liable for all the debts of the partnership. The limited partner is liable only to the extent of his, her, or its contribution or agreed contribution to the partnership. The limited partner is treated as a general partner without limited liability if the name of the limited partner appears in the name of the partnership or if the limited partner exercises control over the partnership business (or in some jurisdictions if the limited partner 'takes part in the management of the partnership business').[69]

28. Limited liability partnerships responded to concerns of professional persons (such as doctors, engineers, lawyers, and accountants) over rising damages awards in tort claims, particularly in the US, that led to insurance becoming unavailable for some risks. A limited liability partnership reduces the scope of exposure to liability risks. Some Canadian jurisdictions have adopted 'partial shield' liability protection under which a partner is not liable for the negligence of a fellow partner unless he was supervising that fellow partner or was negligent himself. Other jurisdictions have adopted 'full shield' liability protection under which the partners are protected from the ordinary debts of the firm including the negligence of their fellow partners (although they remain liable for their own negligence). Most Canadian jurisdictions restrict the formation of limited liability partnerships to regulated professions. British Columbia allows the formation of a limited liability partnership for any type of business.

29. Since partnerships in Canada are not considered separate legal entities, Canada does not have concepts such as partnerships with legal personality or partnerships

68. *See* generally Part II on Partnerships, particularly paras 441, 464–466. Under the laws of some countries silent partners can limit their liability (as in, for instance, Belgium – *see International Encyclopaedia of Laws: Corporations and Partnerships – Belgium* (Deventer: Kluwer, 2006) at para. 34). Perhaps the closest approximation to this in Canadian jurisdictions are provisions that allow a person to make an advance of money by way of a loan on a contract in writing for a share of the profits or a rate of interest varying with the profits. When, however, such an advance is made the lender's interest is subordinated to the interests of other creditors on an insolvency. *See infra* para. 445 and notes 1090 and 1091.

69. *See infra* paras 458, 459.

with reduced legal personality. This can create difficulties with respect to civil actions both by and against a partnership since the rights or obligations are not rights or obligations of the partnership (as there is no such legally recognized entity) but are rights and obligations of individual partners. Concern for multiple actions by or against individual partners (with potentially inconsistent results) has led to rules which tend to force the joinder of all partners to the action. The difficulties so created have, however, been ameliorated in most jurisdictions by rules of court procedure that allow partnerships to both sue and be sued in the name of the partnership. This does not make the partnership a separate legal entity.[70] It is simply a convenient means of joining partners in an action.[71]

§2. Corporations

30. Corporations may be created under general statutes of incorporation or by a special act of the federal Parliament or a provincial legislature. General statutes of incorporation may limit the types of corporations that can be incorporated under the statute. For instance, the CBCA provides that the act does not apply to a body corporate which is a bank, an insurance company, a trust company, or a loan company.[72] In the federal legislative regime for corporations these types of corporations are dealt with under separate statutes.[73]

31. The form of the documents used to incorporate corporations (or companies) in Canada varies from one jurisdiction to another. Under the federal CBCA, and the acts of several of the provinces, the key document is the articles of incorporation. In Nova Scotia, the key documents for incorporation are the memorandum of association and the articles of association. Statutes in a memorandum of association jurisdiction, such as Nova Scotia, provide that the memorandum of association constitutes a contract amongst the members, or shareholders, of the company.[74] In British Columbia the 'memorandum of association' has been replaced with a document called the 'notice of articles' but it is similar, in terms of its contents and function, to a memorandum of association.[75] The province of Prince Edward Island retains incorporation by a document called a 'letters patent'. This approach was, until relatively recently, common in several other jurisdictions in Canada. The letters patent is issued pursuant to the prerogative of the Crown. Thus, incorporation pursuant to the issuance of a letters patent is

70. *See*, for example, *Re Thorne and New Brunswick Workmen's Compensation Board* (1962), 33 D.L.R. (2nd) 167, 48 M.P.R. 56 (N.B.S.C. A.D.).
71. *See infra* para. 443.
72. CBCA s. 3(4).
73. *See* the *Bank Act*, S.C. 1991, c. 46; the *Trust and Loan Companies Act*, S.C. 1991, c. 45; and the *Insurance Companies Act*, S.C. 1991, c. 47.
74. NSCA s. 24(1) provides that the memorandum and articles bind the company and the members as if they had signed and sealed the documents containing covenants on the part of each member to observe all the provisions of the memorandum and the articles subject to the provisions of the act. For the BCBCA *see* s. 19.
75. *See* BCBCA ss 11 and 19.

considered to be incorporation by permission rather than incorporation as of right as is the case under the articles of incorporation or memorandum of association jurisdictions.

32. An essential feature of corporations incorporated under incorporation statutes in Canada is that they are considered legal entities separate from the shareholders or directors and officers of the corporation.[76] Corporations thus have a potential perpetual existence that is not affected by the death or incapacity of shareholders of the corporation. Further, under incorporation statutes in Canada, the liability of the shareholders of the corporation is limited to the contributions the shareholders have made.[77] The main general statutes of incorporation in the provinces of Alberta, British Columbia, and Nova Scotia allow for the incorporation of either companies in which in the liability of shareholders of the corporation is limited to the contributions shareholders have made or 'unlimited liability companies'.[78] Section 51.11 of the British Columbia *Business Corporations Act* (BCBCA),[79] for instance, provides that:

> A company formed under section 10 is an unlimited liability company if its notice of articles contains the following statement:
>
> The shareholders of this company are jointly and severally liable to satisfy the debts and liabilities of this company to the extent provided in section 51.3 of the Business Corporations Act.

The availability of unlimited liability companies in these jurisdictions is directed primarily at investors from the US for whom these unlimited liability companies can provide the tax advantage of flow-through tax treatment under federal tax laws in the US.

33. Corporations incorporated under most general statutes of incorporation in Canada need not have objects clauses. Objects clauses created problems for corporations and third parties dealing with corporations because it was held early on, at least with respect to memorandum of association companies, that acts of the corporation that were beyond the objects of the corporation were ultra vires. Contracts made with a corporation that had acted beyond its powers were considered void.[80] To rectify this problem most general statutes of incorporation in Canada give corporations the powers of natural persons.[81] The articles of incorporation, or the memorandum, may impose restrictions on the business of the corporation but the articles, or memorandum, do not contain objects in the traditional sense. Acts for the purpose of carrying on a business that the corporation is restricted from carrying on are not invalid (or *ultra*

76. With respect to memorandum of association companies this has been the case at least since the decision in *Salomon v. Salomon & Co.*, [1897] A.C. 22, 66 L.J. Ch. 35 (H.L.).
77. *See,* for example, CBCA s. 45(1).
78. *See* the ABCA Part 2.1; BCBCA Part 2.1; and NSCA s. 12.
79. S.B.C. 2002, c. 57, as amended.
80. *See Ashbury Railway Carriage & Iron Co. v. Riche* (1875), L.R. 7 H.L. 653. This was not the case with respect to letters patent companies – *see Bonanza Creek Cold Mining v. The King*, [1916] 1 A.C. 566, 85 L.J.PC. 114, 10 W.W.R. 391, 26 D.L.R. 273.
81. *See,* for example, CBCA s. 15; BCBCA s. 30.

vires the corporation).[82] Instead, the directors or officers who engage in such acts are subject to applications for an injunction or actions for damages.

34. Corporations may be created for purposes other than making profits from carrying on business. For instance, corporate entities may be created with a non-profit or charitable purpose.[83] Cooperative associations may be created and may operate with a typical corporate structure but usually distribute any surplus in the form of reduced prices to its members.[84]

§3. Associations

35. Partnerships, by the definition of 'partnership' in most provincial partnership acts, are formed to carry on business with a view of profit. Corporations are also frequently incorporated for the purpose of carrying on a business for profit. Persons may, however, also associate for the purpose of carrying on non-profit or charitable activities. Non-profit associations and charitable associations can be incorporated or unincorporated.[85]

36. There are advantages to the incorporation of non-profit or charitable associations. These advantages are similar to the advantages of incorporation for the purpose of carrying on business for profit. Unincorporated associations are not recognized legal entities.[86] Thus an unincorporated association cannot enter into legally binding contracts or sue or be sued in its own name. Lacking legal status an unincorporated association cannot own land or an interest in land. To engage in these activities the unincorporated association would have to act through an agent or trustee.

37. Incorporating a non-profit or charitable association not only provides a recognized separate legal personality, but it also provides a continuing existence, not affected by the death or bankruptcy of its members, and limited liability. However, incorporation of non-profit or charitable organizations involves expense and time. Further, the statutory regimes under which such associations can be incorporated may impose restrictions and ongoing requirements that the association may prefer to avoid.[87]

---

82. *See*, for example, CBCA s. 16(3).
83. *See infra* , §3 on 'Associations'.
84. For a discussion of cooperatives legislation in Canada *see* D. Ish, *The Law of Canadian Cooperatives* (Toronto: Burroughs, 1981); D. Ish, *Co-operatives in Principle and Practice* (Saskatoon: Centre for the Study of Co-operatives, University of Saskatchewan, 1992) and *See*, for example, *Canada Cooperative Association Act*, S.C. 1998, c. 1; *The Co-operatives Act*, S.S. c. C-37.3; British Columbia *Cooperative Association Act*, S.B.C. 1999, c. 28.
85. For a detailed discussion of the law of associations *see* D.J. Bourgeois, *The Law of Charitable and Not-for-Profit Organizations*, 3rd ed. (LexisNexis Canada, 2002) and D.J. Bourgeois, *Charities and Not-for-Profit Administration and Governance Handbook*, 2nd ed. (LexisNexis Canada, 2009).
86. *See* Bourgeois, *The Law of Charitable and Not-for-Profit Organizations*, *supra* n. 85, at 50–51.
87. *See* Bourgeois, *The Law of Charitable and Not-for-Profit Organizations*, *supra* n. 85, at 48–54.

38. The federal legislation, and the legislation of several provinces, provides separate statutory regimes for the incorporation of non-profit and charitable associations.[88] For instance, for profit corporations are incorporated federally under the CBCA while non-profit corporations are incorporated under the *Canada Not-for-profit Corporations Act*.[89]

39. The process of incorporation for non-profit or charitable associations varies somewhat from jurisdiction to jurisdiction within Canada. The process is, however, similar to the process described in Part I, Chapter 1 below.[90]

88. *See* the *Canada Not-for-profit Corporations Act*, S.C. 2009, c. 23; *The Non-Profit Corporations Act*, S.S. 1995, c. N-4.2; the *Companies Act*, R.S.A. 2000, c. C-21; the *Companies Act*, R.S.N.B. 1973, c. C-13. These jurisdictions have separate statutes dealing with 'business' corporations.
89. S.C. 2009, c. 23.
90. *See infra* paras 68–70.

Chapter 3. The Historical Background of Corporations and Partnerships

§1. A Brief Canadian Historical Context

40. To follow the historical development of the law of partnerships and corporations in Canada as outlined below it is useful to have a brief background on the development of Canada as a nation. Canada was colonized by both France and England through the seventeenth and eighteenth centuries and further colonized by England during the nineteenth century. The French colony of New France, which primarily occupied the lands to the immediate north and south of the St. Lawrence River in what is now the province of Quebec, was ceded to England in 1763 by the Treaty of Paris at the end of the Seven Years War. Initially English law was imposed on Quebec (the former colony of New France).[91] The *Quebec Act* of 1774, however, restored the French civil law as it had existed in the colony of New France at the end of the war.[92]

41. The *Constitution Act* of 1791 divided Quebec into the provinces of Upper and Lower Canada,[93] the boundary being the present boundary between Ontario and Quebec. The act provided for elected legislative assemblies in both Upper and Lower Canada.[94] It also provided that the laws of Quebec would continue to apply in both Upper and Lower Canada until the laws were altered by the assemblies of the provinces.[95] The French civil law remained in force in Lower Canada (or roughly speaking, modern day Quebec). In 1792, Upper Canada passed an act adopting the laws of England.[96]

42. In other provinces that were originally colonized by the English, the common law rule was that the first settlers of the colony were deemed to have brought English law with them (at least with respect to governing themselves).[97] The date on which the first settlement occurred was factually difficult to determine. Consequently, the date when the first legislative assembly was held was, in some cases, deemed to be

91. English law was imposed by The Royal Proclamation of 1763, a proclamation of the King of England exercising his prerogative power. There is some doubt as to whether the The Royal Proclamation of 1763 did effectively impose English law on Quebec it having done so probably in violation of the standards of international comity. *See* P.W. Hogg, *Constitutional Law of Canada*, 5th ed., (Toronto: Carswell, 2007 Supplemented) at 2.3(b) n. 25 referring to B. Slattery, 'The Land Rights of Indigenous Canadian Peoples as Affected by the Crown's Acquisition of Territories' (D. Phil. Thesis, Oxford University, 1979), at 206.
92. *Quebec Act,* 1774 (UK), R.S.C. 1985, Appendix 11, No. 3.
93. *The Constitution Act*, 1791 (UK), R.S.C. 1985, Appendix 11, No. 3.
94. *Ibid.*, s. 2.
95. *Ibid.*, s. 33.
96. Statutes of Upper Canada 1792 (32 Geo. 111), c. 1, s. 1.
97. *See* P.W. Hogg, *Constitutional Law of Canada*, 5th ed., (Toronto: Carswell, 2007 Supplemented) at 2.2(a).

the date of reception of English law.[98] With respect to the reception of English common law the concept was that the common law was a universally applicable pre-existing body of doctrine that the courts 'discovered'. Thus, the reception of English common law was a continuous process with colonial courts following the decisions of common law courts throughout the British Empire, especially the decisions of the Judicial Committee of the Privy Council in England, and the decisions of the House of Lords which, although not binding, were considered very persuasive.[99]

43. Upper Canada and Lower Canada were united by *The Union Act*, 1840 to form the united province of Canada with a single legislature.[100] A confederation of the province of Canada, Nova Scotia, and New Brunswick was brought about in 1867 under the *British North America Act, 1867* passed by the British Parliament at Westminster.[101] The confederation formed the country of Canada with four provinces, namely, Nova Scotia, New Brunswick, Ontario, and Quebec (the former province of Canada being divided into Ontario and Quebec). Under the *British North America Act, 1867* (since renamed the *Constitution Act, 1867*) legislative powers were divided between the provincial legislatures and the federal Parliament creating the federal state described above.[102] In the years following confederation new provinces were formed and joined in confederation.

§2. Partnerships

44. Initially the partnership law applied in the English-speaking provinces of Canada was English common law. The law of partnerships was codified in the UK in 1890[103] and similar acts were passed in several of the English-speaking provinces of Canada at about the same time.[104] These statutes typically preserved the common law to the extent it was not inconsistent with the act.[105]

45. Statutes providing for the creation of limited partnerships were also enacted. Ontario enacted a limited partnerships act as early as 1849.[106] Other provinces also enacted provisions for the creation of limited partnerships which were generally based on the American Uniform Limited Partnerships Act.[107]

98. *See*, for example, *Young v. Blaikie* (1822), 1 Nfld. L.R. 277 (S.C. Nfld.); *Uniacke v. Dickson* (1848), 2 N.S.R. 287 (S.C.N.S.).
99. *See* Hogg, *supra* n. 97, at 2.2(a).
100. *The Union Act*, 1840 (UK), R.S.C. 1985, Appendix II, No. 4.
101. The *British North America Act, 1867* (UK), R.S.C. 1985, Appendix II, No. 5. Renamed the *Constitution Act*, 1867 by s. 53(2) of the *Constitution Act*, 1982 enacted as Schedule B to the *Canada Act* 1982, (UK) 1982, c. 11.
102. *See supra* Ch. 1, §3 I.
103. The *Partnership Act*, 1890, 53 & 54 Vict. c. 39.
104. *See*, for example, *The Partnership Act*, S.O.1920, c. 41, and the *Partnership Act*, 1894, S.B.C. 1894, c. 36.
105. *See*, for example, the BCPA s. 90.
106. *An Act to Authorize Limited Partnerships in Upper Canada (1849)*, 12 Vict. c. 45.
107. Cites to the current versions of enactments providing for limited partnerships are set out *infra* para. 441, n. 1070.

46. Quebec followed an approach to partnerships closer to the European model. The Quebec Civil Code provides for partnerships '*en nom collectif*' (general partnership), '*en commandite*' (limited partnership), or '*en participation*' (undeclared partnership).[108]

§3. Corporations

47. Early forms of corporations in Canada evolved from grants of crown charters.[109] The Hudson's Bay Company was created through a charter granted by the crown in 1670.[110] Crown charters were also granted in the latter part of the eighteenth and early part of the nineteenth century for projects such as roads, canals, harbours, and later, railways. Some corporations were also incorporated under special acts of colonial legislatures.

48. In 1849 the provinces of Lower Canada and Upper Canada passed statutes allowing for the grant of letters patent to create companies for the building of roads and bridges.[111] In 1850 the United Provinces of Canada enacted a general statute of incorporation for mining, shipbuilding, manufacturing, or chemical concerns.[112] The statute provided for limited liability and an expeditious incorporation process with no dependence on executive discretion (such as pertained to the grant of a letters patent).[113] The corporation created under the act was a separate entity with succession and capable of suing and being sued.[114]

49. In 1864 the United Provinces of Upper and Lower Canada passed a general incorporation statute that provided for the grant of a letters patent on application to the Governor-in-Council.[115] This Act of the United Provinces in 1864 formed the basis of the post-confederation federal statute of 1869.[116] It also formed the basis of provincial legislation in the provinces of Quebec, Ontario, Manitoba, New Brunswick, and Prince

---

108. *See infra* para. 441.

109. For a more detailed history of the development of corporations in Canada *see* R. Risk, 'The Nineteenth-Century Foundations of the Business Corporation in Ontario' (1973) 23 *U.T.L.J.* 270; T. Hadden et al., *Canadian Business Organizations* (Toronto: Butterworths, 1984) at 18–35; B.L. Welling, *Corporate Law in Canada: The Governing Principles*, 3rd ed., (Mudgeerba, Qld., Australia: Scribblers Publishing, 2006) at 47–57; E.E. Palmer, '*The Pre-Confederation History of Corporations in Canada*' in J.S. Ziegel ed., *Studies in Canadian Company Law*, vol. 1, (Toronto: Butterworths, 1967) 33.

110. For a history of the company *see* Peter C. Newman, *Company of Adventurers* (Markham, Ont.: Viking Canada, vol. 1 1985, vol. 2, 1987). The Charter is reproduced at 320 of vol. 1.

111. *An Act to Authorize the Formation of Joint Stock Companies for the Construction of Roads and other Works in Upper Canada*, 1849, 12 Vict., c. 84; and *An Act to Authorize the Formation of Joint Stock Companies in Lower Canada for the Construction of Macadamized Roads, and of Bridges and Other Works of Like Nature*, 1849, 12 Vict., c. 56.

112. *An Act to Provide for the Formation of Incorporated Joint Stock Companies for Manufacturing, Mining, Mechanical, or Chemical Purposes*, 1850, 13 & 14 Vict., c. 28.

113. *Ibid.*, ss I and XI.

114. *Ibid.*, s. II.

115. *An Act to Authorize the Granting of Charters of Incorporation to Manufacturing, Mining, and other Companies*, 1864, 27 & 28 Vict., c. 23.

116. *Canada Joint Stock Companies Letters Patent Act*, 1869, 32 & 33 Vict., c. 13.

Edward Island.[117] The provinces of Nova Scotia, Newfoundland, Alberta, Saskatchewan, and British Columbia adopted the English Act which provided for incorporation through the filing of a memorandum of association.[118]

50. Substantial modifications to corporate legislation in Canada have taken place since the late 1960s. In 1967 the Ontario government appointed a commission chaired by A.F. Lawrence (the 'Lawrence Committee') to review corporate law in Ontario.[119] The commission's report (the 'Lawrence Report') recommended adopting an article of incorporation type of corporate scheme based on an American model. In 1970 Ontario enacted corporations legislation that adopted most of the recommendations of the Lawrence Committee.[120] The federal government set up a task force in 1967 to reconsider the federal corporations legislation. Proposals for revisions to the federal business corporations law (known as the 'Dickerson Report') were released in 1971.[121] This report followed many of the suggestions made by the Lawrence Committee and added other modifications. The proposals in the Dickerson Report were the basis for the enactment of the CBCA which was proclaimed in force in 1975.[122] Many of the modifications in the CBCA were anticipated in British Columbia in amendments to its *Companies Act* in 1973.[123] After the enactment of the CBCA several other provinces began to adopt many of the modifications made in the CBCA.[124]

51. Since most corporate legislation throughout the country have adopted provisions identical to or substantially similar to the provisions in the CBCA, the brief overview of corporate law in Canada presented in this text focuses on the CBCA. Notational references are provided which point out some of the differences between the CBCA and other corporate legislation in Canada.

117. *See* F.W. Wegenast, *The Law of Canadian Companies* (Toronto: Burroughs and Company, 1931) at 20–27.
118. *Ibid.*
119. *Report of the Select Committee on Company Law* (Toronto: Queen's Printer, 1967).
120. *The Business Corporations Act*, S.O. 1970, c. 25.
121. R.W.V. Dickerson et al., *Proposals for a New Business Corporations Act for Canada*, 2 vols (Ottawa: Supply and Services, 1971).
122. S.C. 1974–1975–1976, c. 33 (now R.S.C. 1985, c. C-44).
123. *Companies Act*, S.B.C. 1973, c. 18.
124. For a summary of the pattern of adoption of the CBCA in other jurisdictions in Canada *see* R.J. Daniels, '*Should Provinces Compete? The Case for a Competitive Law Market*' (1991) 36 McGill L.J. 130, at 152–155.

Chapter 4. Sources and Hierarchy of the Law on Corporations and Partnerships

52. The main sources of partnership law in Canada are the partnership acts of the various provinces. The decisions of courts interpreting partnership acts are another important source of partnership law.

53. The main sources of corporate law in Canada are the general statutes of incorporation of the various provinces and the federal CBCA. There are also statutes of incorporation for particular businesses such as banks, insurance companies, and trust companies.[125] In addition, there are special statutes of incorporation under which a single, particular corporate entity is created. This is often the case for municipal corporations or universities. There are numerous decisions of courts interpreting the current federal and provincial statutes of incorporation. There are also numerous decisions of courts interpreting forerunners to the current statutes of incorporation as well as common law court decisions with respect to such matters as the fiduciary duties of directors and officers.

54. There are both federal and provincial statutes of incorporation because section 92(11) of the *Constitution Act* gave the provinces power to incorporate companies having 'provincial objects' while the federal Parliament has a general power to enact legislation with respect to all matters not specifically assigned to the provinces.[126] Although the provinces only have a power to incorporate corporations with 'provincial objects' it was held early on that corporations incorporated under provincial statutes could nonetheless operate outside of the province subject to the laws of the other jurisdiction.[127] Thus there remains very little distinction between the federal and provincial powers to incorporate corporations except perhaps that a federally incorporated corporation, although subject to the laws of other jurisdictions within the country, cannot be precluded from operating in any jurisdiction within the country.[128]

125. For federal legislation providing for the incorporation of companies involved in particular businesses *See*, for example, the *Bank Act*, S.C. 1991, c. 46; the *Insurance Companies Act*, S.C. 1991, c. 47; the *Trust and Loan Companies Act*, S.C. 1991, c. 45. For the province of British Columbia *See*, for example, the *Financial Administration Act*, R.S.B.C. 1996, c. 141, that provides for the incorporation of insurance companies and trust companies. For the province of Saskatchewan *See*, for example, the *Trust and Loan Corporations Act*, 1997, S.S. 1997, c. T-22-2.

126. *See* the *Constitution Act*, 1867, s. 91.

127. *See Bonanza Creek Gold Mining v. The King*, [1916] 1 A.C. 566, 85 L.J.P.C. 114, 10 W.W.R. 391, 26 D.L.R. 273.

128. *See*, for example, *John Deere Plow Co. v. Wharton*, [1915] A.C. 330, 84 L.J.P.C. 64 (P.C.). A province can prohibit the carrying on of a particular business within the province even though that would prevent a federally incorporated company from carrying on that business in the province, as long as the province prohibits all companies, not just federally incorporated companies, from carrying on that business in the province (*see Canadian Indemnity Co. v. A.G.B.C.*, [1977] 2 S.C.R. 504).

55. Other important sources of corporate law in Canada are the securities acts of the provinces. Generally, these acts apply with respect to trading in securities[129] in the province.[130] Securities commissions are created under securities acts in several of the provinces. These securities commissions are given very broad discretionary powers.[131] Provincial securities commissions in Canada have typically also been granted rule-making powers. Rules made under these rule-making powers can often have a substantial impact on corporate transactions that traditionally would have been considered to fall within the confines of 'corporate law'. For instance, National Policy No. 62-202, a joint policy statement issued by the Canadian Securities Administrators,[132] outlines the position of Canadian securities administrators with respect to takeover bid defensive tactics and the response they may take to a takeover defensive tactic of a type that they do not approve of.[133]

129. The term 'security' is very broadly defined and includes both debt and equity securities.
130. The jurisdictional scope of securities regulation in Canada can be quite broad – *See,* for example, *Gregory & Co. Inc. v. The Quebec Securities Commission,* [1961] S.C.R. 584; *R.v. McKenzie Securities Ltd.* (1966), 55 W.W.R. 157 (Man. C.A.); and *In the Matter of Asbestos Corporation Limited* (1988), 11 O.S.C.B. 3419.
131. For instance, they typically have the power to deny corporations or individuals the right to various exemptions provided in securities acts, to order compliance, to order that trading in particular securities cease or that an individual cease trading, and to remove the licence of an individual or corporation to trade in securities. They have the power to require that a person not serve, or no longer serve, as a director or officer of an issuer of securities, and they typically also have the power to impose administrative fines. Securities commissions can typically impose these sanctions where they find it 'in the public interest' to do so.
132. The Canadian Securities Administrators consists of the securities administrators of all the provinces and territories in Canada.
133. National Instrument 54-101 dealing with communications with shareholders and Multilateral Instrument 61-501 (that applies in Ontario and Quebec) dealing with insider bids, issuer bids, business combinations, and related party transactions are other examples of securities administrator rules that have a significant impact on matters that might be said to fall within the scope of traditional corporate law with respect to the relationships between shareholders *inter se* and between shareholders and the corporation.

Chapter 5. International Private Law

§1. Recognition of Foreign Corporations

56. Foreign corporations are recognized in Canada according to the status granted to the corporation by the laws of the foreign country.[134,135] Questions of status are determined according to the law of the corporation's domicile and the domicile of a corporation is the country in which the corporation was incorporated.[136]

57. The law of the domicile of the corporation determines such matters as the existence of the corporation, the legal personality of the corporation, the liability of the corporation's shareholders, which persons are entitled to act on behalf of the corporation, the capacity of the corporation, and its powers.[137] Whether a particular corporation has been amalgamated with another corporation also depends on the law of the domicile of the particular corporation.[138] The law of the domicile of the corporation also determines the internal relationships between shareholders themselves and between shareholders and management of the corporation.[139]

58. The legal status of associations of persons, other than corporations, depends on the law of the country in which the association was formed. A separate legal existence granted to foreign partnerships and unincorporated associations by the laws of the jurisdiction in which the association was formed will be recognized even where such separate legal existence is not granted to similar associations of persons in Canada.[140]

59. The capacity of a foreign corporation to transact business in Canada will depend on the capacity and powers given to the corporation by the law of its domicile and on the constraints imposed by the laws of the jurisdiction in Canada in which the

134. For a general discussion of conflict of law rules as applied in Canada *see* J. Walker & J.-G. Castel, *Canadian Conflict of Laws*, 6th ed., (Markam, Ont.: LexisNexis Canada, 2005) Ch. 30.
135. *See* Walker & Castel, *ibid.*, at 30–31. For instance, in *CPR v. Western Union Telegraph Co.* (1889), 17 S.C.R. 151 at 155 it was noted that: '[t]he comity nations distinctly recognizes the right of foreign incorporated companies to carry on business and make contracts outside of the country in which they are incorporated, if consistent with purposes of the corporation, and not prohibited by its charter, and not inconsistent with the local laws of the country in which the business was carried on, subject always to the restrictions and burthens imposed by the laws enforced therein; for there can be no doubt that a state may prohibit foreign corporations from transacting any business whatever, or it may permit them to do so upon such proper terms and conditions as it may prescribe.'
136. *See*, for example, *Skyline Association v. Small* (1974), 50 D.L.R. (3rd) 217, affirmed 56 D.L.R. (3rd) 471 (B.C.C.A.).
137. *See* the discussion in Walker & Castel, *supra* n. 134, at 30–31 and the references therein.
138. *Ibid.*, at 30–35 and *see National Bank of Greece and Athens SA. v. Metliss*, [1957] 3 All E.R. 608 (H.L.).
139. *See*, for example, *Honsberger v. Weyburn Townsite Co.* (1919), 59 S.C.R. 281.
140. *See* James G. McLeod, *The Conflict of Laws* (Calgary, Alta: Carswell, 1983) at 455 and *See*, for example, *Yon Hellfeld v. Rechnitzer (E.) & Mayer Frere & Co.*, [1914] 1 Ch. 748 (C.A.).

corporation is carrying on business.[141] Corporations 'carrying on business' in a province or territory in Canada must also become registered or licensed in the province or territory within a period of time (usually thirty days) of commencing to carry on business in the province or territory. These registration requirements are typically enforced through a penal sanction and through constraints on unregistered corporations such as inability to maintain a legal action in the province, or acquire or hold land or any interest in land within the province.[142]

§2. Continuance

I. Import

60. Several general statutes of incorporation in Canada allow corporations incorporated in other jurisdictions to become incorporated under the particular statute. The process is referred to as 'continuance' and provisions that allow for corporations incorporated under the legislation of other jurisdictions to be 'continued' under the particular statute are commonly referred to as 'import' provisions. For instance, the CBCA provides that a corporation incorporated otherwise than under an Act of the federal Parliament may, if so authorized by the laws of the jurisdiction where it is incorporated, apply to be 'continued' under the CBCA.[143] Once the corporation completes the process of continuance it becomes a corporation to which the CBCA applies as if the corporation had been incorporated under the CBCA.[144]

61. When a corporation is continued under the CBCA rights and obligations it had prior to the continuance survive after the continuance. In particular:[145]

- the property of the corporation before the continuance continues to be the property of the corporation;
- the corporation continues to be liable for the obligations it was liable for before the continuance;
- causes of action, claims, or liability to prosecution survive the continuance;

141. *See* McLeod, *supra* n. 140, at 460–461 and Walker & Castel, *supra* n. 134, at 30–31.
142. For extra-provincial registration requirements *See,* for example, ABCA ss 276–296; BCBCA ss 375–399; MCA ss 187–199; *Extra-Provincial Corporations Act* (Ontario), R.S.O. 1990, c. E-27.
143. CBCA s. 187(1). *See also* ABCA s. 188(1); BCBCA s. 302; MCA s. 181(1); NBBCA s. 126(1); NWTBCA s. 190(1); OBCA s. 180(1); PEICA s. 85(1); QBCA ss. 288–296; SBCA s. 181(1); YBCA s. 190(1). There are no import continuance provisions under the NCA or the NSCA.
144. CBCA s. 187(5). *See also* ABCA s. 188(5); BCBCA s. 305; MCA s. 181(7); NBBCA s. 126(5); NWTBCA s. 190(4); OBCA s. 180(5); PEICA s. 85(4); SBCA s. 181(5); YBCA s. 190(5).
145. CBCA s. 187(7). *See also* ABCA s. 188(7); BCBCA s. 305; MCA s. 181(9); NBBCA s. 126(7); NWTBCA s. 190(7); OBCA s. 180(7); PEICA s. 85(5); SBCA s. 181(7); YBCA s. 190(7). Generally, the concept is that the corporation has not at any point ceased to exist but has simply continued its existence under the laws of the importing jurisdiction. Thus, arguably all the prior rights and obligations would continue to exist even if the legislation did not specifically deem this to be the case.

- civil, criminal, or administrative actions survive the continuance; and
- convictions, rulings, or orders against the corporation before the continuance can be enforced against the corporation after the continuance.

The general statutes of incorporation of several other jurisdictions set out roughly corresponding provisions.[146]

II. Export

62. Several general statutes of incorporation in Canada also allow for a corporation incorporated under the particular statute to be continued under the laws of incorporation of another jurisdiction. This type of continuance provision is commonly referred to as an 'export' provision. For instance, the CBCA provides that a corporation may be continued under the laws of another jurisdiction if:[147]

- the continuance is authorized by the shareholders;
- it is established to the satisfaction of the Director (the administrator of the CBCA) that the proposed continuance will not adversely affect creditors or shareholders of the corporation; and
- the laws of the other jurisdiction in which the corporation will be continued meet certain specified conditions.

63. Under the CBCA the continuance is approved by the shareholders when it is approved by a special resolution[148] of shareholders at a meeting for which the notice requirements of the act have been complied with.[149] With respect to approval of the continuance by shareholders, each share of the corporation carries the right to vote whether or not it otherwise carries the right to vote.[150] The shareholders are entitled

146. *See* the provisions of other statutes referred to in the notes above in this section on import continuance.
147. CBCA s. 188(1), (10). *See also* ABCA s. 189(1), (9); BCBCA s. 308–311; MCA s. 182(1), (11); NBBCA s. 127(1), (8); NWTBCA s. 191(1); OBCA s. 181(1), (9); PEICA s. 86(1), (6); QBCA ss. 297–303; SBCA s. 182(1), (9); YBCA s. 191(1), (9). There are no export continuance provisions under the NCA or the NSCA.
148. A 'special resolution' is a resolution passed by not less than two-thirds of the votes cast by the shareholders who voted in respect of the resolution or which is signed by all the shareholders entitled to vote on the resolution [CBCA s. 2(1)].
149. CBCA s. 188(3), (5). *See also* ABCA s. 189(2), (4); BCBCA s. 308(2); MCA s. 182(4), (6); NBBCA s. 127(2), (4); NWTBCA s. 191(4); OBCA s. 181(2), (3); PEICA s. 86(2); SBCA s. 182(3), (5); YBCA s. 191(2), (4). Notice requirements for meetings are discussed *infra* para. 176.
150. CBCA s. 188(4). *See also* ABCA s. 189(3); MCA s. 182(5); NBBCA s. 127(3); NWTBCA s. 191(4); SBCA s. 182(4); YBCA s. 191(3). If the articles of incorporation will be altered in the process of the continuance in a way that prejudicially affects the rights of the shares of a particular class or series then the holders of the shares of the particular class or series will be entitled to vote separately as a class on the resolution with respect to the continuance – *See*, for example, CBCA s. 176 and *infra* paras 134, 193, 194.

to exercise a 'dissent' right under which shareholders who dissent to the resolution in writing at or before the meeting to approve the resolution are entitled to be paid the fair value of their shares.[151] The notice of the meeting must also state that a dissenting shareholder is entitled to be paid the fair value of her or his shares.[152]

64. The specified conditions under the CBCA with respect to laws of the jurisdiction under which the corporation is to be continued are that:[153]

- the property of the corporation before the continuance will continue to be the property of the corporation;
- the corporation will continue to be liable for the obligations it was liable for before the continuance;
- causes of action, claims, or liability to prosecution will survive the continuance;
- civil, criminal, or administrative actions will survive the continuance; and
- convictions, rulings, or orders against the corporation before the continuance will be enforceable against the corporation after the continuance.

The general statutes of incorporation in several other jurisdictions set out roughly corresponding provisions with respect to the continuance of a corporation under the laws of another jurisdiction.[154]

151. CBCA s. 190(1)(d). *See also* ABCA s. 191(1)(d); BCBCA s. 309; MCA s. 184(1)(d); NBBCA s. 131(1)(e); NWTBCA s. 191(2) and s. 193; OBCA s. 185(1)(d); SBCA s. 184(1)(d); YBCA s. 193(1)(d). The PEICA does not provide dissent rights on an export continuance.
152. CBCA s. 188(3). *See also* ABCA s. 189(2); MCA s. 182(4); NBBCA s. 127(2); NWTBCA s. 191(2); OBCA s. 181(2); SBCA s. 182(3); YBCA s. 191(2).
153. CBCA s. 188(10). *See also* ABCA s. 189(9); BCBCA s. 310; MCA s. 182(11); NBBCA s. 127(8); NWTBCA s. 191(9); OBCA s. 181(9); PEICA s. 86(6); SBCA s. 182(9); YBCA s. 191(9).
154. *See* the provisions of other statutes referred to in the notes in this section on export continuance.

Chapter 6. The Labour Law Connection: Co-determination and Corporate Structure

65. There is no general requirement for, or provision for, employee co-determination within the corporate structure set out in most incorporation statutes in Canada.[155] Indeed aspects of both corporate law and labour law in Canada tend to complicate employee representation in the management of corporations.[156] As a result employee representation on the boards of directors of corporations in Canada tends to be a relatively rare phenomenon.

66. There have been occasional employee buy-outs of corporations.[157] Some start-ups of new business are also employee owned.[158] Employee owned businesses may be organized as private corporations or as employee or 'worker' cooperatives under legislation governing cooperative associations.[159] Otherwise employees may own shares in corporations through employee stock option plans, but use of these plans does not typically result in a significant increase in employee participation in the management of corporations.[160]

67. Statutes have been enacted in some Canadian jurisdictions directed at encouraging investment by employees through tax incentives.[161] Although there is evidence of an increased interest in worker cooperatives[162] there has not, as yet, been a dramatic increase in employee participation in management decision-making in Canada.

---

155. The exceptions are the ABCA s. 106(9) and SBCA s. 101(8) that allow the articles to provide for the election or appointment of directors by creditors or employees of the corporation. ABCA s. 122(4) provides that in determining whether a transaction is in the best interests of the corporation such a creditor or employee appointed director may give special, but not exclusive, consideration to the interests of those who elected her or him.
156. *See* C.S. Axworthy, '*Corporation Law as if Some People Mattered*' (1986) 36 U. Toronto L. J. 392 at 399–404; and *see* C.S. Axworthy & D. Perry, '*The Law of Worker Ownership*' (1989) 27 Osgoode Hall L. J. 647 at 648–649. In *Peoples Department Stores v. Wise* (2002), 244 D.L.R. (4th) 564 (S.C.C.) at para. 42 the Supreme Court of Canada held that directors owe their fiduciary duties to the corporation and that meant not just the shareholders but others including 'employees, suppliers, creditors, consumers, governments and the environment'. *See also infra* para. 304.
157. Some of these are noted in R.J. Long, '*The Incidence and Nature of Employee Profit Sharing and Share Ownership in Canada*' in *Industrial Relations* (Laval, Que.: Department of Industrial Relations, University of Laval, 1992) 463 at 467–468.
158. *Ibid.*
159. *Ibid.*
160. *See* Axworthy and Perry, *supra* n. 156, at 684–686.
161. These are reviewed in Long, *supra* n. 157, at 468–470.
162. *See* Long, *supra* n. 157, at 468.

Part I. Corporations (Companies)

Chapter 1. Widely Held Corporations

§1. Formation

I. Formal Requirements for Incorporation

A. Filing Requirements

68. In Canada, there are three ways to effect incorporation, namely, by articles of association, memorandum of association or letters patent. The articles of association system is the most frequently used now. The memorandum of association form of statute remains in use in Nova Scotia. The BCBCA has features that reflect an earlier memorandum of association form of statute. Articles of incorporation and memorandum of association are forms of a registration system whereby incorporation is made by deposit of documents. A letters patent, however, is granted pursuant to a discretionary act of an administrator. Until recently both Prince Edward Island and Quebec retained a letters patent approach to incorporation. Until 2011 Quebec provided for incorporation either by way of letters patent or, as under the CBCA, the filing of articles of incorporation. Legislation in Quebec that took effect in 2011 removed incorporation by way of letters patent and required existing letters patent companies to be continued within five years using the articles of incorporation approach. This has left Prince Edward Island as the only remaining jurisdiction in Canada to provide for incorporation by way of letters patent.

69. Under the CBCA, a corporation can be incorporated by one or more individuals or bodies corporate by signing and filing articles of incorporation[163] with a public officer, called the Director, together with a notice of the registered office of the corporation,[164] a notice of directors of the corporation,[165] and a Canada-biased search of name report called a 'NUANS' report (Newly Upgraded Automated Name Search).

163. CBCA s. 5.
164. CBCA ss 7 and 19.
165. CBCA ss 7 and 106.

An application for incorporation can be done electronically.[166] Forms of these documents are prescribed by regulation. Articles must contain the following information:[167]

- name of the corporation;
- the province in Canada where the registered office is to be situated;
- description of shares and classes of shares;
- restrictions, if any, on the transfer of shares;
- number of directors;
- restrictions, if any, on the business of the corporation; and
- any additional provisions permitted by-law or that can be inserted in the by-laws of a corporation.

As to additional provisions that can be inserted in the articles, one might consider including provisions for private corporations[168] to avoid the application, wholly or in part, of provincial securities acts. As most corporations in Canada are close corporations, articles may contain provisions such as:

- a limit of fifty shareholders;
- a restriction on the right to transfer shares; and
- a prohibition against any distribution of securities to the public.

A public corporation may constrain the issue, transfer, or ownership of its shares where such constraints are necessary to qualify under a prescribed Canadian law to receive licences, permits, grants, or other benefits by reason of a level of Canadian ownership or control.[169] A corporation imposing such constraints may sell the shares held by non-Canadian shareholders as if it were the owner thereof.[170] In such circumstances very specific and technical rules apply.

70. In a memorandum of association system, there is usually a Registrar, instead of a Director, who performs the same functions as the Director under the CBCA. BCBCA[171] allows one or more natural persons to form a company by entering into an incorporation agreement and filing an incorporation application.[172] The incorporation agreement must contain the agreement of each incorporator to take one or more shares of the company.[173] The incorporation application must set out the names and addresses of the incorporator, set out the proposed name for the company and contain a notice of articles.[174] The notice of articles must set out the name of the company, the name

166. *See* CBCA s. 258.1.
167. CBCA s. 6.
168. Corporate statutes in Canada generally do not use terms such as 'private corporation' or 'private company'. Instead the CBCA refers to 'distributing corporations' and 'non-distributing corporations'. In very general terms, a 'distributing corporation' is a corporation that has distributed securities to the public.
169. *See,* for example, CBCA s. 174.
170. *See,* for example, CBCA s. 46.
171. S.B.C. 2002, c. 57.
172. BCBCA s. 10(1).
173. BCBCA s. 10(2).
174. BCBCA s. 10(3).

and address of each of the directors, the registered office, the records office, the authorized share structure, and the rights and restrictions for each class or series of shares.[175] The company must have articles that set rules for its conduct.[176] The articles may set restrictions on the business the company can carry on and the powers the company can exercise.[177] The current statute in British Columbia was enacted in 2002. It repealed the former *Company Act* under which a corporation was incorporated by the filing of a memorandum and articles. The 2002 Act replaces the memorandum with a document described as a 'notice of articles'. Under the 2002 Act the company must have articles governing its conduct but, unlike the previous *Company Act*, the articles do not have to be filed. One must not confuse the articles under the BCBCA with the articles of incorporation of the CBCA. The articles under the BCBCA and Nova Scotia Companies Act (NSCA) are closer to the by-laws of a CBCA corporation.

In the letters patent approach in Prince Edward Island the 'Minister of Justice and Public Safety and Attorney General' may, by letters patent, grant a charter to one or more persons as shareholders in a company. An application signed by the applicants is sent to a government official called the 'Director of Corporations'. The application must contain the corporate name, the description of the share capital, the corporate purposes, the place in the province of its registered office, the names, and addresses of each of the applicants, the names of those who will be the first or provisional directors, and the names and addresses of the persons who have subscribed for shares.[178] The main difference between a letters patent system and the other two systems is that in articles of incorporation and memorandum of association jurisdictions the incorporation is a right whereas the obtaining of letters patent is subject to a governmental discretionary power.

B. *Notification, Registration, Incorporation, and Publicity*

71. When documents sent to the Director are in accordance with the CBCA, and accompanied by the prescribed fees (CAD 250, or CAD 200 for an online application), the Director must then register the articles and issue a certificate of incorporation.[179] First, the Director endorses on the two copies of the articles the word 'Filed' and the date of filing, issues in duplicate the appropriate certificate, and attaches it to each of the copies of the articles. The Director then registers one of the certificates with the articles and sends to the corporation the other copy of the articles and the certificate. Finally, the Director publishes in the *Canada Gazette*, or in a periodical created by the law, a notice of the issue of the certificate.[180] In memorandum of association and letters patent jurisdictions, similar steps are taken.

175. BCBCA s. 11.
176. BCBCA s. 12.
177. BCBCA s. 12(2).
178. *See*, for example, the Prince Edward Island *Companies Act*, R.S.P.E.I. 1974, c. C-14, as amended, ss 1, 4, and 6.
179. CBCA s. 8.
180. CBCA s. 262.

72. A CBCA corporation has the capacity and the power to carry on business throughout Canada.[181] Provincial statutory provisions and ordinances of the territories, however, provide that a corporation not incorporated under the laws of the province must register or obtain a licence for doing business.[182] Registration is on a form generally provided for by the province. Moreover, any extra-provincial corporation must also appoint an agent for service resident in the province for the purpose of service of process, notices, and other proceedings.[183] Penalties are imposed if a corporation fails to observe the extra-provincial registration requirements. The penalties may be in the form of a fine, or an inability to carry on business or maintain an action in the province.[184] There is some question as to the constitutional validity of some penalties if imposed on federal corporations when these penalties may affect the status and powers of these corporations.[185] Some statutory provisions relating to extra-provincial corporations specifically exclude federal corporations in whole or in part from the application of the statute.[186]

73. The capacity and powers of provincial corporations to carry on business outside the incorporating province are granted by the province that has conferred the incorporation, usually to the extent that the law of any jurisdiction outside the province permits it.[187] Provincial statutes recognize the right of extra-provincial corporations to carry on business in the province subject to the registration requirements noted above.

C. Contracts Made on Behalf of a Corporation (Company) Before Incorporation

74. Incorporation of a federal corporation is a right and not a privilege. Therefore, a certificate of incorporation may generally be obtained in a couple of days and sometimes less (possibly in as little as a few hours). However, there may be circumstances in which it is useful to enter into contracts prior to incorporation ('pre-incorporation contracts'). Section 14 of the CBCA recognizes the validity of pre-incorporation contracts and sets out rules as to the liability of promoters and the corporation with respect to the pre-incorporation contracts once the corporation comes into existence.

75. A promoter who enters into, or purports to enter into, a written contract on behalf of a corporation before it comes into existence is bound by (and entitled to the benefit of) that contract[188] unless there is an express clause in the contract to the contrary.[189] The corporation may, within a reasonable time after it becomes incorporated, adopt the written contract and be bound by it.[190] When the corporation so adopts the

181. CBCA s. 15(2).
182. *See,* for instance, BCBCA s. 375 and NBBCA s. 196. *See also supra* para. 59.
183. *See,* for example, BCBCA ss 376(1)(b) and 386 and NBBCA s. 196.
184. *See,* for example, BCBCA ss 426(1)(b) and 428(3) and NBBCA ss 213 and 214.
185. *See,* for example, *John Deere Plow v. Wharton,* [1915] A.C. 330, 84 L.J.PC. 64 (P.C.).
186. *See,* for example, NBBCA s. 213(3).
187. *See,* for example, BCBCA s. 32 and OBCA s. 16.
188. CBCA s. 14(1).
189. CBCA s. 14(4).
190. CBCA s. 14(2).

contract, the promoter ceases to be bound by the contract unless a court decides otherwise.[191] The contract entered into by the promoter must be in written form before section 14 of the CBCA applies. In the case of oral contracts the common law prevails. Under the common law a corporation could not ratify a contract entered into on its behalf before it came into existence. Thus, it was impossible for third parties to contract with a corporation before its incorporation.[192] To make a pre-incorporation contract enforceable by or against the corporation under the common law the corporation and third party would have to enter into a new contract after the corporation came into existence through the process of incorporation.[193]

76. Even though statutory provisions with respect to pre-incorporation contracts have been adopted in most Canadian jurisdictions, there remain some differences in wording. Some provinces cover both oral and written contracts,[194] whereas others follow the CBCA model.[195] Nova Scotia and Prince Edward Island have not yet enacted statutory provisions with respect to pre-incorporation contracts and the common law rules, discussed above, still apply. The British Columbia *Business Corporations Act* takes a different approach. Like the CBCA it expressly permits a company to adopt a pre-incorporation contract, but instead of a presumption of promoter liability it deems the promoter to warrant that the company will come into existence and will adopt the contract within a reasonable period of time. It makes the promoter liable for damages for a breach of that warranty.[196]

II. Initial Subscribers

A. Number and Character of Incorporators

77. In Canadian corporate law there is no need for a minimum number of subscribers for incorporation greater than one. For instance, section 5(1) of the CBCA simply says that one or more individuals aged 18 or more, of sound mind, and not bankrupt, may be incorporators by signing articles of incorporation and sending them

191. CBCA s. 14(3).
192. *See Kelner v. Baxter*, (1866) L.R. 2 C.P. 174.
193. *See Howard v. Patent Ivory Mgf. Co.* (1888), 38 Ch. D. 156. The common law was not quite as restrictive as suggested in the short note above. A corporation might be able to take advantage of a pre-incorporation contract on the basis of several theories. For instance, it might be said that the promoter was a trustee of a chose in action in favour of the corporation as beneficiary, that the company was the assignee of rights under the contract, that an offer was made to the promoter as agent for the third party to make an offer to the company, or that the contract was a provisional contract to become binding on the incorporation of the company. The performance of the terms of the original attempted contract might allow the court to infer a subsequent contract based on the post-incorporation dealings between the corporation and the third party. If the corporation or the third party performed, or partly performed, the contract to the benefit of the other person a court might rectify the consequent enrichment applying restitutionary principles.
194. OBCA s. 21 and NBBCA s. 12.
195. *See,* for example, MBCA s. 14; SBCA s. 14; and ABCA s. 14.
196. BCBCA s. 20.

to the Director.[197] One or more bodies corporate may also incorporate a corporation under the CBCA.[198]

78. Prince Edward Island requires that any incorporator be an individual thus precluding a body corporate from being an incorporator.[199]

B. Initial Share Capital

79. When a corporation is incorporated, there is no need for an initial share capital in the corporation. Section 104 of the CBCA requires only that an organizational meeting be held at which its directors may authorize the issue of securities.

80. Incorporators must subscribe for at least one share under the BCBCA[200] and the Prince Edward Island *Company Act*.[201]

C. Contribution in Kind

81. Directors of a corporation have the power to issue shares for money or other consideration in property or past services.[202] Where the issuance is for a consideration other than money, one must determine the fair equivalent of a money consideration.[203]

82. Directors are jointly and severally liable to the corporation for the difference if the consideration received is less than the fair equivalent of money had the shares been issued for money at that time.[204]

D. Other Material Formation Requirements

83. At the issuance of a certificate of incorporation by the Director, a corporation comes into existence and may carry on business. A meeting of its board of directors must then be held to complete the internal organization. At this meeting, the directors may make by-laws, adopt forms of securities certificates and corporate records, appoint officers and an auditor, make banking arrangements, and transact any other business.[205]

84. Even if this organizational meeting is not held, a corporation may nevertheless carry on business because the CBCA provides that an act of a corporation is not invalid only because it is contrary to the corporation's articles or to the act.[206] The doctrine of constructive notice (deemed public knowledge of the corporate charter) has been abolished[207] and the indoor management rule has been codified from the case law.[208] This codified indoor management rule provides that, where a third party has contracted

197. CBCA s. 5(1).
198. CBCA s. 5(2).
199. PEICA s. 6.
200. BCBCA s. 10(2).
201. PEICA s. 6(i).
202. CBCA s. 25(1), (3).
203. CBCA s. 25(3) and (4).
204. CBCA s. 118(1).
205. CBCA s. 104(1).
206. CBCA s. 16(3).
207. CBCA s. 17.
208. CBCA s. 18.

with the corporation in good faith, the corporation cannot claim against the third party that its internal rules have not been complied with. Only Prince Edward Island has not abolished the constructive notice doctrine.

III. Essential Elements of the Legal Person

A. Registered Office

85. Every corporation must have a registered office located in Canada.[209] Incorporators must file a notice of the specific address of the registered office with the articles of incorporation.[210] The act requires a corporation to prepare and maintain corporate records (articles, by-laws, unanimous shareholders' agreement, notices of directors and place of registered office, minutes of meetings, securities register, and accounting records) at its head office or in any other place in Canada designated by its directors.[211] The registered office is important because every notice or service on a corporation may be made to the registered office as it appears on the last notice sent to the Director.[212]

86. The articles indicate the province in which the registered office is located.[213] The directors can change the address of the registered office within the province.[214] A change of the province within which the registered office is located requires an amendment of the articles.[215] A special resolution is needed to make the change.[216] The articles of amendment are then sent to the Director who issues a certificate of amendment.[217] The fees payable upon delivery of articles of amendment are CAD 200.[218]

87. The registered office of a provincial corporation must be located inside the incorporating province.[219] A directors' resolution with a notice of the change to the government is usually sufficient.[220] The CBCA now allows the directors to change the place of the registered office within the province that the articles say the registered office is to be situated.[221] In Yukon, directors may change the registered office by

209. CBCA s. 6(1)(b) and s. 19.
210. CBCA s. 19(2).
211. CBCA s. 20(1).
212. CBCA s. 254.
213. CBCA s. 6(1)(b).
214. CBCA s. 19(3).
215. CBCA s. 173(1)(b).
216. A special resolution requires the approval of two-thirds of the votes cast (*see* CBCA s. 2(1)). In some jurisdictions the special resolution requires more than a two-thirds majority (*See,* for example, NSCA s. 87 where three-quarters of the votes cast is required for approval).
217. CBCA ss 177–178.
218. As to the procedure to be followed by the Director, *see* para. 71.
219. *See,* for example, BCBCA s. 34; OBCA s. 14(1); and NBBCA s. 17(1).
220. *See,* for example, NSCA s. 79.
221. CBCA s. 19(3).

passing a resolution with respect to the change and sending a notice of the change to the Registrar.[222]

B. *Name*

88. The corporate name is the only real source of delay in the incorporation process. This problem can, however, be solved, except in Nova Scotia and Prince Edward Island, by the choice of a designating number assigned to a corporation by the Registrar (or, under the CBCA the Director).[223] The choice of a business name may be the most difficult part of an incorporation. Incorporators may refer the question to a specialized search house. In any case, the Director requires that articles be accompanied by a computerized name search under the NUANS system, which must be dated not more than ninety days prior to the receipt of the articles. If for any reason an interested party is not ready to file the articles, a name may be reserved for up to ninety days for an intended corporation or for a corporation about to change its name.[224]

89. The following is a brief overview of the main rules set out in the CBCA, or regulations under the CBCA, with respect to the choice of a corporate name. A name must include an expression or a term such as corporation or limited (or an abbreviation or the French equivalent) to reflect the limited liability of the members of a corporation.[225] A corporate name may be in English, French or a combined English and French form.[226] A name can neither be a prohibited name nor can a name be deceptively misdescriptive according to the rules prescribed by regulation.[227] It cannot be confusingly similar to a trademark or another business name.[228] There will be confusion, *inter alia*, if the name is likely to lead to the inference that the business carried on by the corporation is connected with the business of another corporation or sponsored, controlled, or affiliated with a political, academic, or professional organization when such is not the case. A few names such as 'United Nations', 'Royal Canadian Mounted Police', and 'Parliament Hill' are prohibited in a corporate name.[229] As for deciding if a corporate name is confusing with a trademark, official mark, or trade name, regard must be had to the circumstances.[230] These circumstances, among others, include the inherent distinctiveness of the name, the length of time the name has been used, the nature of the goods or services, the degree of resemblance between the names, and the geographical area of use.[231] Moreover, a name must be distinctive. In other words, it cannot be too general, only descriptive of goods or services provided, or primarily or only a family name or geographic name used alone.[232]

222. YBCA s. 22.
223. CBCA s. 11(2).
224. CBCA s. 11(1).
225. CBCA s. 10(1).
226. CBCA s. 10(3).
227. CBCA s. 12(1).
228. CBCA Regulations s. 18.
229. CBCA Regulations s. 25.
230. CBCA Regulations s. 19.
231. CBCA Regulations s. 19.
232. CBCA Regulations s. 30.

90. A corporate name can be changed voluntarily by a corporation at any time by way of amendment of its articles following the procedure already referred to in paragraph 88 above. A change of a corporate name must comply with the rules discussed above for the choice of a corporate name. The Director has the right to require a change of corporate name where it is not in accordance with the act.[233] If the corporation does not comply with the request of the Director to change its name, then the Director may revoke its corporate name, assign a new corporate name[234] and issue a certificate of amendment.[235]

91. Section 10(5) of the CBCA requires the use of the corporate name in legible characters in all contracts, invoices, negotiable instruments, and orders for goods or services issued or made for the corporation. A corporation may be identified under a name other than its corporate name and may use different business names for its commercial enterprises but must also put its corporate name on documents as noted above.

92. In British Columbia, the Registrar can order a company to change its name if it contravenes any of the prescribed requirements for corporate names.[236] Also, section 158 of the BCBCA makes an officer or a director personally liable to indemnify persons who contract with the company and who suffer loss or damage as a result of being misled by the fact that the company did not use its name as required by the statute. To be liable, a director or an officer must knowingly permit the company not to display or use its name as it should. The CBCA only provides for a fine against the corporation in such circumstances.[237]

C. Objects Clause

93. Under most general statutes of incorporation in Canada a corporation is not required to have an objects clause. Section 15 of the CBCA provides that, subject to the act, a corporation has the rights, powers, and privileges of a natural person. It also has an extraterritorial capacity to operate outside Canada so far as the law of extraterritorial jurisdictions permit.[238] It is not necessary to adopt a by-law in order to confer any particular power on a corporation or its directors.[239] These provisions are intended to abolish, or render inoperative, the doctrine of *ultra vires*.[240] Section 16(3) of the CBCA provides that any act of a corporation is not invalid by reason only that the act is contrary to its articles or the CBCA.

94. Section 6(1)(f) of the CBCA, however, authorizes a corporation to insert in its articles any restriction on the businesses it may carry on. This provision is useful for incorporators or shareholders who, for any reason, want to restrict the powers and

233. CBCA s. 12(2).
234. CBCA s. 12(5).
235. CBCA s. 13.
236. BCBCA s. 28.
237. CBCA s. 251.
238. CBCA s. 15(3).
239. CBCA s. 16(1).
240. The doctrine of *ultra vires* rendered acts not set out in the corporation's objects invalid. *See* the discussion *supra* para. 33.

the capacity of a corporation. Section 16(2) of the CBCA says that a corporation cannot carry on a business or exercise a power that it is restricted by its articles from carrying on or exercising. Section 16(3), however, provides that no act of a corporation is invalid by reason only that the act is contrary to the corporation's articles or to the act. Thus, an act of the corporation, such as the entering into of a contract on behalf of the corporation by its directors or officers, is not invalid by reason only that it contravenes the restrictions in the articles. A third party or the corporation can still enforce the contract. Persons such as shareholders may, however, still pursue an action, perhaps as a derivative action, against the directors or officers who engaged in the act contrary to the restriction.

95. The Prince Edward Island letters patent system requires that a corporation insert in its constitution its objects or purposes.[241] The *ultra vires* doctrine has, however, been held not to apply to a letters patent company so acts contrary to the objects of the company are not invalid.[242] If the company entered into a contract contrary to its objects, the contract would not for that reason alone be invalid and either the company or a party with whom the company entered into the contract could enforce it. Acts contrary to the objects of a letters patent company would, however, be beyond the authority of the directors or officers allowing an action against directors or officers who engaged in such acts. A company incorporated under the NSCA has the powers of a natural person but the memorandum can put restrictions on the objects and powers of the company and there is no equivalent of section 16(3) of the CBCA that overrides the *ultra vires* doctrine so acts by the company contrary to the restrictions in the memorandum may be *ultra vires* the company.[243] A company incorporated under the BCBCA also has the powers of a natural person and while the articles may contain a restriction on the objects or powers of the company, no act of the company contrary to such a restriction is invalid merely because the act contravenes such a restriction.[244]

96. The practice of a profession governed by a statutory licensing regime can only be carried on in corporate form if that licensing act expressly permits it.[245] Where professional corporations are permitted they are often regulated by special rules departing from general corporation statutes, especially as to the liability of professionals.

241. PEICA s. 6(c).
242. *See*, for example, *Bonanza Creek Gold Mining Co. v. The King*, [1916] 1 A.C. 566.
243. Restrictions on the objects and powers of the company may be put in the memorandum of a company incorporated under the NSCA pursuant to s. 10(a)(ii) of the NSCA. Section 26(4) of the NSCA sets out wide powers for the company and s. 26(8) says that 'subject to this Act, a company has the capacity, rights, powers and privileges of a natural person'.
244. Section 30 of the BCBCA says that a company incorporated under the BCBCA 'has the capacity and the rights, powers and privileges of an individual of full capacity'. Section 12(2)(a) allows for restrictions on the business that may be carried on by the company and on the powers that the company may exercise, but s. 33(2) says that 'no act of a company … is invalid merely because the act contravenes [such a restriction]'.
245. *See*, for example, OBCA s. 3.1.

D. Commercial or Civil Character

97. Share capital companies are, in essence, of a commercial character. For instance, section 4 of the CBCA says that the act deals with the law of 'business corporations'. Non-profit corporations are discussed above in paragraphs 35–39.

§2. Capital and Shares

I. Nominal, Issued, Paid-Up, Minimum, and Authorized Capital

A. Classes and Series of Shares and Capital Accounts

98. The CBCA does not distinguish between big and small or widely held and closely held corporations, and this is reflected in the incorporation process. As to capital, there is no statutory requirement for a minimum or authorized capital. Section 6(1)(c) of the CBCA simply states that the articles must set out classes and any maximum number of shares that a corporation is authorized to issue. Thus, there can be an unlimited authorization of share capital unless a limit on the authorized share capital is set out in the articles. As shares must be fully paid before their issuance,[246] there is no need for a distinction between paid-up capital and capital that is not fully paid up. The CBCA thus basically deals with capital accounts and stated capital accounts.

99. The capital account is the sum of each of the stated capital accounts of a corporation. There is a duty to maintain a separate stated capital account for each class and series of shares issued by a corporation.[247] To each such capital account a corporation must credit all the consideration received on the issue of each share of the class or the series related to the particular stated capital account.[248] By doing so a corporation follows a good accounting practice and all sums paid in consideration of the issuance of a share in money, goods, or past services, will be part of its capital. No dividend can be paid from any consideration received for an issuance of shares. There are a few exceptions to this requirement to add the full amount of the consideration to the stated capital account. They relate to non-arm's length transactions, amalgamations, arrangements and to bodies corporate continued under the CBCA.[249] In these circumstances, a corporation may credit only a part of the consideration received to a stated capital account.

100. A board of directors usually has the power to issue, allot, and determine the price of shares.[250] Shares are non-assessable and shall not be issued until fully paid in money, property, or past services.[251] Where issuance is for goods or past services, the consideration must be valuable in money and the value must not be less than the

246. CBCA s. 25(3).
247. CBCA s. 26(1).
248. CBCA s. 26(2).
249. CBCA s. 26(3) and (7)–(10).
250. CBCA s. 25(1).
251. CBCA s. 25(2).

fair equivalent of the money that a corporation would have received if these shares were issued for money.[252]

101. Only Quebec, Nova Scotia, and Prince Edward Island provide for the issuance of partly paid shares and directors may call on shareholders for the whole or any part of the amount unpaid with respect to shares.[253] Some jurisdictions state that no share is transferable until all payable calls have been fully paid in[254] whereas Nova Scotia gives the directors the power to refuse a transfer where all payable calls have not been paid in.[255] Shareholders remain liable for any amounts unpaid with respect to their shares.[256]

B. Alteration of Capital

102. The share capital may be altered by increasing or reducing the share capital. A stated capital account may be increased by the issuance of shares, or by the addition of an amount of money. It can be decreased by eliminating part of the capital or by reducing the number of shares.

103. Two situations may arise when a stated capital account is increased by the issuance of shares. If the number of shares of a class is unlimited, any consideration for shares issued is simply added to this stated capital account. If, however, the articles set out a maximum number of shares in that class, and all the shares have been issued or their number is insufficient for any reason, one must either make an amendment of the articles to increase the limit on the number of shares of the class that may be issued or abolish the limit on the number of shares that may be issued. A corporation may also want to add to its stated capital account any amount coming from an increase in its realizable assets. To do so its articles must be amended.

104. A decrease in a stated capital account may occur through a reduction in the maximum number of shares of a class. This can be done by way of an amendment to the articles. Section 38 of the CBCA allows a corporation to reduce its stated capital account for any purpose, provided that its articles are amended. Capital may be decreased in cases where, for instance, a corporation wants to distribute to its shareholders an amount of money not exceeding the stated capital or where this stated capital does not represent the realizable value of the assets of the corporation.

105. A corporation may accept a shareholder's gift of its own shares and then reduce its stated capital account.[257] The same rule prevails in Quebec when the donated shares are fully paid.[258] Capital may also be reduced when a corporation acquires its own shares. Unlike other reductions of capital for which an amendment of the articles

252. CBCA s. 25(3).
253. *See* QBCA s. 53; NSCA s. 48; PEICA s. 41.
254. *See* PEICA s. 47. QBCA s. 84 provides that, 'a share may not be transferred until all instalments payable up to the time of transfer have been fully paid'.
255. *See* s. 39 of the 2nd schedule of the NSCA.
256. *See* PEICA s. 56 and NSCA s. 64. QBCA ss 75–80 set out provisions for dealing with unpaid amounts on shares.
257. CBCA s. 37.
258. QBCA s. 99.

is required pursuant to section 38 of the CBCA, an amendment of the articles to reduce capital is not required in respect of an acquisition by the corporation of its own shares.

106. The CBCA relaxes the hitherto complex and rigid rule restricting the corporation from acquiring its own shares. Section 39 of the CBCA sets out rules to be followed by a corporation where it purchases, redeems, or otherwise acquires its own shares. An adjustment of a stated capital account must be made to reflect the decrease in value of the account. As shares are issued without a par value and for a consideration fixed by the board of directors which may fluctuate from issue to issue depending on the circumstances of the issue, one cannot reduce the stated value of the capital account by a particular price paid for an issue of shares. Therefore, the value of a share of a class must be fixed by a formula. This formula is the average price obtained by dividing the total amount paid for all the shares of the class by the number of shares of that class. This average price is used for adjustment of the stated capital account. The stated capital account is reduced by an amount equal to the number of shares acquired by the corporation multiplied by this average price.

107. Sections 34–36 of the CBCA govern purchases or redemptions by a corporation of its own shares. Various requirements are set out depending on the form of the acquisition. Acquisitions by the corporation of its own shares are also subject to solvency tests.[259] A purchase by a corporation of its own shares involves an agreement between the corporation and its shareholder.[260] If the solvency test is met, it is simply a matter of contract. Section 35 of the CBCA specifically refers to an acquisition of shares in the course of a settlement or compromise, to an elimination of fractional shares, to a non-assignable contract between a corporation and a director, officer, or employee by which the corporation purchases their shares and to an acquisition to comply with a right to dissent of a shareholder[261] or a court order.[262] The distinction between the requirements of section 35 of the CBCA and the general rule in section 34 of the CBCA is that the solvency test is less rigorous in the situations referred to in section 35 of the CBCA. Section 36 of the CBCA provides that the redemption price, or a formula to calculate the price, must be inserted in the corporate articles. Section 36 also sets out a solvency test. This solvency test is less rigorous than the general test set out in section 34 of the CBCA.

108. In British Columbia one finds the same categories of reduction of capital. For redemption, purchase, or acquisition of its own shares, the law is roughly the same except that the BCBCA does not go as far as the CBCA in that there is a less detailed solvency test. A company must not make a payment, or provide any other consideration, to acquire its shares if there are reasonable grounds for believing that the company is insolvent, or the making of the payment, or providing of the consideration, would render the company insolvent.[263] 'Insolvent' is defined as 'unable to pay the company's debts as they become due in the ordinary course of its business'.[264] The words 'ordinary course of its business' were intended to limit the solvency test to the payment of debts

259. Solvency tests are discussed *infra* paras 123–126.
260. CBCA s. 34.
261. CBCA s. 190.
262. CBCA s. 241.
263. BCBCA s. 74.
264. BCBCA s. 1(1).

as they come due but not requiring that assets be greater than liabilities. In Nova Scotia acquisitions by a corporation of its own shares are dealt with in the same way as in the CBCA except that a general reduction of capital may be made only with an approval of a court[265] and section 51 of the NSCA requires a special resolution of shareholders. The Prince Edward Island Companies Act (PEICA) says nothing about acquisitions by a corporation of its own shares other than a general rule as to reduction of capital which requires that a by-law be approved by a special resolution of the shareholders and that a supplementary letters patent must afterwards be issued.[266]

C. Pre-emptive Rights to Subscribe for Shares

109. A pre-emptive right of subscription is not a statutory right everywhere in Canada. Pre-emptive rights exist only in New Brunswick (except for corporations listed on a stock exchange).[267] In other jurisdictions, the law is either silent or makes pre-emptive rights optional. For instance, section 28 of the CBCA provides that if the articles so provide, no share of a class shall be issued unless the shares have first been offered to the shareholders of that class. Those shareholders have a pre-emptive right to acquire the shares on a pro rata basis according to their holding of shares of that class. The terms and price of the offer to those shareholders must be the same as the terms and the price offered to the public or other shareholders. A pre-emptive right is a limitation on the general power to issue shares which is conferred on the directors by section 25 of the CBCA. Even if set out in the articles, however, a pre-emptive right is not absolute. If shares of a class are to be issued for a consideration other than money, as a share dividend or pursuant to the exercise of a conversion privilege, option or, right previously granted, then there is no pre-emptive right.

D. Issue of Shares at a Premium and at a Discount

110. Pursuant to section 24 of the CBCA only shares without nominal or par value can be issued. Thus, under the CBCA shares with nominal or par value are not permitted. The rationale for this is that par value shares are arbitrary and misleading because an uninformed shareholder may be left with a false impression about the real value of his or her investment. No par shares give greater flexibility to a corporate financial structure and eliminate accounting problems associated with surpluses. Further, the concept of par value is neither useful nor necessary for preference or redeemable shares. With par value shares prohibited, there is no possibility for the issuance of shares at a premium or a discount, because premiums or discounts are calculated as differences between the par value and the price paid for the shares. Nevertheless, section 41 of the CBCA allows payment of a reasonable commission in consideration of a purchase or an agreement to purchase shares of a corporation. Consequently, a form of discount from the price determined by the directors may be given even with respect to no par value shares.

265. *See* NSCA s. 58.
266. *See* PEICA ss 35–36.
267. NBBCA s. 27.

111. However, the concept of par value shares is still in use in Canada. The provinces of Quebec,[268] Nova Scotia,[269] New Brunswick,[270] British Columbia,[271] and Prince Edward Island[272] provide for shares with or without nominal or par value. Under the statutes in these jurisdictions par value shares can be issued at a premium but not at a discount. Issuance of par value shares at a discount is expressly prohibited by these statutes[273] except for Prince Edward Island which allows allotment at a discounted price if it is confirmed at a shareholders' meeting.[274]

E. *Public Issue Requirements (Prospectuses) and Promoters*

112. Securities regulation is a matter of provincial jurisdiction. Every corporation intending to make a public distribution of its shares or other securities, unless entitled to rely on certain specific exemptions, must prepare a prospectus and obtain a provincial securities commission authorization (called a receipt) in each province where the shares are to be distributed. Exemptions are provided in some circumstances depending on the nature of the securities or the nature of the distribution.

113. A preliminary prospectus is submitted to a securities commission for vetting before the final prospectus is submitted. This preliminary prospectus must contain most of the information required in the final prospectus. This technique allows a corporation to announce its intent to issue shares to the public and to forward this prospectus to any person. Also, a corporation may solicit prospective subscribers although it cannot accept any undertaking on their part.

Securities regulations also provide for 'short-form' (or 'simplified') prospectuses and preliminary 'short-form' (or 'simplified') prospectuses. A short-form prospectus can be used if a corporation has satisfied certain disclosure requirements (such as the electronic filing of a current annual information form, current financial disclosure, information circulars for annual meetings, and timely disclosure) and has equity securities listed and posted for trading on the Toronto Stock Exchange, Tier 1 or Tier 2 of the TSX Venture Exchange, Aequitas NEO Exchange Inc. or the Canadian Securities Exchange. A preliminary short-form prospectus is to be submitted for vetting before submitting a final short-form prospectus. In some circumstances a shelf prospectus can also be used. A shelf prospectus is a special type of short-form prospectus. The shelf prospectus can be used to issue securities in tranches over the course of two years following the filing of the shelf prospectus.

114. A prospectus must meet the requirements of the law as to the information to be disclosed and certificates warranting the completeness and accuracy of the information must be provided. The prospectus must disclose all material facts likely to affect the value of or market price of the securities. A prospectus is a very detailed document. The information required in a prospectus generally includes such things as

268. QBCA s. 43.
269. NSCA s. 10.
270. NBBCA s. 22(1).
271. BCBCA s. 52.
272. PEICA s. 6.
273. *See* QBCA s. 52; NSCA s. 110(2); and BCBCA s. 64.
274. PEICA s. 30.

the distribution spread, the distribution plan, the use of the net proceeds from the distribution, the risk factors and the speculative nature of the enterprise if any, the capital structure of the issuer, its operations, the amount of each of the dividends paid or other distributions made by the issuer during its last three financial years, details of executive remuneration, the indebtedness of senior executives, the number of escrowed shares, any recent material contracts, and the principal holders of securities. A prospectus must also set forth the audited financial statements of the corporation for each of the last three financial years and the auditor's report. Where a material change occurs that is likely to affect the value or the market price of the securities, an amendment to a prospectus must be made. If there is a misrepresentation in any prospectus, the issuer or any participating underwriter is liable for this misrepresentation and any purchaser has a right of action for damages or may elect to exercise a right of rescission. This is so unless the securities holder had knowledge of the misrepresentation at the time of purchase.

115. A receipt for the final prospectus must be issued by securities commissions in each of the provinces where the shares are to be issued before the issuer can issue its shares to the public. Securities commissions have a discretion to refuse a receipt for a prospectus. The scope of the commission's discretion is typically prescribed by the securities act or regulations under which the commission operates. A securities commission can refuse to issue a receipt for non-compliance with the disclosure requirements. Securities commissions also have some discretion to assess the merits of the investment offered by the securities. For instance, a securities commission may refuse to give a receipt if they believe that the issuer does not appear to have the financial resources necessary to ensure the viability of its business, or if persons having a determining influence over the affairs of the corporation do not appear to have the integrity to safeguard the interests of security holders.

A warning must appear on the first page of a prospectus saying that no securities commission has in any way passed upon the merits of the securities offered in a prospectus. The distribution of securities under the prospectus must be terminated within one year from the date of the receipt for a prospectus but a distribution may be extended (usually for another year) if an updated prospectus is submitted to the requisite securities commissions.

116. The name of any promoter of an issuer or of any of its subsidiaries within the two preceding years must be indicated in the prospectus, and the prospectus must indicate the nature and amount of any consideration received by the promoter or to be received by the promoter from the issuer or any of its subsidiaries. The nature and the amount of any assets, services, or other consideration received and to be received by the issuer or any of its subsidiaries from the promoter must also be disclosed. The same rule applies where any assets have been acquired within the past two years or are to be acquired by the issuer or by any of its subsidiaries from the promoter. A securities commission may also request a promoter to complete a form whereby questions about experience, residence, professional references, previous registrations, or refusals of registrations for trading in securities, infractions of federal laws, civil proceedings, and bankruptcy are asked. Securities commissions may require that before a first public distribution a specified number of shares held by a promoter, or other person, be non-transferable by the promoter, or other person. These shares are held in escrow for a fixed period. In National Policy 46-201 the Canadian Securities Administrators have provided guidelines on the escrow of shares in initial public offerings.

117. Where a corporation wants to distribute its shares to the public in two or more provinces, it must conform to the law of each jurisdiction. This would require the filing of a prospectus in each province and the obtaining of a receipt for the prospectus, after examination, in each jurisdiction. However, Multilateral Instrument 11-102 provides a 'passport system' for multi-jurisdictional filings. If the issuer indicates on the electronic filing system ('SEDAR') that it is filing under Multilateral Instrument 11-102 the principal regulator can issue a receipt for the preliminary prospectus, and subsequently the prospectus, on behalf of the other jurisdictions participating in the passport system and in which the securities are to be distributed. Multilateral Instrument 11-202 sets out how the principal regulator will be identified. Ontario is not a party to Multilateral Instrument 11-102 but under National Policy 11-102 where a prospectus is filed in Ontario it will provide a receipt on behalf of other jurisdictions in which the prospectus is filed.

118. The system of distributing additional securities of reporting issuers requires a prospectus unless the securities are distributed pursuant to an exemption from the prospectus requirement. This may require repetition of information already published in other documents.

F. Stock Exchange Introduction Requirements

119. Before the mid-1990s there were five stock exchanges in Canada, namely the Toronto Stock Exchange (the largest stock exchange in Canada), the Montreal Stock Exchange, the Alberta Stock Exchange, the Winnipeg Stock Exchange, and the Vancouver Stock Exchange. By mergers and agreements these were reduced to two exchanges – the Toronto Stock Exchange and the Montreal Exchange. Another exchange, the Canadian Securities Exchange, began operations in 2003. A number of alternative trading systems have developed in recent years as well.

The Toronto Stock Exchange is the major exchange on which corporate shares are listed. The Montreal Exchange is a financial derivatives exchange. The Toronto Stock Exchange (TSX) has its own regulations and is subject to the jurisdiction of the provincial securities commission where it is located. A stock exchange must be recognized by the securities commission of the province in order to carry on business in that province.

120. The TSX has a main exchange (the TSX exchange) and a venture exchange (the TSX Venture exchange). The listing requirements for TSX Venture Exchange are less stringent than the TSX exchange. To list the applicant must meet criteria enacted by the stock exchange in terms of number of shareholders, liquid assets, earnings, and solvency.

121. The listing criteria vary according to the nature of the business of the corporation. For instance, the Toronto Stock Exchange lists corporations in three main categories: industrial (general), mining, or oil and gas.[275] It also has criteria for structured products (such as exchange traded funds) and capital pool companies. The usual minimum listing requirements for an industrial corporation that has been operating

275. *See* TSX Company Manual, s. 307.

profitably are: net tangible assets of CAD 2 million, adequate working capital to carry on business and pre-tax earnings from ongoing operations of at least CAD 200,000 in the immediately preceding fiscal year and pre-tax cash flow of CAD 500,000 in the immediately preceding fiscal year.[276] Notwithstanding the fact that a corporation meets the minimum requirements of a stock exchange, the stock exchange has a discretion to consider any relevant factor in assessing the merits of a listing application and may refuse to grant a listing.[277] For instance, the listing could be refused if the background and experience of the management in the context of the business of the company were considered inadequate.[278]

G. Forbidden Reductions of Capital and Acquisitions of Shares by the Corporation Itself

122. Generally in Canadian corporate law the holding by a corporation of its own shares is either prohibited or exceptional.[279] Where permitted, a corporation may hold its shares for someone in the capacity of legal representative, by way of security for a transaction entered into in the ordinary course of business[280] or, under a prescribed Canadian law, to receive licences, permits, grants, or other benefits by reason of a level of Canadian ownership or control.[281] Other cases of acquisition by a corporation of its own shares must lead to a cancellation of the shares so acquired.[282]

123. For a corporation to reduce its capital or acquire its own shares, there must be reasonable grounds to believe that the corporation is not insolvent or will not become insolvent following the reduction of capital or acquisition of shares. The solvency of the corporation is determined according to criteria set out in the CBCA. Several solvency tests are set out depending on the circumstances but there are common elements to these solvency tests. First, a corporation must be able to pay its liabilities when they become due and second, the realizable value of its assets must at least be sufficient to pay all its liabilities. The refinements in the various solvency tests are built around the second of the two above-noted tests.

124. A corporation may reduce its stated capital for any purpose so long as it is or remains solvent.[283] The solvency test provided by the CBCA in this situation is the least stringent of all the solvency tests. To reduce its stated capital, the corporation must have reasonable grounds to believe that it is able, and would remain able after the reduction, to pay its liabilities as they become due and that the realizable value of its assets will stay equal to or higher than the aggregate of its liabilities.[284]

---

276. *See* TSX Company Manual, s. 309.
277. *See* TSX Company Manual, s. 306 and s. 313.
278. *See* TSX Company Manual, s. 311.
279. A subsidiary is also not permitted to hold shares of its holding corporation – *see infra* para. 389.
280. CBCA s. 31.
281. CBCA s. 32.
282. CBCA s. 39(6).
283. Reductions of stated capital were discussed *supra* para. 104.
284. CBCA s. 38.

125. The CBCA is very flexible with respect to the acquisition by a corporation of its own shares. The only condition is the corporation's solvency.[285] The solvency test varies according to the circumstances of the acquisition. This solvency test is divided into two parts. The first one, always present, is that the corporation be able to pay its liabilities as they become due. The second test varies according to the nature of the acquisition and is based on the realizable value of the corporation's assets. The most stringent situation is where corporations generally purchase their shares,[286] in which case the realizable value of the corporation's assets must not be less than the aggregate of the liabilities of the corporation and the stated capital of all classes of the corporation's shares. As noted above,[287] section 35 of the CBCA allows a corporation, *inter alia*, to acquire its shares in specific situations such as the compromise of a debt or the fulfilment of a non-assignable contract of purchase of shares owned by a director. In these circumstances the second part of the solvency test, as to the realizable value of assets, requires that the corporation be able to pay, on a redemption of shares or liquidation of the corporation, all amounts that would be due to the holders of shares having the right to be paid prior to the holders of the shares to be acquired. Where there is a redemption of shares,[288] the second part of the solvency test, as to the realizable value of assets, requires that the corporation be able to pay, on a redemption of shares or liquidation of the corporation, all amounts that would be due to the holders of shares having the right to be paid ratably with or prior to the holders of the shares to be acquired.

126. The restrictions on the reduction of capital and acquisition of shares in the CBCA are similar to those found in all Canadian jurisdictions except in Prince Edward Island which does not have specific rules about the acquisition of shares.[289] Under the Quebec Business Corporations Act (QBCA) the solvency test for an acquisition of shares is whether 'there are reasonable grounds for believing that [the corporation] is, or would after the payment be, unable to pay its liabilities as they become due'.[290] The QBCA solvency test for a reduction of capital is similar considering whether 'there are reasonable grounds for believing that [the corporation] is, or would after the reduction be, unable to pay its liabilities as they become due'.[291]

In British Columbia, the law with respect to the redemption, purchase, or acquisition by a company of its own shares, is roughly the same as the federal law except that the BCBCA does not go as far as the CBCA in terms of the solvency requirements.[292] A court may declare that a corporation is insolvent or will become insolvent upon an acquisition of shares.[293]

285. On the acquisition by a corporation of its own shares *see supra* para. 107.
286. CBCA s. 34.
287. *See supra* para. 107.
288. CBCA s. 36.
289. *See,* for example, OBCA s. 30(2) and NBBCA s. 33(2).
290. *See* QBCA s. 95.
291. *See* QBCA s. 101.
292. *See* the discussion in para. 108 above.
293. BCBCA s. 78(2).

In Prince Edward Island, shares are subject to redemption in accordance with the provisions of issue attaching to the shares or with the consent of the holders thereof.[294]

II. Classes of Shares

127. Specific rights, privileges, restrictions, and conditions of each class or series of shares must be set out in the articles of association, memorandum of association, notice of articles, or letters patent as the case may be. Any change to these rights, privileges, restrictions, or conditions must be made by amendment of the corporate charter and with separate consent of the shareholders affected in a manner different from others.[295]

A. Bearer or Registered Form

128. Section 24(1) of the CBCA provides that shares of a corporation shall be in registered form, thereby precluding the use of bearer form share certificates. This is because bearer form share certificates were not commonly used in Canada at the time of the enactment of the CBCA. However, a foreign corporation, continued under the CBCA, may issue share certificates in bearer form if, before its continuation, its charter granted such a right to its shareholders.[296] Section 48(4) of the CBCA states that a security is in registered form if it specifies a person entitled to the security and that a transfer of the security may be recorded in a securities register. This section also provides that a security is in registered form if it bears a statement that it is in registered form. To be able to exercise rights attaching to shares a shareholder must be registered in the records of the corporation.[297]

129. Some Canadian jurisdictions still recognize share warrants,[298] namely New Brunswick[299] and Nova Scotia.[300] Share warrants may be issued to a bearer by a corporation for any of its fully paid shares. The bearer is then entitled to the shares specified in the share warrant.[301] As a bearer, by definition, is not registered in corporate records, the right to payment of a dividend is normally obtained by delivery to a corporation of a coupon or any other document detachable from the warrant.[302] A bearer of a share warrant can also be registered as a shareholder in the corporate records by the surrender of the share warrant.[303]

294. PEICA s. 88.
295. *See,* for example, CBCA ss 173 and 176; and BCBCA s. 54.
296. CBCA s. 187(9).
297. CBCA s. 51.
298. The term share warrants here refers to warrants as evidence of title to the shares as opposed to a right to buy shares (another common use of the term share warrant). *See infra* para. 142.
299. NBBCA s. 51.
300. NSCA s. 47.
301. NBBCA s. 51(1) and NSCA s. 47(1).
302. NBBCA s. 51(1) and NSCA s. 47(1).
303. NBBCA s. 51(3) and NSCA s. 47(3).

B. *Presumption of Equality of Shares and Classes of Shares*

130. In Canadian corporate law the rights of shareholders are presumed to be equal unless an inequality is created by the corporate charter. Where a corporation has only one class of shares, all the shareholders' rights are equal in all respects, including the right to vote at shareholders' meetings, to receive any dividend declared, and to receive the remaining property of the corporation on dissolution.[304] Where the articles provide for more than one class of shares, the rights, privileges, restrictions, and conditions attaching to the shares of each class must be set out in the articles.[305] Given the presumption of the equality of share rights even shares which are in separate classes will have the same rights unless specific rights for particular classes are set out in the articles. For instance, if nothing appears in the description of a particular class as to the voting rights of that class, shares of that class will have the right to vote at each meeting of shareholders. The only exception is where it is specifically provided that a particular class of shares will have voting rights to the exclusion of all other classes.

The CBCA does not list features of different classes of shares. Instead, the determination of rights and restrictions is left to drafters of the initial articles or to shareholders and the features of different classes of shares can be virtually limitless. The only requirement is that a corporation's share capital must contain the three fundamental rights: i.e., to vote, to receive dividends, and to share in the remaining assets on winding-up.[306] It is not mandatory for these three rights to be attached to any one class. For instance, a corporation could have three classes of shares, the first one with only the right to vote, the second one with only the right to receive dividends, and the third one with only the right to have the remaining assets on the dissolution.

131. In corporate jargon the terms 'common shares' and 'preference shares' are often referred to. The CBCA, however, does not make such a distinction. The use of the words 'common shares', usually refers to the fact that these shares have a right to one vote per share at a shareholders' meeting, the right to receive dividends after the payment of preferred dividends on classes of shares having preferred dividend rights and the right to get the remaining corporate assets after payment of liabilities and payments to holders of shares of classes having preference rights on liquidation. 'Preference shares' are shares with special rights or restrictions concerning voting, dividends and winding-up of a corporation.

C. *Voting Rights*

132. Unless the articles provide otherwise, every share has one vote at every meeting of shareholders.[307] As noted above, the CBCA is very flexible and authorizes a corporation to stipulate special rights or restrictions. This also applies to voting. Thus, the articles may provide for multiple voting for a class of shares or, on the other hand, may provide that the particular class of shares will have no vote at all at ordinary shareholders' meetings.

304. CBCA s. 24(3).
305. CBCA s. 24(4).
306. CBCA s. 24(4).
307. CBCA s. 140.

133. Multiple voting shares are used where promoters or a group of shareholders want to retain control over the corporation. The interests of non-voting or subordinate voting shares are protected by class voting rights[308] provided under corporate statutes and, in the case of reporting issuers,[309] by securities commission requirements that may include disclosure, formal valuation, and/or majority of the minority approval of certain transactions.[310]

134. All but one class of shares may be denied voting rights at every shareholders' meeting. Nevertheless, the CBCA makes a few exceptions in order to protect shareholders in particular circumstances. A class vote in respect of certain fundamental changes in rights and priorities is provided for by section 176 of the CBCA. Whether or not those shares usually carry the right to vote, they are entitled to a separate vote when the corporate articles are to be amended in a way that creates rights or privileges equal or superior to the shares of such a class. This is also true if this amendment alters a priority given by the articles. Other situations requiring a separate vote of a particular class, whether or not it otherwise carries the right to vote, include the increase of any maximum number of shares of a class having a preferential dividend, the removal of a right to an accrued or cumulative dividend, the granting, to any class having inferior rights to the shares of the particular class, of rights equal or superior to the shares of the particular class. The CBCA also provides for voting rights to all the shareholders, whether or not their shares otherwise carry the right to vote, where there is a proposal for an amalgamation,[311] a continuance by export,[312] an extraordinary sale, lease or exchange of all or substantially all the corporate assets other than in the ordinary course of business,[313] or a liquidation and dissolution of the corporation.[314]

135. The NSCA does not provide the above-noted special voting rights but a ratification by a court must be obtained with respect to an extraordinary sale of assets other than in the ordinary course of business.[315] Under the Newfoundland Corporations Act (NCA) an extraordinary sale not in the ordinary course of business does not require the consent of shareholders not usually having voting rights but all of them have a right to dissent and may require the acquisition of their shares by the corporation.[316] This latter right is also granted in Nova Scotia.[317] Quebec, British Columbia, Prince Edward Island, and the Northwest Territories companies statutes do not allow voting rights to shareholders not usually having such a right to vote for liquidation and winding-up of a corporation. The PEICA does not provide a voting right for any shareholder with respect to an extraordinary sale, lease, or exchange of all or substantially all the corporate assets not in the ordinary course of business.

308. *See* para. 192 below.
309. A 'reporting issuer' is an issuer of securities (such as a corporation) which has distributed securities to the public or has securities listed and posted for trading on a stock exchange.
310. *See* Multilateral Instrument 61-501 (applicable in Ontario and Quebec).
311. CBCA s. 183.
312. CBCA s. 188.
313. CBCA s. 189(3).
314. CBCA s. 211.
315. NSCA s. 26(9).
316. NCA s. 303.
317. Section 2 of the 3rd Schedule under the NSCA.

136. Subject to the foregoing, a corporation may provide in its articles that holders of some classes of shares will have the right to vote only in specified circumstances. For instance, one might give a class of preference shares a right to vote where preferential dividends are in arrears for more than a predetermined period. Occasionally a non-voting class of shares with a preferential dividend right is given the right to elect a stated number of directors if the preferential dividend goes into arrears for a specified period of time or by a specified amount. The articles may also give a specific class an exclusive right to elect a fixed number of directors and, therefore, secure representatives for this class on the board of directors.

D. Dividend Rights

137. Where the articles provide for only one class of shares, each share has an equal right to receive any dividend declared by the corporation. Similarly, where the articles do not specify differing dividend rights for different classes, each share has an equal right to receive any dividend declared by the corporation. A dividend may be declared or paid where the statutory test as to solvency is met, namely, that there are reasonable grounds to believe that the corporation will be able to pay its liabilities as they become due and that the payment of the dividend will not cause the realizable value of the corporate assets to be less than the aggregate of liabilities and stated capital of all classes.[318]

If so stipulated, dividends may be preferential or not, fixed or not, or cumulative or not. A dividend is preferential if it must be paid to a class before any amount is paid to other classes. A preference may also be established among classes. A dividend is fixed where corporate articles specify a particular amount or percentage to be paid to a class. A cumulative dividend carries forward to a subsequent period for any given period in which it is not paid. In other words, if the dividend is not paid then the fixed sum accumulates and the accumulated sum must be paid upon a subsequent declaration of dividends before any dividend can be paid in respect of shares carrying subordinate dividend rights. However, if a dividend is not cumulative, the right to claim it is lost for any year in which the corporation does not declare a dividend.

138. If a corporation uses a share capital structure which discriminates between classes with respect to the right to dividends, it is important to state in detail the rights of each class or series of shares. Even though there is a rule as to equality of rights, the case law is far from clear and an incomplete drafting may cause interpretation problems. For instance, a fixed dividend must be stipulated to be preferential because, in the absence of such a preference, the right may be meaningless. If there is no preference, the class will participate equally with other classes up to this fixed amount precluding any advantage that may have been intended by stipulating a fixed amount. However, the words fixed dividends, may either be related to a maximum or not. Whenever a maximum is specified it is important to give a preference, for this is a giving up of the right to participate equally in any dividend declared (the preferential right being given in exchange for relinquishing the right to share equally in the payment of dividends). If the fixed dividend is not intended as a maximum, it is necessary to add that the shares are entitled to participate beyond that amount because the case law

318. CBCA s. 42.

is to the effect that the shares are not otherwise entitled to participate.[319] As to a cumulative dividend right, some case law establish a presumption of a cumulative right if the corporate articles are silent.[320] Thus, if a corporation does not want to pay cumulative dividends, its articles must so state. Also, if one wishes to make dividends only partially cumulative, such as making dividends cumulative only if the profits of the corporation stay above a specified level or where the cumulative dividend is to be reduced by half if it is not declared by a specified time, then the articles must so stipulate. A corporate constitution may set out a discretionary dividend by which its board of directors may declare and allocate a dividend to particular classes of shares.[321]

E. Rights on Winding-Up

139. A preference over other classes of shares as to the repayment of capital upon a liquidation, or upon a dissolution, or winding-up, of a corporation or for any other purpose may be inserted in the articles. Whenever such a preference is established, one must indicate a method whereby the amount to be paid on those shares will be determined. Again, here it is important to determine exactly what is planned. This right is a preferential return of capital and the terms 'preferential' and 'capital' may be open to interpretation. One might provide a preference only as to a reimbursement of the amount paid for the shares without a participation in a distribution of the surplus assets after this reimbursement. The case law has, however, stated that shares are to participate in any surplus assets of the corporation if this right has not been specifically removed.[322] Furthermore, a corporation may provide in its articles for a preference for an amount not necessarily equal to the amount paid for the share. For example, it may set out a clause whereby the preference is up to twice the value of the share. A formula should also indicate what is to be considered capital. For instance, it might be an amount paid for the share, an average value of the share according to the stated capital account or the value of the share according to the corporate assets.

F. Conversion Rights

140. Shares may be issued on the basis that corporate holders may have an option to convert their shares into shares of another class according to terms set out in the articles. Usually this right is set out as a ratio at which preferred shares can be converted into common shares. These shares are often convertible until a predetermined time. A corporation may also state that the conversion will be automatic or that shares will be redeemed after some preset date. Convertible shares are useful for a corporation because the flexibility provided to the holders of such shares makes it easier to raise capital.

---

319. *International Power Co. v. McMaster University*, [1946] S.C.R. 178.
320. *See Webb v. Earle* (1875), L.R. 20 Eq. 556.
321. *R. v. McClurg*, [1990] 3 S.C.R. 1020.
322. *International Power Co. v. McMaster University*, [1946] S.C.R. 178.

G. Certificates and Share Warrants

141. Section 49 of the CBCA provides that a shareholder is entitled to a share certificate or to a non-transferable written acknowledgement of his or her right to obtain such a share certificate. Pursuant to the CBCA, a share certificate must state on its face the name of the corporation, the words 'Incorporated under the *CBCA*', the name of the person to whom it was issued, the number and class of shares, and the designation of any series that the certificate represents.[323] Furthermore, if there is more than one class of shares, a certificate shall state the rights, restrictions, and other characteristics of shares or indicate that the corporation will furnish the shareholder, on demand and free of charge, the full text of it.[324] Share certificates are negotiable instruments[325] but they cannot be issued to bearer. Section 24 of the CBCA requires shares to be in a registered form. Share certificates may, however, be endorsed in blank and this includes an endorsement to bearer.[326] Such an endorsement does not cause the certificate to be in bearer form because section 48(6) of the CBCA states that a security is in bearer form only if it is payable to bearer according to its terms and not by reason of endorsement.

142. As noted above,[327] shares must be in registered form and, therefore, share warrants are not recognized by the CBCA. The term 'warrant' is used in the Canadian securities market, but does not refer to a property right in shares. Instead, it is used to represent the fact that a holder of the warrant is entitled to buy shares of the corporation at a specific price and in a specified period of time. The warrant, by itself, is a security and can be traded on a stock exchange or on an over-the-counter market.

143. As seen earlier, some Canadian jurisdictions provide for share warrants.[328] A share warrant is not a share certificate but a document entitling a bearer to the shares specified therein. Shares may be transferred by delivery of the warrant.[329]

H. Shares in Series

144. The articles of a corporation may authorize an issue of one or more series of shares, being part of one or more classes of shares.[330] Series are a division of a class of shares. The articles may confer on the board of directors the power to fix the designation, rights, privileges, restrictions, and conditions attaching to shares of each series. There are a few limitations to this rule. The first one is that the shares of any series of the same class cannot have priority of payment as to dividends and return of capital over other series and must be shared ratably unless there is enough money to satisfy all rights of all the series of a class, including accumulated sums.[331] This means,

323. CBCA s. 49(7).
324. CBCA s. 49(13).
325. CBCA s. 48(3).
326. CBCA s. 65(5).
327. *See supra* para. 128.
328. *See supra* para. 129.
329. NBBCA s. 51(2) and NSCA s. 47(2).
330. CBCA s. 27.
331. CBCA s. 27(2).

for instance, that if a payment of a cumulative dividend cannot be made in full, each series of shares of the same class will participate pro rata in the amounts to be paid whatever the rate of dividend stipulated for any series. The second limitation is that already issued series within a class cannot be superseded as to dividends or return of capital priority by the issue of a new series within that class.[332] Therefore, new series subsequently issued cannot have dividend or return of capital paid before already issued series have been paid. Subject to the foregoing, the articles may set out different voting rights, dividend, or return of capital rates, and so on, for holders of different series of shares within the same class.

145. For issues of series, a board of directors has discretion to fix the characteristics of all series, subject to the limitations of the CBCA or those which may be inserted in the corporate articles. Once these characteristics are determined by resolution of the board of directors, it is necessary to file articles of amendment to designate the series before any of the shares can be issued.[333] No shareholders' meeting is needed to ratify the issue of a series of shares of a class. This makes the issuance of shares in series an efficient tool for corporate financing because directors may take into account the current financial state of the corporation as well as the state of the financial market for fixing, with a minimum of delay, marketable characteristics for a series.

146. In Ontario, section 25 of the Ontario Business Corporations Act (OBCA) is stricter than the CBCA as it applies the pro rata payment rule even to declared, but not paid, non-cumulative dividends and prohibits any priority as to dividends and return of capital between shares of series of the same class. The Nova Scotia *Company Act* does not regulate the issue of shares in series.

III. Transfer of Shares

A. Registration

147. If a shareholder disposes of its shares freely or in return for payment, a transferee who would like to become a registered shareholder must have those shares registered in the corporate records. Between the parties, the sale or donation is completed by endorsement of the share certificates by the transferor and delivery of the share certificates to the transferee.[334] Registration of shareholders is, however, required for the full exercise of the rights attached to shares. A corporation may treat a registered shareholder as the person exclusively entitled to vote, receive notices or dividends, and to otherwise exercise the rights and powers of a shareholder.[335]

332. CBCA s. 27(3).

333. CBCA s. 27(4).

334. CBCA ss 60 and 64.

335. CBCA s. 51(1). Provincial and territorial securities transfer legislation, discussed briefly below, contains a similar provision. *See*, for example, the *Securities Transfer Act*, SBC 2007, c. 10, s. 64 and the *Securities Transfer Act*, S.O. 2006, c. 8, s. 64.

B. Sales or Gift of Shares

148. Under the CBCA share certificates are transferable by endorsement and enables a transferee to become a registered holder without a new certificate being issued in his or her name. Where a person named in a share certificate presents the share certificate for registration, an issuer shall register the transfer if everything seems in accordance with the act.[336] The fact that a transfer comes from a sale or a gift does not matter. A corporation must usually register any person who asks to be registered if the shares are duly endorsed by an appropriate person, the endorsement seems genuine and effective, the transfer is rightful or to a bona fide purchaser and the corporation has no duty or has discharged its duty regarding adverse claims as to the registration.[337] An issuer may require an assurance that each endorsement is genuine by requiring a guarantee of the person endorsing.[338] This includes, among other things, evidence of appointment of a fiduciary, or of an administrator, or representative of a deceased person.

149. Jurisdictions across the country have passed securities transfer legislation.[339] These statutes follow a uniform *Securities Transfer Act* developed by the Uniform Law Conference of Canada[340] and are modelled on Article 8 of the US *Uniform Commercial Code*. Under these provincial and territorial securities transfer acts title to a security can be represented in a certificate (referred to as a 'certificated security') but can be represented without a certificate (referred to as an 'uncertificated security'). The provincial and territorial securities transfer acts deal with such matters as what constitute notice of an adverse claim, rules for effective endorsements, warranties that apply in securities transactions whether the securities are held directly or indirectly through one or more nominees, seizure of securities, enforceability of securities contracts, evidence in legal proceedings concerning securities, and conflict of laws. They also deal with transfers of certificated and uncertificated securities, registration of transfers, and rights of persons who hold securities indirectly through one or more nominees.

C. Stock Exchange Requirements

150. With respect to the Toronto Stock Exchange, every listed company must maintain a transfer agent in one or more of Vancouver, Calgary, Toronto, Montreal, or Halifax where all the issued securities of a listed class must be directly transferable. Transfer facilities may be maintained in more than one such city but transfer certificates must be interchangeably transferable and identical.[341] A transfer agent must keep a

---

336. CBCA s. 76(1).
337. CBCA s. 76.
338. CBCA s. 77(1).
339. *See*, for example, the *Securities Transfer Act*, SA 2006, c. S-4.5; the *Securities Transfer Act*, SBC 2007, c. 10; the *Securities Transfer Act*, S.O. 2006, c. 8.
340. *See* http://www.ulcc.ca/en/home/530-josetta-1-en-gb/uniform-actsa/securities-transfer-act/1124-securities-transfer-act.
341. *See* TSX Company Manual, s. 347.

ledger listing the names of security holders, and must also issue new certificates and cancel old certificates.[342]

151. For a stock exchange, the CBCA enacts special rules as to delivery of securities to a shareholder. Delivery is made to a shareholder in two steps. In the first step a selling broker acquires possession of the securities or there is an acknowledgement to the selling broker that the securities are held for him or her. In the second step the selling broker delivers the shares, or like shares, to the buying broker. This second step may also be made by effecting clearance of the sale in accordance with the rules of the stock exchange on which the transaction took place.[343] The buying broker may then register the shares in the corporate records in the name of the shareholder or register himself or herself as holder of the shares. In this latter registration, shares are said to be held in a 'street name' or 'street form'.

152. Publicly traded shares are now usually held in a depository institution and share transfers are recorded as entries in the books of the depository institution. Consequently, share certificates do not need to be transferred. The depository institution holds the shares as nominee for the beneficial owner. The depository will often hold the securities on behalf of a brokerage firm that, in turn, holds the securities as nominee for its clients. The Canadian Depository for Securities provides depository, settlement, and clearing services in Canada.

153. The CBCA and provincial securities laws provide that a broker cannot exercise voting rights with respect to these shares but must carry out the written instructions of the beneficial owner.[344] National Instrument 54-101 created by the Canadian Securities Administrators and adopted in every provincial and territorial jurisdiction in Canada deals with shareholder communication in the context of the largely nominee ownership of securities through a securities depository system. It provides a system for communicating with the beneficial owners of securities who object to having the issuer know of their beneficial ownership and their contact information (referred to as 'objecting beneficial owners') and also for communicating with beneficial owners of securities who do not object to the issuer knowing of their beneficial ownership and contact information (referred to as 'non-objecting beneficial owners'). For objecting beneficial owners meeting materials are sent indirectly through intermediaries. For non-objecting beneficial owners meeting materials can be sent directly.

D. *Protection of Shareholders in a 'Tender Offer' (or 'Takeover Bid')*

154. This topic is discussed below in §5.IV.

E. *Insider Trading*

155. While corporate statutes in Canada have addressed insider trading, insider trading is primarily dealt with in provincial securities legislation. The discussion that

342. *See* TSX Company Manual, s. 348.
343. CBCA s. 71(1).
344. CBCA s. 153. *See also* NI 54-101.

follows focuses, therefore, on the insider trading provisions in provincial securities acts.

Provincial securities acts provide for penal, administrative, and civil sanctions for insider trading. In 2004, a provision prohibiting insider trading was also added to the federal criminal code based on the federal criminal law power.[345] Enforcement under the federal criminal code provision is, therefore, limited to penal sanctions. The potential penal sanctions under the federal criminal provisions on insider trading are, however, significantly more substantial than the potential penal sanctions under provincial securities acts.

1. The Prohibition of Insider Trading or Informing

156. Towards the end of the 1960s the province of Ontario adopted what is now referred to as a 'person-connected' approach to the prohibition of insider trading and other provinces later followed this approach. Under the person-connected approach the legislation attempts to define the persons who are subject to a prohibition from trading when they have access to undisclosed material information. Some jurisdictions have shifted to an 'information-connected' approach that does not focus on defining persons subject to a prohibition from trading but instead more generally prohibits trading by persons who have knowledge of undisclosed material information and who knew or ought to have known that information was not publicly disclosed. While it has been suggested that an information-connected approach be considered in Canada, Canadian provinces have yet to adopt an information-connected approach. Most provincial securities acts in Canada, therefore, identify the types of persons who are subject to a prohibition of insider trading and do so by describing such persons as being in a 'special relationship' with a 'reporting issuer'. These persons are prohibited from purchasing or selling securities of the reporting issuer with knowledge of a 'material change' or 'material fact' with respect to the reporting issuer that has not been generally disclosed.[346] A person in a special relationship is also prohibited from informing others of a material change or material fact with respect to the reporting issuer.[347]

2. 'Reporting Issuer', 'Material Change', and 'Material Fact'

157. A 'reporting issuer' is generally defined as an issuer of securities (such as shares or debentures that a corporation might issue) that has issued securities under a prospectus or similar disclosure document, or that has securities listed and posted for

345. *See* S.C. 2004, c. 3, s. 5 which added s. 382.1 to the *Criminal Code*, R.S.C. 1985, c. C-46.

346. *See* ASA s. 147(2); BCSA s. 57.2(2); MSA s. 112(2); NBSA s. 147(2); NSA s. 77(1); NSSA s. 82(1); OSA s. 76(1); SSA s. 85(3). *See also* QSA s. 187 for similar but differently worded provisions.

347. *See* ASA s. 147(3); BCSA s. 57.2(3), (4); MSA s. 112(3); NBSA s. 147(4); NSA s. 77(2); NSSA s. 82(2); OSA s. 76(2); SSA s. 85(4) & (5). *See also* QSA ss 188 and 189 that are of similar effect but worded differently.

trading on a stock exchange.[348] A 'material change' is typically defined as a change in the business, operations, or capital of the issuer that would reasonably be expected to have a significant effect on the market price or value of any of the securities of the issuer.[349] A 'material fact' is typically defined as a fact that significantly affects, or could reasonably be expected to significantly affect, the market price or value of any of the securities of the issuer.[350]

3. 'Special Relationship'

158. The term 'special relationship' is given a very broad scope. It includes 'insiders', 'affiliates', and 'associates' of a reporting issuer.[351] 'Insiders' are defined as directors or officers of an issuer, a person (which includes a corporation) who (or which) has control or direction over securities carrying more than 10% of the voting rights on the issuer's outstanding securities, and includes the directors and senior officers of such a person.[352] An 'affiliate' is a parent of the issuer or a subsidiary of the issuer. Two subsidiaries of the same parent are also said to be 'affiliated'.[353] An 'associate' of an issuer is a person who is a partner of the issuer, a trust, or estate in which the issuer has a substantial beneficial interest (or for which the issuer acts as trustee), or another issuer in respect of which the issuer in question beneficially owns or controls more than 10% of the voting rights attached to outstanding voting securities of that other issuer.[354]

159. The term 'special relationship' also includes officers and employees of the reporting issuer.[355] Persons engaging in business or professional activities on behalf of the reporting issuer, and the directors, officers, and employees of those persons, are

348. *See* ASA s. 1(ccc); BCSA s. 1(1) 'reporting issuer'; MSA s. 1(1); NBSA s. 1(1); NSA s. 2(1)(oo); NSSA s. 2(1)(ao); OSA s. 1(1); Q.S.A. s. 5 'reporting issuer', and s. 68; SSA s. 2(1)(qq).

349. *See* ASA s. 1(ff); BCSA s. 1(1) 'material change'; MSA s. 1(1); NBSA s. 1(1) 'material change'; NSA s. 2(1)(w); NSSA s. 2(1)(v); OSA s. 1(1) 'material change'; SSA s. 2(1)(y). Under the QSA the term 'privileged information' is used. 'Privileged information' is defined in s. 5 of the QSA as 'any information that has not been disclosed to the public and that could affect the decision of a reasonable investor'.

350. *See* ASA s. 1(gg); BCSA s. 1(1); MSA s. 112(1); NBSA s. 1(1); NSA s. 2(1)(x); NSSA s. 1(1)(w); OSA s. 1(1); SSA s. 2(1)(z). With respect to the QSA *see supra* n. 349.

351. *See* ASA s. 9(a); BCSA s. 3(a); MSA s. 112(1) 'person or company in a special relationship with a reporting or other issuer' (a); NBSA s. 147(1) 'person in a special relationship with an issuer' (a); NSA s. 77(5)(a); NSSA s. 82(5)(a); OSA s. 76(5)(a); SSA s. 85(1)(a)(i).

352. *See* ASA s. 1(aa); BCSA s. 1(1); MSA s. 1(1); NBSA s. 1(1); NSA s. 2(1)(s); NSSA s. 2(1)(r); OSA s. 1(1); SSA s. 2(1)(w).

353. *See* ASA ss 2–4; BCSA s. 1(2)–(4); MSA s. 1(2)–(4); NBSA s. 1(2)–(4); NSA s. 2(2)–(4); NSSA s. 2(2)–(4); OSA s. 1(2)–(4); SSA s. 2(2)–(4).

354. *See* ASA s. 1(c); BCSA s. 1(1); MSA s. 1(1); NBSA s. 1(1); NSA s. 2(1)(b); NSSA s. 2(b); OSA s. 1(1); SSA s. 2(b).

355. *See* ASA s. 9(c); BCSA s. 3(c); MSA s. 1(1); NBSA s. 147(1) 'person in a special relationship with an issuer' (c); NSA s. 77(5)(c); NSSA s. 82(5)(b); OSA s. 76(5)(c); SSA s. 85(1)(a)(iii). *See also* QSA s. 189(4).

also in a special relationship with the reporting issuer.[356] Also, insiders, affiliates, and associates of a person proposing to make a takeover bid or engage in a reorganization, amalgamation, arrangement, or similar business combination with a reporting issuer are in a special relationship with that reporting issuer, as well as the directors, officers, and employees of such persons.[357] Persons engaging in business or professional activities on behalf of persons proposing to engage in a takeover or other business combinations are also included in the term special relationship as well as their directors, officers, and employees.[358]

160. Persons who know of material changes or material facts which they acquired while formerly in any of the relationships described above are also considered to be in a special relationship with the reporting issuer.[359] A potentially infinite chain of tippees is also caught under the term 'special relationship'. The term includes a person who knows of a material change or material fact with respect to a reporting issuer having acquired the knowledge from another person who is in any of the relationships described above, or from another person who received the information where it originated from a person in any of the relationships described above, and that person knew, or ought to have known, that the person communicating the information was in one of the above-noted relationships or that the information originated from a person in one of the above-noted relationships.[360]

4. Penal, Civil, and Administrative Sanctions

161. There are penal, civil, and administrative sanctions available with respect to insider trading or informing others of material inside information. The penal sanctions are imprisonment or fines. In some jurisdictions the fine can be up to three times the profit derived from insider trading.[361] A civil action for damages can be brought by a person who purchased securities of the reporting issuer from a person in a special relationship with the reporting issuer or can be brought by a person who sold securities

356. *See* ASA s. 9(b), (c); BCSA s. 3(b), (c); MSA s. 112(1) 'person or company in a special relationship with a reporting or other issuer' (b), (c); NBSA s. 147(1) 'person in a special relationship with an issuer' (b), (c); NSA s. 77(5)(b), (c); NSSA s. 82(5)(b), (c); OSA s. 76(5)(b), (c); SSA s. 85(1)(a)(ii)(iii). *See also* QSA s. 189(4).
357. *See* ASA s. 9(a)(ii), (c); BCSA s. 3(a)(ii), (iii), (c); MSA s. 112(1) 'person or company in a special relationship with a reporting or other issuer' (a)(ii), (c); NBSA s. 147(1) 'person in a special relationship with an issuer' (a)(ii), (iii), (c); NSA s. 77(5)(a)(ii), (iii), (c); NSSA s. 82(5)(a)(ii), (iii), (c); OSA s. 76(5)(a)(ii), (iii), (c); SSA s. 85(1)(a)(i)(B), (C) and (a)(iii).
358. *See* the provisions cited *supra* n. 356.
359. *See* ASA s. 9(d); BCSA s. 3(d); MSA s. 112(1) 'person or company in a special relationship with a reporting or other issuer' (d); NBSA s. 147(1) 'person in a special relationship with an issuer' (d); NSA s. 77(5)(d); NSSA s. 82(5)(d); OSA s. 76(5)(d); SSA s. 85(1)(a)(iv). *See* QSA s. 189(4) and (6) for provisions which may have much the same effect.
360. *See* ASA s. 9(e); BCSA s. 3(e); MSA s. 112(1) 'person or company in a special relationship with a reporting or other issuer' (e); NBSA s. 147(1) 'person in a special relationship with an issuer' (e); NSA s. 77(5)(e); NSSA s. 82(5)(e); OSA s. 76(5)(e); SSA s. 85(1)(a)(v). *See also* QSA s. 189(5) and (6).
361. *See*, for example, BCSA s. 155(5)(b).

of the reporting issuer to a person in a special relationship with the reporting issuer.[362] An action can also be taken against a person who informed another of an undisclosed material change or material fact while in a special relationship with a reporting issuer by a person who traded with a person who obtained the undisclosed information.[363] The reporting issuer, a security holder of the reporting issuer or a securities commission in the applicable province, can bring an action for any benefit received by an insider, associate, or affiliate from trading on, or informing with respect to, an undisclosed material fact or material change.[364] Administrative sanctions include cease trade orders and the removal of exemptions provided by the applicable securities act.[365]

5. Defences

162. Certain defences to allegations of insider trading or informing are available. Where a person in a special relationship informs another of an undisclosed material change or material fact there is a defence where such disclosure was in the necessary course of business or was necessary to effect a takeover bid, reorganization, amalgamation, arrangement, or similar business combination.[366] There is also a defence with respect to trading on, or informing of, an undisclosed material fact or material change where the accused can show that he or she reasonably believed the information had been generally disclosed.[367] In the case of a civil action for damages there is the additional defence that the plaintiff knew, or ought to have known, of the undisclosed material change or material fact.[368] There are also exemptions from the prohibition of insider trading or informing for situations in which the person who allegedly traded or informed cannot be said to have taken advantage of the information.[369]

---

362. *See* ASA s. 207(2); MSA s. 113(1); NBSA s. 157(2); NSA s. 134(1); NSSA s. 142(1); OSA s. 134(1); SSA s. 142(1); QSA s. 226. Section 136 of the BCSA allows a person to bring an action, subject to specified restrictions, to recover losses incurred in relation to a transaction where there has been a contravention of the prohibition of insider trading or informing commencing from the time of the contravention to the time of the material change or material fact is generally disclosed.
363. *See* ASA s. 207(3); MSA s. 113(2); NBSA s. 157(3); NSA s. 134(2); NSSA s. 142(2); OSA s. 134(2); SSA s. 142(2); and QSA s. 227. For the BCSA *see supra* n. 362.
364. *See* ASA ss 207(5), 208(1); BCSA ss 136.1, 137(1); MSA ss 113(4), 114 (a security holder can apply for leave to have the securities commission bring an action); NBSA ss 157(6), 158(1); NSA ss 134(4), 135(1); NSSA ss 142(4), 143(1); OSA ss 134(4), 135(1); QSA ss 228, 229, 233; SSA ss 142(4), 143(1).
365. ASA s. 198(1); BCSA s. 161(1); MSA s. 148(1); NBSA s. 184(1); NSA ss 127(1), 128; NSSA s. 134(1)(b), 134(2); OSA s. 127; QSA ss. 264, 265; SSA s. 134.
366. *See* ASA s. 147(3); BCSA s. 57.2(3)(b); MSA s. 112(3); NBSA s. 147(4); NSA s. 77(2); NSSA s. 82(2); OSA s. 76(2); QSA s. 188(2); SSA s. 85(4).
367. *See* ASA s. 147(6); MSA s. 112.2; NSA s. 77(4); NSSA s. 82(4); OSA s. 76(4); QSA ss 187(1) and 188(1); SSA s. 85(6).
368. *See* ASA s. 207(2)(b); MSA s. 113(1)(b); NBSA s. 157(2)(b); NSA s. 134(1)(b); NSSA s. 142(1)(b); OSA s. 134(1)(b); SSA s. 142(1)(b).
369. *See*, for example, ASA s. 147(5) and (6); BCSA s. 57.2(3), (4), (5) and (6); NBSA s. 147.1; Ontario *Securities Act Regulation* 1015, s. 175.

6. Insider Reporting

163. There are also insider reporting requirements. 'Insiders', defined as noted above,[370] are required to file reports within ten days of becoming an insider. They are required to disclose any direct or indirect beneficial ownership of, or control, or direction over, securities of the reporting issuer of which they are an insider.[371] Where there is a change in this direct or indirect beneficial ownership of, or control, or direction over, securities of the reporting issuer, the insider is required to file a report of the change, or changes, within ten days of the change.[372]

7. Insider Trading Provisions in Incorporation Statutes

164. As noted above, the statutes of incorporation in several jurisdictions within Canada also have provisions with respect to insider trading. For instance, the CBCA has civil liability provisions that apply where an 'insider', purchases or sells a security of the corporation with knowledge of confidential information that, if generally known, might reasonably be expected to affect materially the value of any of the securities of the corporation. A civil action for damages can be brought against the person trading on the information by the person with whom the trade was made or by the corporation for any benefit received by the insider.[373] Insiders are also prohibited from short selling securities of the corporation or directly or indirectly buying a put or selling a call with respect to any of the shares of the corporation or its affiliates.[374] The term 'insider' is broadly defined in the CBCA and generally includes the same persons that are included in the definition of 'special relationship' in most provincial securities acts (also including an infinite chain of tippees as most provincial securities acts do).[375]

165. Section 382.1 of the federal *Criminal Code* also prohibits insider trading. It is generally consistent with provincial securities act provisions in terms of what it prohibits. As with provincial securities acts, it takes a person-connected approach identifying the kinds of persons who are subject to a trading, or informing, prohibition. Like the provincial provisions, it prohibits trading on the basis of material information concerning an issuer, or any of the securities of an issuer, that has not been generally disclosed. Like the provincial provisions, it also prohibits a person with knowledge

370. *See supra* para. 158.

371. *See* ASA s. 182; BCSA s. 87(2); MSA s. 109; NBSA s. 135; NSA s. 107; NSSA s. 113; OSA s. 107(1); QSA s. 96; SSA s. 116. *See also* National Instrument 55-104 on 'Insider Reporting Requirements and Exemptions'.

372. *See* ASA s. 182; BCSA s. 87(2); MSA s. 109; NBSA s. 135; NSA s. 107; NSSA s. 113; OSA s. 107(2); QSA s. 97; SSA s. 116 and *see* National Instrument 55-104 ('Insider Reporting Requirements and Exemptions').

373. CBCA s. 131.

374. CBCA s. 130.

375. CBCA s. 131(1).

of such information from informing others of that information (often referred to as 'tipping').[376]

IV. (Mortgage) Debentures and Other Securities

A. Options and Rights

166. A corporation may issue certificates, warrants, notes, and any other title attesting that a holder has a right of conversion, an option, or a right to acquire securities of the corporation.[377] A conversion privilege, right, or option must be described in the creating title. This title of conversion may be stipulated as being transferable or not, and may be in registered or bearer form. It may be an independent and distinct right or be attached to another security from which it may be separable or not separable. As noted above,[378] a preferred share can be given a right to be converted into a common share. In a security representing a corporate debt, a conversion or any option, or right may be set out in a trust indenture or in a warrant indenture. This trust or warrant indenture will indicate in detail all terms and conditions about the rights given to the debt security.

B. Trust Indenture

167. A corporation has the right to borrow funds by any means since it generally has the capacity and the powers of a natural person.[379] Such a right to borrow is a vital part of corporate financing along with the issuance of shares. When significant sums of money are borrowed, a trust indenture is often used. A trust indenture is any deed, indenture, or instrument made by a corporation for the purpose of issuing debt obligations and which appoints a person as a trustee for the holders of the debt obligation issued.[380] A debt obligation may be a bond, a debenture, a note, or any other evidence of indebtedness or guarantee of a corporation, whether secured or unsecured. Bonds and debentures are commonly used. Bonds are usually issued in units to raise a collective sum from several lenders. They are secured by specific properties of a corporation. It is a form of long-term debt bearing a fixed rate of interest and is not usually repayable until the term expires unless an event of default specified in the indenture so provides. It is the same with debentures except that they are typically secured by a floating charge over the corporate assets (or a charge on all present and after-acquired property). Bonds and debentures may be convertible into shares at the request of a holder by following the rules set out in the trust indenture. The validity of a trust indenture is not affected

376. *See* S.C. 2004, c. 3, s. 5 which added s. 382.1 to the *Criminal Code*, R.S.C. 1985, c. C-46. For a further discussion of s. 382.1 of the *Criminal Code* and a comparison to the provisions in provincial securities acts *see* Mark R. Gillen, *Securities Regulation in Canada*, 3rd ed., (Toronto: Carswell, 2007) 375–391.

377. CBCA s. 29.

378. *See supra* para. 140.

379. CBCA s. 15.

380. CBCA s. 82(1).

by the fact that there is only one holder of all the securities issued under it. A trust indenture may be made with only one lender and then it is more a form of guarantee than a way of financing as such.

168. The CBCA regulates trust indentures with a view to providing full and fair continuing disclosure to holders in order to protect their interests. The CBCA codifies the common law. Duties are imposed on trustees to avoid conflicts of interest, act honestly in good faith with a view to the best interests of the holders of the debt obligation and exercise the care, diligence, and skill of a reasonably prudent trustee.[381] This codification is significant because under the common law these duties can be varied by the terms of the trust but no deviation from these duties is permitted under the CBCA provisions. A trustee may require evidence from the issuer relating to compliance with any condition of the trust indenture.[382] He or she has the duty to give the holders of debt obligations notice of any event of default arising under the trust indenture unless he or she reasonably believes that it is in the best interests of the holders to withhold such notice.[383]

169. Debt obligations issued under a trust indenture or otherwise are securities and thus a bond or a debenture, not in bearer form, must be registered in a securities register.[384] These securities are negotiable instruments governed by the securities transfer code of the CBCA. Where securities are issued under a trust indenture, a trustee is usually responsible for keeping the records.

170. Section 39(11) of the CBCA makes it clear that a debt obligation issued is not redeemed by reason only that the indebtedness evidenced by a security has been repaid. Section 39(12) of the CBCA adds that a corporation acquiring its debt obligation may either cancel it or reissue it for an existing or future debt. Provincial statutes contain similar rules.[385] Such rules are useful, for instance, where a corporation has a fluctuating loan such as a bank line of credit.

171. Unlike the CBCA, Quebec law does not describe rules as to powers and duties of a trustee nor rules about securities registers. This is left to practice and usual civil law contractual rules. The standard of conduct of a trustee has not been codified and, therefore, is not mandatory, so securities holders are less protected. These remarks also apply for New Brunswick, Nova Scotia, and Prince Edward Island.

172. Contracts and property matters fall within provincial powers under the term 'property and civil rights' in section 92(13) of the *Constitution Act* and thus are within the exclusive jurisdiction of each province. A trust indenture, or any other deed, securing a corporate debt must then conform to particular provincial rules about security interests, including registration of movable or immovable security.

381. CBCA s. 91.
382. CBCA ss 86 and 89.
383. CBCA s. 90.
384. CBCA s. 50(1).
385. *See*, for example, OBCA ss 43 and 44; NBBCA s. 38; and BCBCA s. 104.

§3. Shareholders, Management, and Control

I. Shareholder Control Mechanisms (Rights and Remedies)

A. *Shareholder Meetings*

1. Generally

173. Shareholders do not have day-to-day control of the running of the corporation. That power is entrusted to the managers (the directors and officers).[386] This separation of ownership and control creates a danger that the managers will use their powers to favour their own interests at the expense of the shareholders. At least in theory, shareholder meetings are thus an important mechanism for ensuring that the corporation is run by the managers (directors and officers) in the best interests of the shareholders. It is at a shareholders' meeting that shareholders elect the directors, who in turn are empowered to appoint the officers. Shareholders also appoint the auditor and approve the annual financial statements. In addition, shareholders must approve a variety of corporate 'fundamental changes', including amalgamation, sale of all or substantially all of the corporation's assets, change in the jurisdiction of incorporation, changes to the corporation's constitution, and winding-up. Shareholders may also ratify certain actions that might otherwise constitute wrongdoing by a corporate fiduciary. Further, shareholders have a right to discuss corporate business at a shareholders' meeting. These and other entitlements detailed below are designed to foster shareholder democracy and give shareholders ultimate control over the behaviour of corporate managers.

The reality, however, is that it is the managers who control the 'proxy machinery'. That is, they decide when corporate meetings are called, what issues are placed on the agenda, and what goes into the circular soliciting proxies from shareholders. Further, many individual ('retail') shareholders take little or no interest in matters of corporate governance, and either vote their proxies in favour of management nominees (or management initiatives) or simply discard their form of proxy. Traditionally, institutional investors (like banks, trust companies, pension funds, mutual funds, and insurance companies) have also taken little interest in corporate governance and have tended to sell their shareholdings when dissatisfied with management (the so-called Wall Street Rule). Thus, shareholder meetings and shareholder voting requirements have not always exerted the strictest discipline over corporate managers.

As in the US, however, institutional investors have taken a more active role in shareholder meetings and in matters of corporate governance. The result is that shareholder meetings and shareholder votes have taken on a new significance as a means for disciplining corporate managers and ensuring that the business is run in the interests of the shareholders.

386. CBCA s. 102(1) ('the directors shall manage, or supervise the management of, the business and affairs of a corporation').

2. Annual Meetings

a. The Requirement to Hold an Annual Meeting

174. Every corporation is required to have an annual meeting within eighteen months of incorporation and within fifteen months of its last annual meeting.[387] Corporate legislation requires that at least three items of business be dealt with at the annual meeting:

(1) the election of directors;[388]
(2) the appointment of the auditor;[389]
(3) shareholder approval of the corporation's financial statements and auditor's report (if there is one).[390]

Other items of business may also be dealt with at the annual meetings.[391]

b. Quorum

175. Unless the by-laws otherwise provide, a quorum of shareholders consists of holders of a majority of shares entitled to vote at the meeting, represented either in person or by proxy.[392]

c. Notice Requirements

176. Canadian corporate statutes typically require that notice of the time and place of the meeting must be sent to shareholders. The federal legislation, for example, requires that for a public corporation notice must be sent to shareholders at least twenty-one days, and not more than sixty days before the meeting.[393] A private corporation can, in its articles or by-laws, provide for a shorter notice period.[394] Notice must also be given to each director of the corporation, and to the auditor.[395] Shareholders and others entitled to notice may waive notice of the meeting, and attendance at the meeting is deemed to be a waiver unless the person attends the meeting for the purpose of objecting to the transaction of business on the ground that the meeting is not lawfully called.[396]

---

387. CBCA s. 133(1).
388. CBCA s. 106(3).
389. CBCA s. 162(1).
390. CBCA s. 155(1).
391. The CBCA indicates that all business transacted at an annual meeting, aside from the three items of business referred to above, 'is deemed to be special business' [CBCA s. 135(5)].
392. CBCA s. 139(1).
393. CBCA s. 135(1) and CBCA Regulations s. 44.
394. CBCA s. 135(1.1).
395. *Ibid.*
396. CBCA s. 136.

d. Resolution in Lieu of Meeting

177. The requirements for an annual meeting of shareholders may be satisfied by a resolution in writing signed by all the shareholders entitled to vote at an annual meeting.[397] This right is of utility only for private companies in which there are comparatively few shareholders.

3. Special Meetings

a. Special Meetings Are Discretionary

178. The corporation may also hold a special meeting at which any proper corporate business may be transacted.[398] Special meetings are typically called when there is a need to obtain shareholder approval of a corporate fundamental change, such as an amalgamation.

b. Quorum

179. The quorum for a special meeting is the same as a quorum for a general meeting.[399]

c. Notice

180. The same notice requirements apply in the case of special meetings as apply in the case of an annual meeting.[400]

d. Resolution in Lieu of Meeting

181. A resolution in writing signed by all the shareholders entitled to vote on the resolution is as valid as if it had been passed at a meeting of shareholders.[401]

4. Judicially Ordered Meetings

182. When it is impracticable to call a meeting in the normal manner (e.g., where the number of shareholders has been reduced below a quorum, or the directors cannot agree on whether to call a meeting[402]), a court may order that a shareholders' meeting be held.[403] Indeed, the court has a residual discretion to order a shareholders'

---

397. CBCA s. 142(1)(b).
398. CBCA s. 133(2). All business transacted at a special meeting is 'special business' [CBCA 135(5)].
399. *See supra* para. 175.
400. *Supra*, para. 176.
401. CBCA s. 142(1)(a).
402. *See*, for example, *Re Canadian Javelin and Boon-Strachan Coal Co. Ltd.* (1976), 69 D.L.R. (3rd) 439 (Que. S.C.).
403. CBCA s. 144(1).

meeting 'for any other reason [the] court thinks fit'.[404] In general, the most common situation for a judicially ordered meeting is where the board of directors has split into irreconcilable factions,[405] or in a small private corporation where a quarrel among shareholders has resulted in the inability to muster a quorum to hold a shareholders' meetings.[406]

5. Who May Call a Shareholders' Meeting

183. Directors are entitled to call either an annual or a special meeting of shareholders,[407] and will normally do so. Shareholders holding at least 5% of the issued voting shares of a corporation may, however, require the directors to call a meeting.[408] The exercise of this right is infrequent.

6. Shareholder Proposals

a. Nature of Shareholder Proposals

184. A shareholder is entitled to submit a proposal to the directors. So long as the proposal relates in a significant way to the business or affairs of the corporation,[409] and meets other statutory requirements,[410] the directors must submit the proposal (and a supporting statement not exceeding 500 words) to shareholders for consideration at a shareholders' meeting.[411]

---

404. *Ibid.* It is a discretion that 'should be exercised cautiously, however, given the general scheme of the CBCA, which is to repose in the directors of a corporation the general power to manage its business and affairs, including the primary responsibility for determining when shareholders will be consulted and asked to act at meetings' (*see Airline Industry Revitalization Co. v. Air Canada* (1999), 45 O.R. (3rd) 370 (S.C.) at 388). It has also been said that a narrow interpretation of the court's power to order a meeting 'reflects the courts' policy of not interfering in internal corporate affairs' (*see Montreal & Canadian Diocese of the Russian Orthodox Church Outside of Russia Inc. v. Protection of the Holy Virgin Orthodox Church (Outside Russia) in Ottawa, Inc.* (2002), 30 B.L.R. (3rd) 315 at 317 (Ont. C.A.).
405. *See*, for example, *Re Canadian Javelin and Boon-Strachan Coal Co. Ltd.* (1976), 69 D.L.R. (3rd) 439 (Que. S.C.).
406. *See*, for example, *B. Love Ltd. v. Bulk Steel & Salvage Ltd. (No. 2)* (1982), 40 O.R. (2nd) 1, 141 D.L.R. (3rd) 621. Courts are, however, reluctant to order shareholder meetings where the effect would be to favour one faction over another in a battle for control. *See*, for example, *Re Morris Funeral Service Ltd.* (1957) 7 D.L.R. (2nd) 642 (Ont. C.A.); and *Re Barsh and Feldman* (1986), 54 O.R. (2nd) 340 (Ont. H.C.).
407. CBCA s. 133.
408. CBCA s. 143.
409. CBCA s. 137(5)(b.1).
410. For example, the proposal must be submitted at least ninety days before the anniversary date of the previous annual meeting, must not be substantially the same as a similar proposal put before shareholders within the preceding five years and the proposal did not receive the prescribed minimum support at the meeting and must not be for the purposes of securing publicity (CBCA s. 137(5) and CBCA Regulations ss 49–51).
411. CBCA s. 137(1), (2), and (3) and s. 48 of the regulations under the CBCA.

b. Types of Proposals

185. In general, there are five different types of shareholder proposals. Shareholders may:

(1) make nominations for directors (although this right is restricted to shareholders holding 5% or more of the shares of the corporation (or 5% of a class of voting shares));[412]
(2) propose a change in the company's articles of incorporation (the primary constitutional document of the company);[413]
(3) propose a change in the company's by-laws (the secondary constitutional document of the company);[414]
(4) propose a liquidation and dissolution of the corporation;[415]
(5) make a proposal relating to any other proper corporate matter (the 'residual category').[416]

c. Effect of Shareholder Proposal

186. Directors nominated and elected through the shareholder proposal mechanism are validly elected directors. Similarly, where shareholders confirm a proposal to amend the articles of incorporation or by-laws, or to liquidate and dissolve the corporation, it would appear that the resolution is binding upon the directors. There is doubt, however, as to the effect of a shareholder proposal in the residual category. Because Canadian corporate law statutes give the directors the power to manage the business and affairs of the corporation,[417] it would appear that a proposal falling in this category constitutes only a recommendation to the directors, and that the directors may, but need not follow such recommendation.

d. Frequency and Success Rate of Shareholder Proposals

187. Shareholder proposals are a relatively infrequent occurrence. In addition, shareholder proposals routinely garner the support of only a small percentage of shareholders. The utility of the proposal mechanism in enhancing shareholder democracy has, therefore, been minimal. This may change, however, as institutional shareholders begin to use the proposal mechanism when dissatisfied with management performance (as many have done in the US).

412. CBCA s. 137(4).
413. CBCA s. 175(1).
414. CBCA s. 103(5).
415. CBCA s. 211(1).
416. *See supra* para. 184.
417. CBCA s. 102(1).

7. The Shareholder's Right of Discussion at Shareholders' Meetings

a. The Right of Discussion

188. In the federal legislation, a shareholder entitled to vote at an annual meeting may discuss at the annual meeting any matter in respect of which he/she would have been entitled to submit a proposal.[418] Some of the provincial statutes extend the right to discussion to special meetings as well.[419] Because there is also a common law right to discussion, it may be that shareholders in federal companies also have a right of discussion at special meetings.[420]

b. Right of Discussion Not Unlimited

189. Shareholders are not entitled to engage in a filibuster. While a majority of shareholders may not deny any individual shareholder her right of discussion, the majority (or the Chairperson), acting in good faith, may end discussion after a reasonable period of time.[421] The right, therefore, only protects the making of 'reasonable arguments for a reasonable time'.[422]

c. The Right of Discussion and Shareholder Democracy

190. While in theory the right of discussion is designed to further shareholder democracy, in practice its utility is limited. Relatively few shareholders take advantage of the right. Moreover, the courts have tended not to give the right of discussion an expansive interpretation.[423] In the main it has been used to ask embarrassing questions of management when corporate performance has been poor.

8. Conduct of the Chairperson at a Shareholders' Meeting

191. The Chairperson of a shareholders' meeting presides in a fiduciary capacity and must conduct the meeting accordingly. The Chair may, therefore, for example, not arbitrarily refuse to entertain discussion on a motion, or abruptly end a meeting before all business has been transacted.[424] In the latter case, the shareholders may appoint a new chair from among themselves and continue the meeting.[425]

The Chair can accept the registered shareholder as the person entitled to vote voting shares and has no obligation to go behind the legal (or registered) title to shares

418. CBCA s. 137(1)(b) limits this right to the annual meeting.
419. *See*, for example, OBCA s. 99(1)(b).
420. *See*, for example, *Wall v. London and Northern Assets Corp.*, [1898] 2 Ch. 469 (C.A.).
421. *See*, for example, *Wall v. London and Northern Assets Corp.*, [1898] 2 Ch. 469 (C.A.).
422. *Ibid.*
423. *See*, for example, *Turner v. Canadian Pacific Ltd.* (1979), 27 O.R. (2nd) 549, 107 D.L.R. (3rd) 142 (H.C.), although *see also infra* para. 191.
424. *See*, for example, *National Dwelling Society v. Sykes*, [1894] 3 Ch. 159; *Re Bomac Batten Ltd. and Pozhke* (1983), 43 O.R. (2nd) 344 (O.H.C.J.).
425. *Ibid.*

to inquire as to their beneficial ownership.[426] A Chair can also be a person who has an interest in the result of voting on a resolution at a meeting of shareholders.[427] If the Chair does have an interest in the result of voting on a resolution, the Chair must, nonetheless, act in an even-handed manner.[428]

9. Shareholder Voting Rights

a. Types of Shareholder Resolutions

192. 'Ordinary' shareholder resolutions are passed by a simple majority of shareholders voting in respect of the resolution (rather than all the shareholders of the company).[429] 'Special' resolutions must be passed by two-thirds of the voting shareholders.[430]

b. Circumstances in Which Shareholders Vote

193. Shareholders elect the directors of the company by ordinary resolution,[431] and may also cast some or all of them out of office by an ordinary resolution prior to the expiry of their terms.[432] Shareholders must also approve a variety of corporate fundamental changes by special resolution. These include amalgamation,[433] amendment to the articles of incorporation,[434] sale of all or substantially all of the assets of the company,[435] reduction of stated capital,[436] winding-up,[437] and continuance (reincorporation) in another jurisdiction.[438] Shareholders may also vote by a simple majority to 'ratify' action taken by corporate fiduciaries which might otherwise constitute an actionable wrong, although under Canadian law ratification is no longer dispositive of the issue of liability.[439]

426. *See Re Marshall* (1981), 129 D.L.R. (3rd) 378.
427. *See Blair v. Consolidated Enfield Corp.* (1993), 15 O.R. (3rd) 783.
428. On the duties of the Chair *See,* for example, *Hastman v. St. Elias Mines Ltd.*, 2013 BCSC 1069 and *Hadjor v. Homes First Society* (2010), 70 B.L.R. (4th) 101 (Ont. S.C.J.) (both of which cite with approval the Australian case of *Australian Olives Ltd. v. Stout*, [2007] FCA 2090 (Aus. F.C.)).
429. CBCA s. 2(1).
430. *Ibid.*
431. CBCA s. 106(3).
432. CBCA s. 109.
433. CBCA s. 183.
434. CBCA s. 173.
435. CBCA s. 189(3)–(9).
436. CBCA s. 38.
437. CBCA s. 211.
438. CBCA s. 188.
439. *Infra* paras 195–194, 220 and 309.

c. Shareholders Entitled to Vote

194. Generally, unless the articles of incorporation otherwise provide, each share of the corporation entitles the holder to one vote at a meeting of shareholders.[440] Frequently, the articles will in fact enfranchise some shareholders (e.g., common shareholders) but not others (e.g., preferred shareholders). Even shareholders who are not given the right to vote in the articles, however, may be given special statutory rights to vote in certain situations. Thus, for example, the federal legislation enfranchises all shareholders in connection with an amalgamation,[441] a sale of all or substantially all the assets of the corporation,[442] and a change in the jurisdiction of incorporation.[443] Further, class voting entitlements will arise when a class of shareholders stands to be affected by a corporate fundamental change in a manner different from other classes of shareholders. Thus, an otherwise non-voting class of shareholders is entitled to vote separately as a class in relation to an amalgamation,[444] a sale of all or substantially all of the assets of the corporation,[445] and amendments to the articles of incorporation that prejudice the rights of holders of the shares of the non-voting class.[446]

d. 'Majority of the Minority' Voting Entitlements

195. The common law rule of general application is that all shareholders may vote their shares to approve corporate transactions, even though they have a particular interest in the subject matter of the transaction. Thus, for example, where a director sold a steamship to the company, he was allowed to use his own votes to approve the transaction.[447] In an increasing number of contexts, however, the statutes, the securities administrators, and the courts have excluded interested shareholders from voting their shares.

e. Statutory 'Majority of the Minority' Voting Requirements

196. The Ontario legislation requires a 'majority of the minority' vote to approve a going private transaction, although this provision does not appear in the federal or other provincial legislation.[448] More generally, corporate legislation typically indicates that no provision in a resolution relieves a director or officer from the duty to comply with the act or regulations (including the fiduciary duty) or relieves him from the

440. CBCA s. 140(1).
441. CBCA s. 183(3).
442. CBCA s. 189(6).
443. CBCA s. 188(4).
444. CBCA s. 183(4).
445. CBCA s. 189(7).
446. CBCA s. 176. Provincial legislation typically contains similar requirements.
447. *Northwest Transportation Company, Limited v. Beatty* (1887), 12 App. Case 589 (EC.). *See also Pender v. Lushington* (1877), 6 Ch.D. 70.
448. OBCA s. 190.

consequences of breach.[449] These statutory provisions make a significant change in the common law entitlement of shareholders (including interested shareholders) to relieve corporate fiduciaries from liability for breach of duty. On an ad hoc basis, the courts have also sometimes invalidated (or depreciated the evidentiary weight of) shareholder approvals secured only by the votes of interested shareholders.[450]

f. Administrative 'Majority of the Minority' Voting Requirements

197. Provincial securities regulators also sometimes require a majority of the minority voting approval for 'reporting issuers' (public companies).[451] Such approval is required, for example, in connection with a 'related party transaction' in which a controlling shareholder has a special interest in the subject matter of the transaction.[452] The stock exchanges will also in some circumstances require listed companies to obtain a majority of the minority approval for certain transactions, such as the issuance of shares to a non-arm's length party or an issuance that materially affects the control of the company.[453]

g. Permitted Limitations on the Right to Vote

198. A corporation may issue non-voting shares, although it must have at least one class of voting shares.[454] Shares can carry multiple or fractional votes. Authority is divided on the issue of whether the corporation may limit any shareholder to a stated maximum number of votes.[455] There is authority, however, for the view that voting rights may not depend on the identity of the shareholder.[456] Thus, where shares carried

449. *See*, for example, CBCA s. 122(3). *See also* CBCA s. 242, which provides that shareholder approval is not fatal to the maintenance of a derivative action, oppression application, or winding-up action, although the court may take shareholder approval into account.

450. *See*, for example, *Wedge v. McNeil* (1981), 126 D.L.R. (3rd) 596 (P.E.I.S.C.), rev'd on other grounds (1982), 142 D.L.R. (3rd) 133 (P.E.I.C.A.); *Re Northwest Forest Products Ltd.*, [1975] 1 W.W.R. 724 (B.C.S.C.); *Clemens v. Clemens Bros. Ltd.*, [1976] 2 All E.R. 268 (Ch.D.). Majority of the minority voting approvals have most frequently been required in the case of 'arrangements' under corporate legislation. *See*, for example, *Re Standard Manufacturing Co. and Baird* (1984), 45 Nfld. & P.E.I.R. 159, 5 D.L.R. (4th) 697 (Nfld. T.D.).

451. The term 'reporting issuer' is defined in, e.g., ASA s. 1(ccc); BCSA s. 1(1) 'reporting issuer'; NBSA s. 1(1); NSA s. 2(1)(oo); NSSA s. 2(1)(ao); OSA s. 1(1); QSA s. 5 'reporting issuer', and s. 68; SSA s. 2(1)(qq).

452. *See* the Canadian Securities Administrators Multilateral Instrument 61-101, Part V generally and, in particular, para. 5.6 which has been adopted by the securities regulators in the provinces of Ontario and Quebec.

453. *See*, for example, TSX Company Manual, ss 601–604.

454. CBCA s. 24(4).

455. Cf. *Jacobsen v. United Canso Oil & Gas Ltd.* (1980), 11 D.L.R. 313, [1980] 6 W.W.R. 38 (Alta. Q.B.); *Jacobsen v. United Canso Oil & Gas Ltd.* (1980), 12 B.L.R. 113, 40 N.S.R. (2nd) 692 (S.C.).

456. *Bowater Canadian Limited v. R.L. Crain and Craisec Ltd.* (1987), 62 O.R. (2nd) 752 (C.A.).

ten votes per share when held by the original owner, but only one vote per share if sold, the court held that this 'step-down' in voting rights was illegal.[457]

h. 'Coattails' Attached to Non-voting Shares

199. The Toronto Stock Exchange will refuse to list any class of non-voting shares that do not have 'coattail' protection. A coattail requires that where a takeover bid is made for the voting shares and the non-voting either become convertible into the voting shares or are given an identical offer. Thus, the purpose and effect of the requirement is to ensure that any takeover premium paid to the voting shareholders is shared with non-voting shareholders.[458]

i. Cumulative Voting

200. The articles of the corporation may provide for cumulative voting for directors in which each shareholder receives votes equal to the number of votes attached to each share held times the number of directors to be elected.[459] Cumulative voting tends to ensure the representation of minority constituencies on the board of directors, but is not common in public companies.

10. The Proxy Voting System

a. Generally

201. In public companies, relatively few shareholders will appear in person at a shareholder meeting. Most shareholders who vote do so by proxy. The proxy rules are designed to foster shareholder democracy. Thus, the rules aim at ensuring that shareholders who do not attend shareholders' meetings nonetheless receive adequate information with which to vote. They are also designed to ensure that management's views and those of any dissident shareholders seeking proxies from shareholders are adequately put before shareholders prior to voting.

b. Right to Appoint a Proxy

202. The corporate statutes entitle all shareholders entitled to vote at a meeting of shareholders to vote by proxy,[460] although a proxy is only valid in respect of the meeting for which it is given.[461]

---

457. *Ibid.*
458. *See* TSX Company Manual, s. 624(l).
459. CBCA s. 107.
460. CBCA s. 148(1).
461. CBCA s. 148(3).

c. The Mandatory Solicitation Requirement

203. Management must solicit proxies from shareholders for its proposed nominees for directors and for proposed corporate initiatives,[462] although there are typically exemptions from this requirement for small (or private) companies.[463] The solicitation must be accompanied by a management proxy circular, which contains detailed information about the identities and qualifications of management nominees for director and about proposed management initiatives (including any management conflicts of interest).[464] The purpose of the mandatory solicitation and proxy circular requirements is to expose management nominees and proposed management initiatives to shareholder scrutiny.

d. The Dissident Circular Requirement

204. Any shareholder soliciting proxies from other shareholders is required to assemble a 'dissident's proxy circular', which contains detailed information about (among other things) the identity of the dissident shareholders, reasons for opposing management and any conflicts of interest on the part of the dissident shareholders.[465]

e. Meaning of 'Solicitation'

205. The corporate statutes typically define 'solicitation' to include, among other things, a request not to execute or to revoke a proxy, and communicating with a shareholder under circumstances reasonably calculated to result in the procurement, withholding, or revocation of a proxy.[466] In practice, this exposes shareholders to the danger that informal communications among shareholders for the purpose of discussing management initiatives will be construed to be 'solicitations' requiring a dissident's

462. CBCA s. 149. Section 55 of the regulations under the CBCA adopts the form for the management proxy circular set out in Form 51-102F5 of National Instrument 51-102 developed by the Canadian Securities Administrators.
463. *See*, for example, CBCA s. 149(2) (mandatory solicitation requirement does not apply to a corporation that is not a 'distributing corporation' (which, in common (non-legal) parlance, is a public corporation) and has fifty or fewer shareholders); OBCA s. 111 (mandatory solicitation requirement does not apply to a private company).
464. CBCA s. 150(1)(a).
465. CBCA s. 150(1)(b). For a public corporation s. 57 of regulations under the CBCA adopts as the form for a dissident proxy circular the information circular form set out in Form 51-102F5 of National Instrument 51-102 developed by the Canadian Securities Administrators.
466. CBCA s. 147. Contrasting views on how far this definition extends may be found in *Western Mines Ltd. v. Sheridan*, unreported, 10 Oct. 1975, B.C.S.C., and *Brown v. Duby* (1980), 28 O.R. (2d) 745 (H.C.). Some scope for shareholder communication without the requirement of a dissident's proxy circular has been provided by amending the definition of 'solicitation' to allow for: (i) a public announcement by a shareholder of how the shareholder intends to vote and the reasons for that decision, or (ii) a communication for the purposes of obtaining the number of shares required for a shareholder proposal (*see* the discussion of shareholder proposals in paras 183–188 above).

proxy circular. This has the effect of chilling inter-shareholder communications, and tends to impede, rather than advance, the achievement of shareholder democracy.

f. Reimbursement for Proxy Solicitation Expenditures

206. Management is entitled as a matter of course to have the corporation pay its proxy solicitation expenses.[467] There is no entitlement for dissident shareholders to corporate reimbursement of proxy solicitation expenses.

B. *The Statutory Derivative Action*

1. Common Law Background and Inspiration for the Statutory Derivative Action

207. At common law, where those in charge of the corporation (i.e., directors, officers, or controlling shareholders) engaged in wrongdoing at the expense of the minority, the minority often found itself with little recourse in the courts. In the 1843 case of *Foss v. Harbottle*,[468] the court ruled that where there was a wrong done to the corporation, the corporation itself was the only proper plaintiff. No action could be brought by a minority shareholder seeking redress for the wrong done to the corporation. Thus, if those in control refused to bring an action (which they might well do, if the action would be against themselves or their friends), the minority had no recourse. Over time, three exceptions to the rule developed, but they were very narrowly cast. It was held that a shareholder could sue to redress a wrong to the corporation where:

(1) the act complained of was *ultra vires* the company (i.e., exceeded the objects or powers reserved in the company's constating documents);
(2) the act in question was required to be sanctioned by more than a simple majority of shareholders; and
(3) the act constituted a 'fraud on the minority'.[469]

In addition, a shareholder could maintain a 'personal' action where the harm was done to him personally,[470] although this is not an exception to the rule in *Foss*; it merely recognizes that where the action is the shareholder's, and not the corporation's, the rule in *Foss* has no application. The 'fraud on the minority' exception to the rule in *Foss* was rarely invoked and was essentially limited to cases in which corporate assets (or in some cases corporate opportunities) were appropriated. Thus, at common law, the legal position of the minority shareholder was an unenviable one. This prompted the legal reforms discussed in the following paragraphs.

467. *See*, for example, *Peel v. London and N.W. Railway Co.*, [1907] 1 Ch. 5 (C.A.).
468. (1843), 2 Hare 461, 67 E.R. 189.
469. *Edwards v. Halliwell*, [1950] 2 All E.R. 1064 (C.A.).
470. *Ibid.*

2. The Statutory Derivative Action

208. Canadian corporate law statutes now specifically provide that in respect of any wrong to the corporation, a shareholder (or other 'complainant'[471]) may bring an action in the name of and on behalf of the corporation or any of its subsidiaries.[472] Such an action is known as a 'derivative action', and in the normal case any recovery that results from the suit is paid to the corporation rather than the suing shareholder.

3. Utility of the Derivative Action

209. Directors' and officers' duties are owed to the corporation.[473] Thus, the derivative action provides a specific statutory means for a shareholder to ensure that any breach of duty owed to the corporation by a director or officer can be remedied even if the directors decide not to sue.[474] It is thus an important means whereby fiduciary standards of conduct can be enforced.

4. Derivative Versus Personal Actions: To Whom Is the Duty Owed?

210. There is a fundamental distinction between derivative and personal actions. A derivative action arises where there is an injury to the corporation. Thus, where a duty owed to the corporation is breached, and a complainant seeks redress for the wrong, the appropriate form of the action is derivative, and any remedy will flow in favour of the corporation (rather than the shareholder bringing the suit in the name of the corporation). Since directors' and officers' fiduciary duties are normally owed to the corporation (rather than individual shareholders), breach of such duties will give rise to a derivative action. By contrast, in a personal action, the duty sued upon is owed directly to the individual suing. Thus, for example, where the corporation refuses to accept proxies validly submitted by a shareholder, this is a breach of a statutory duty to the individual shareholder, rather than the corporation, and the form of the action is personal. Any remedy will flow to the individual plaintiff.[475]

5. Derivative Versus Personal Actions: Who Suffers the Harm?

211. An alternative way of stating the difference between derivative and personal actions is that only in connection with the latter does the plaintiff suffer particular

---

471. *See infra* para. 213.
472. *See*, for example, CBCA s. 239(1). A complainant may in fact apply to bring an action, or merely intervene in an action, 'for the purpose of prosecuting, defending or discontinuing the action on behalf of the body corporate' (*see infra* para. 213). Note that a corporation is a 'subsidiary' of another corporation if the latter possesses sufficient votes to elect a majority of the board of directors (CBCA s. 2(1)).
473. On the duties of directors and officers *see infra* §3.II.C, paras 297–310.
474. The decision of whether or not to sue ordinarily belongs to the directors, as part of their mandate to manage the business and affairs of the corporation. *See*, for example, CBCA s. 102(1).
475. *See* generally *Farnham v. Fingold* (1973), 33 D.L.R. (3rd) 156 (Ont. C.A.); *Goldex Mines Ltd. v. Revill* (1973), 54 D.L.R. (3rd) 672 (Ont. C.A.).

harm not shared by other shareholders. Where the corporation refuses to accept valid proxies, for example, the shareholder whose proxies are refused suffers particular harm not shared by the other shareholders. By contrast, where the directors breach their fiduciary duty by paying themselves excessive remuneration, all shareholders suffer indirect harm from the injury to the corporation. However, none suffers a particular harm. Thus, the appropriate form of the action is derivative.

6. Overlap Between Derivative and Personal Actions

212. The courts have indicated that in some cases, either a derivative or a personal action may arise out of the same wrongdoing. Thus, for example, the Ontario Court of Appeal has indicated that violation of either a common law or statutory duty of disclosure would find either a derivative or personal action.[476] Further, in private corporations with a small number of shareholders, a wrong to the corporation committed by a shareholder or director often arises out of a personal dispute between the principals. In such cases, the courts are more likely to find that the action is personal in character, even where there is a breach of a duty formally owed to the corporation. Finally, as noted in §3.I.C below,[477] there is confusion over whether an action with a derivative character can be commenced under the oppression remedy. Many courts have allowed such actions, effectively allowing the complainant to circumvent the requirement (noted below) to obtain leave to commence a derivative action.

7. Standing to Bring a Derivative Action

213. Any 'complainant' may bring a derivative action.[478] The term complainant is defined to mean a present or former security holder of the corporation, a present or former director or officer of the corporation, the Director, and 'any other person who, in the discretion of a court, is a proper person'.[479] Holders of securities include holders of debt obligations.[480] Despite this broad definition, there are apparently no cases involving derivative actions in which the plaintiff has been anyone other than a shareholder. To some extent, this likely reflects the influence of the common law, under which non-shareholder constituencies had no standing to bring a derivative action. It also likely reflects the fact that most derivative actions are suits complaining of breach of a duty owed to the corporation by an officer or director, and courts in the past often

476. *Goldex Mines Ltd. v. Revill* (1973), 54 D.L.R. (3rd) 672 (Ont. C.A.).
477. Paragraph 225.
478. CBCA s. 239(1).
479. CBCA s. 238.
480. CBCA s. 2(1). A shareholder seeking standing to bring a derivative action does not have to have been a shareholder at the time the act that forms the basis of the complaint occurred. *See Richarson Greenshields of Canada Ltd. v. Kalmacoff* (1995), 22 O.R. (3rd) 577.

held that 'the corporation' means the shareholders, and, more recently, have held that 'the corporation' includes the shareholders.[481]

It is at least clear that the statutory grant of standing to non-shareholder constituencies was poorly thought out by the statutory draftspersons and the result is unnecessary uncertainty about who may claim standing to commence a derivative action.

8. The Leave Requirement

214. In order to bring a derivative action, a shareholder must obtain leave of a court. The leave requirement serves a number of purposes:

- it is designed to ensure that the right to bring a derivative action is not abused by opportunistic plaintiffs bringing meritless 'nuisance' suits in order to extort a settlement from the corporation (in order to avoid bad publicity, the costs and nuisance of defending the suit and others);
- it is also designed to give the court an opportunity to 'block actions to recover small amounts, particularly actions really instituted to harass and embarrass directors or officers who have committed an act which, although unwise, is not material';[482]
- it further gives the court an opportunity to consolidate similar actions brought in respect of the same alleged wrongdoing, avoiding multiple actions; and
- finally, the leave requirement was intended to ensure that the directors of the corporation have notice of the allegations of wrongdoing.

Proper notice gives the directors the opportunity to correct the source of complaint. It also gives them the opportunity to consider whether the corporation itself should commence suit (i.e., directly, rather than derivatively), and/or time to prepare a submission opposing the granting of leave. These rationales for the leave requirement are reflected in three conditions precedent for bringing a derivative action. These are:

(1) the complainant must give reasonable notice to the directors of the corporation (or its subsidiary) of her intention to seek leave to commence a derivative action, and the directors do not bring an action;
(2) the complainant must be acting in good faith; and

---

481. *See*, for example, *Bonisteel v. Collis Leather Co. Ltd.* (1919), 45 O.L.R. 195 (S.C.). In *Peoples Department Store v. Wise*, [2004] 3 S.C.R. 461, 244 D.L.R. (4th) 564 the Supreme Court of Canada indicated that directors owe their duties to 'the corporation' and 'the corporation' includes a broader set of interests than just those of shareholders. The decision of the Court stated (at para. 42) that: 'an accurate statement of the law that in determining whether [the directors] are acting with a view to the best interests of the corporation, it may be legitimate, given all the circumstances of a given case, for the board of directors to consider, *inter alia*, the interests of shareholders, employees, suppliers, creditors, consumers, governments, and the environment.'

482. R. Dickerson et al., *Proposals for a New Business Corporations Law for Canada, vol. 1*, (Ottawa: Ministry of Supply and Services Canada, 1971) at para. 482.

(3) it must appear to be in the interests of the corporation (or its subsidiary) that the action be brought.[483]

These are considered in turn.

9. The Requirement of Reasonable Notice

215. The courts have been very generous in interpreting the notice requirement. A very general description of the causes of complaint will generally suffice.[484]

10. The Requirement That the Complainant Be Acting in Good Faith

216. In general, the courts have not been particularly quick to find an absence of good faith. So long as the applicant shows a reasonable chance for success in the action,[485] and there is no ulterior motive for bringing the action (such as gaining a tactical advantage in an intra-corporate dispute[486]) the courts will find that the applicant is acting in good faith.

11. The Requirement That the Action Appears to Be in the Interests of the Corporation

217. As with the other requirements for leave, the courts have been quite generous and have not been quick to find that the action is not in the interests of the corporation. So long as the suit is not frivolous or vexatious, and has a reasonable chance of success, the courts will find that it appears to be in the interests of the corporation.[487]

12. Powers of Court in Connection with a Derivative Action

218. In connection with a derivative action the court may at any time make any order it thinks fit, including an order authorizing the complainant or any other person to control the conduct of the action, an order giving directions for the conduct of the action, or an order directing that any amount adjudged payable by a defendant in the action be paid directly to former or present security holders of the corporation.[488] The last power was given in recognition of the fact that, particularly in the context of a small private company with few shareholders, a wrong done to the company may

483. CBCA s. 239(2).
484. *See*, for example, *Re Northwest Forest Products Ltd.*, [1975] 4 W.W.R. 724 (B.C.S.C.). Some statutes are more specific about the notice that must be given. For example, the OBCA provides that the directors must have received fourteen days notice [OBCA s. 246(2)]. For a discussion of the requirements for leave to bring a derivative action *see Primex Investments Ltd. v. Northwest Sports Enterprises Ltd.*, [1995] B.C.J. No. 2262 (B.C.S.C.).
485. *See*, for example, *Appotive v. Computrex Centres Ltd.* (1981), 16 B.L.R. 133 (B.C.S.C.).
486. *See*, for example, *Vedova v. Garden House Inn Ltd.* (1985), 29 B.L.R. 236 (Ont. H.C.).
487. *See*, for example, *Re Marc-Jay Investments v. Levy* (1974), 50 D.L.R. (3rd) 45 (Ont. H.C.); *Appotive v. Computrex Centres Ltd.* (1981), 16 B.L.R. 133 (B.C.S.C.).
488. CBCA s. 240.

result in harm to a small and discrete set of plaintiffs and remedial efficacy will best be served by making an award directly to security holders. It is also in recognition of the fact that where corporate controllers are the wrongdoers, the minority suing for redress may never see the benefit of damages paid into the corporation if the wrongdoers are inclined to repeat their wrongful conduct. Finally, grant of this power to the court recognizes that sometimes it is past, rather than current security holders who are (in whole or in part) the true victims of the wrongdoing.[489]

13. Costs

219. In a derivative action, the complainant may be saddled with the expense and burden of the action, while any award is normally made to the corporation (and any benefit from the action is thus shared with all other shareholders). The potential risk to the shareholder plaintiff is large, given that in Canadian law the normal rule is that the losing side pays the costs of the winning side. Thus, there is a very real question of what incentive a shareholder has to commence a derivative action. Clearly, the cost rules are of great importance in this regard, and the statutory cost rules are designed in a number of ways to minimize the burden of suing. A complainant need not give security for costs to commence a derivative action.[490] Further, a court can at any time order a corporation to pay the complainant 'interim' costs, but the complainant may nonetheless be held accountable to repay these costs if he loses the action.[491] In addition, both at common law[492] and pursuant to statutory authorization[493] a court may award the plaintiff a partial or complete indemnity for costs against the corporation, so that the corporation pays all costs even if the derivative suit ultimately fails to bear fruit. An indemnity has, however, been awarded in only a small handful of cases involving private corporations.[494] Thus, although this power may gain importance in relation to derivative suits involving public companies, this is not yet the case.

14. Effect of Shareholder Ratification

220. Where shareholders ratify or otherwise indicate their approval of the impugned conduct, this is not a sufficient ground by itself for a court to deny leave to commence a derivative action or find against a plaintiff in a derivative action.[495] The

489. *See,* for example, *Regal (Hastings) Ltd. v. Gulliver*, [1942] 1 All E.R. 378 (H.L.).
490. CBCA s. 242(3).
491. CBCA s. 242(4). On an application for interim costs the court will assess whether there is sufficient merit to the case and whether the complainant's financial circumstances are such that but for an interim order for costs would preclude the claim from being pursued. *See Alles v. Maurice* (1992), 5 B.L.R. (2nd) 146 (Ont. Gen. Div.).
492. *Wallersteiner v. Moir (No. 2)*, [1975] 1 All E.R. 849 (C.A.). *See also* the discussion of the *Wallsteiner* case in the Canadian case of *Discovery Enterprises Inc. v. Ebco Industries Ltd.* (1999), 70 B.C.L.R. (3rd) 299 (B.C.C.A.).
493. CBCA s. 240(d).
494. *See,* for example, *Turner v. Mailhot* (1985), 50 O.R. (2nd) 561 (H.C.).
495. CBCA s. 242(1). *See also* CBCA s. 122(3).

court may, however, take such approval into account in making any order in connection with a derivative action.[496]

15. Court Approval Needed to Discontinue a Derivative Action

221. Any discontinuance or settlement of a derivative action must be approved by a court.[497] This requirement is designed to prevent what has sometimes been referred to as 'double looting'. Double looting occurs where the person bringing the derivative action accepts, in effect, a 'bribe' (which may come, for example, in the form of an attractive lawyer's fee or lucrative consulting contract) in order to settle the action on terms favourable to the defendant(s).

C. The Oppression Remedy

1. Background

222. The statutory oppression remedy was first adopted in the English *Company Act* of 1948. It was a response to the perceived inadequacy of the common law of fiduciary duties in protecting minority shareholders. In 1973, British Columbia was the first province in Canada to adopt the oppression remedy.[498] The catalyst that initiated widespread provincial adoption of the oppression remedy, however, was the federal adoption of the oppression remedy in 1975.[499] As in the UK, the purpose of the oppression remedy was to augment common law fiduciary duties in order to improve the lot of the minority shareholder.[500] In each of the provincial and federal corporation statutes, the statutory oppression remedy applies only to corporations incorporated under the particular statute in question.

2. Standing

223. There is some uncertainty as to standing to claim relief under the oppression remedy. A 'complainant' is given standing to claim relief under the oppression remedy. 'Complainant' is defined to include a present or former registered security holder (which includes a holder of a debt obligation) of the corporation or any of its affiliates, a present or former director or officer of the corporation or any of its affiliates, the Director, or 'any other person who, in the discretion of the court, is a proper person

---

496. CBCA s. 242(1).
497. CBCA s. 242(2).
498. *Companies Act*, S.B.C. 1973, c. 18, s. 221.
499. *Canada Business Corporations Act*, S.C. 1974–1975–1976, c. 33, s. 234.
500. R. Dickerson, et al., *Proposals for a New Business Corporations Law for Canada*, vol. 1 (Ottawa: Ministry of Supply and Services Canada, 1971), para. 485. In *BCE Inc. v. 6796508 Canada Inc.* (2008), [2008] 3 S.C.R. 560, 301 D.L.R. (4th) 80 the Supreme Court of Canada (at paras 45, 58, and 59) observed that the oppression remedy: (i) focuses on harm to the legal and equitable interests of a wide range of stakeholders affected by oppressive acts of a corporation or its directors; (ii) it gives a court a broad jurisdiction to enforce not just what is legal but what is fair; (iii) it is fact specific; and (iv) what is just and equitable is judged by the reasonable expectations of the stakeholders in the context and in regard to the relationships at play.

to make an application under this Part'.[501] The oppression provision itself, however, creates a cause of action only where the interests of 'any security holder, creditor, director or officer' have been interfered with.[502] Since it is a general rule of private law that only the person who suffers injury may bring an action, any complainant who is not included in the latter list of persons would appear, in fact, to have no standing under the oppression remedy. Creditors, at least, have been granted standing under the oppression provision.[503] The corporation itself has been granting standing as a 'complainant' under the oppression remedy in some cases.[504]

3. Substantive Grounds for Relief

224. The federal legislation contains the following grounds for relief:

(2) Grounds – If, on an application under subsection (1), the court is satisfied that in respect of a corporation or any of its affiliates

(a) any act or omission of the corporation or any of its affiliates effects a result,
(b) the business or affairs of the corporation or any of its affiliates are or have been carried on or conducted in a manner, or,

---

501. CBCA s. 238. The Director under the CBCA has set out the circumstances in which the Director may bring a court action under the oppression remedy in 'The Oppression Remedy Guidelines Respecting the Exercise of the Director's Discretion under s. 241 of the Canada Business Corporations Act (CBCA)' (1 Feb. 1996).

502. CBCA s. 241(2). There must be some nexus between the applicant and the harm done (*see HSBC Capital Corporation Inc. v. First Mortgage Alberta Fund (V) Inc.* (1999), 72 Alta. L.R. (3rd) 356 (Q.B.)). A bidder in a takeover bid may have standing under the oppression remedy but the bidder must show its interests have been interfered with in its capacity as a shareholder not just as a bidder. *See*, for example, *Golden Star Resources Ltd. v. IAM Gold Corp.* (2004), 49 B.L.R. (3rd) 36 (S.C.J.)). Wrongfully dismissed employees have successfully invoked the oppression remedy where they were also shareholders *and* where the loss of employment was linked to the employee's status as a shareholder (*See*, for example, *Flatley v. Algy Corp.* (2000), [2000] O.J. No. 3787 (S.C.J.); and *Clitheroe v. Hydro One Inc.*, [2002] O.J. No. 4383 (S.C.J.)).

503. *See*, for example, *Bank of Montreal v. Dome Petroleum Ltd.*, unreported, 14 Aug. 1987, summarized at (1987), 5 A.C.W.S. (3rd) 430; *R. v. Sands Motor Hotel Ltd.*, [1985] 1 W.W.R. 59 (Sask. Q.B.); and *First Edmonton Place Ltd. v. 315888 Alberta Ltd.* (1988), 60 Alta. L.R. (2nd) 122 (Q.B.). A court may allow an oppression claim where corporate conduct was engaged in during and after trial that would reasonably be expected to hinder the satisfaction, or even partial satisfaction of the judgment (*see Levy-Russell Ltd. v. Shieldings Inc.* (1998), 41 B.L.R. (2nd) 142 (Ont. Gen. Div.) aff'g (1998), 41 O.R. (3rd) 54 (Ont. Gen. Div.); and *Downtown Eatery (1993) Ltd. v. Ontario (2001)*, 54 O.R. (3rd) 161 (C.A.)). A court will not, however, routinely convert debt actions into oppression applications (*see Royal Trust Corp. of Canada v. Hordo* (1993), 10 B.L.R. (2nd) 86 (Ont. Gen. Div.); and *Greka Energy Corp. v. Northsun Energy Ltd.* (2001), 21 B.L.R. (3rd) 10 (S.C.)). Principles of standing for creditors under the oppression remedy were summarized in *Sidaplex-Plastics Suppliers, Inc. v. Elta Group Inc.* (1995), 131 D.L.R. (4th) 399 (Ont. Gen. Div.), aff'd in part (1998), 40 O.R. (3rd) 563 (C.A.).

504. *See*, for example, *Gainers Inc. v. Pocklington* (1993), 7 B.L.R. (2nd) 87 (Alta. Q.B.); *Calmont Leasing Ltd. v. Kredl*, [1993] 7 W.W.R. 428, aff'd [1995] 8 W.W.R. 179 (C.A.); and *Dylex Ltd. (Trustee of) v. Anderson* (2003), 63 O.R. (3rd) 659 (S.C.J.).

(c) the powers of the directors of the corporation or any of its affiliates are or have been exercised in a manner that is oppressive or unfairly prejudicial to or that unfairly disregards the interests of any security holder, creditor, director or officer, the court may make an order to rectify the matters complained of.[505]

In the BCE case[506] the unanimous judgment of the Supreme Court of Canada said that there are:

> two related inquiries in a for oppression: (1) Does the evidence support the reasonable expectation asserted by the claimant? and (2) Does the evidence establish that the reasonable expectation was violated by conduct falling within the terms 'oppression', 'unfair prejudice' or 'unfair disregard' of a relevant interest?

4. Overlap with Directors' and Officers' Fiduciary Duties

225. The oppression remedy may, for example, be invoked where there is conduct of the directors that is oppressive. A significant part of the common law of fiduciary duties deals with the duties of the directors.[507] Thus, there is a significant overlap between the oppression remedy and the common law of fiduciary duties. This overlap is intensified due to the fact that the conduct of the corporation's agents (e.g., officers) can be characterized as conduct of the corporation. For this reason it is now common in any action alleging breach of fiduciary duty to also allege oppression. Particularly in view of the fact that many courts have held that the oppression remedy extends to derivative causes of action[508] and the fact that the oppression remedy supplies broader substantive grounds for relief than common law fiduciary duties, the oppression remedy is gradually swallowing up the concept of fiduciary duties.[509]

5. Overlap with the Statutory Derivative Action

226. One question that has not been entirely resolved under the oppression remedy is whether a suit of a derivative character (i.e., breach of a duty owed to the company) can be pursued under the oppression remedy. The draftspersons of the oppression remedy appear to have intended that derivative suits be actionable only with leave of the court pursuant to the derivative leave provisions, except where the wrong to the company was a wrong to minority shareholders.[510] In many cases, courts permitted derivative suits to proceed under the oppression remedy without raising the

505. By comparison, the B.C. legislation makes only 'oppressive' and 'unfairly prejudicial' conduct actionable [BCBCA s. 227(2)].
506. *Supra* n. 500.
507. On the duties of directors and officers *see infra* §3.II.C, paras 297–310.
508. *See infra* para. 226.
509. *See infra* para. 226.
510. R. Dickerson, *Proposals for a New Business Corporations Law for Canada*, vol. 1 (Ottawa: Ministry of Supply and Services Canada, 1971) at para. 484.

issue. In some cases courts held that derivative suits could not be commenced under the oppression remedy,[511] while in others, courts held that they may be.[512] The latter view appeared to dominate, despite the fact that this largely rendered the provision requiring leave for a derivative action meaningless. The result was that whenever there was a breach of a duty owed to the company, counsel often commenced an application under the oppression provision in preference to seeking leave to commence an action under the derivative leave provision because broader relief is available under the oppression remedy than in connection with a derivative action and because there are broader substantive grounds for claims under the oppression remedy. In the 2015 Ontario Court of Appeal decision in *Rea v. Wildeboer*[513] there was a move to reconciling the overlap. The court in that case suggested that the oppression remedy would apply where a wrong to the corporation 'also directly affected the complainant in a manner that was different from the indirect effect of the conduct on similarly placed complainants'.[514] If, therefore, an alleged wrong to the corporation did not have a unique effect on the complainant relative to similarly placed complaints, then the appropriate means of pursuing the claim would be by way of seeking leave to bring a derivative action,

6. De Facto Fiduciary Duty of Controlling Shareholders

227. The courts have effectively used the oppression remedy to create a fiduciary duty for controlling shareholders. This issue is explored below in §3.I.D.

7. Meaning of 'Oppressive, or Unfairly Prejudicial to or That Unfairly Disregards the Interests of'

228. Although the courts have held that 'oppressive', 'unfairly prejudicial', and 'unfairly disregards the interests of' constitute separate and progressively broader grounds of liability,[515] it is the widest standard that is of greatest importance. The courts

511. *See*, for example, *Attorney General of Canada v. Standard Trust Co.* (1991), 5 O.R. (3rd) 660 (Ont Ct. J.).
512. *See*, for example, *Sparling v. Javelin International Ltd. (No. 1)*, [1986] R.J.Q. 1073 (Que. Sup. Ct.). There are competing cases in British Columbia on whether an action that is derivative in nature (in that the complainant's loss derives from the loss to the corporation) can be pursued in an oppression application. The cases are reviewed in *Pasnak v. Chura*, [2003] B.C.J. No. 1591 (B.C.S.C.) (which concluded that derivative claims may not be pursued in an oppression application).
513. 2015 ONCA 373.
514. *Ibid.*, at para. 29.
515. *See*, for example, *Re Abraham and Inter Wide Investments Ltd.* (1985), 51 O.R. (2nd) 460 (H.C.).

have consistently held that standard to be one of 'fairness',[516] although mere prejudice (or disregarding the interests of the petitioner), without unfairness, will not give rise to relief.[517] Although the courts have frequently drawn on the common law of fiduciary duties in determining whether conduct is actionable under the oppression remedy, they have repeatedly held that they are not limited to the common law, and that it should be interpreted broadly and remedially to carry out its purpose.[518] Further, at least in relation to private corporations, the courts have held that they may consider more than simply the strict legal rights of the parties, and that a violation of legitimate shareholder expectations may ground a breach of the section. In this respect, the courts have adopted the principles espoused by the House of Lords in *Ebrahimi v. Westbourne Galleries Ltd.* in which Lord Wilberforce stated that 'a limited company is more than a mere judicial entity, with a personality in law of its own: that there is room in company law for recognition of the fact that behind it, or among it, there are individuals, with rights, expectations and obligations *inter se* which are not necessarily submerged in the company structure'.[519] Although some courts have held that it is necessary to show an

516. *See*, for example, *Re Ferguson and Imax Systems Corp.* (1983), 43 O.R. (2nd) 128. Although some cases have found certain conduct not oppressive, but nonetheless unfairly prejudicial or unfairly disregarding the interests of the petitioner, it is not clear how much of a true distinction exists between the different grounds of liability. For example, in one much-quoted early English case, the court held that oppressive conduct 'should at the lowest involve a visible departure from the standards of fair dealing, and a violation of the conditions of fair play on which every shareholder who entrusts his money to a company is entitled to rely'. *Elder v. Elder & Watson Ltd.*, [1952] S.C. 49 (Scot. Sess.). This essentially enunciates the standard of 'fairness' that has come to be the common interpretation of the more broadly drafted Canadian oppression provision.
517. *See*, for example, *O'Connor v. Winchester Oil & Gas Inc.*, [1986] 2 W.W.R. 737 (B.C.S.C.); *Brant Investments Ltd. v. KeepRite Inc.* (1987), 37 B.L.R. 65 (Ont.H.C.). Some courts have said that the complainant must show bad faith where there has been no illegal act in the conduct of the affairs of the corporation (*See*, for example, *Mahoney v. Taylor* (1996), [1996] B.C.J. No. 1479 (B.C.S.C.); and *Saarnok-Vuus v. Teng* (2003), [2003] B.C.J. No. 353 (B.C.S.C.)).
518. *See*, for example, *Re Ferguson and Imax Systems Corp.* (1983), 43 O.R. (2nd) 128 (C.A.). In the *BCE* case, *supra* n. 500, the Supreme Court of Canada (at para. 58) noted that the oppression remedy 'gives a court broad, equitable jurisdiction to enforce not just what is legal but what is fair'.
519. See *Ebrahimi v. Westbourne Galleries Ltd.*, [1973] A.C. 360, [1972] 2 All E.R. 492 (H.L.) at [1972] 2 All E.R. 500. The *Embrami* reasonable expectations test has been followed by the Supreme Court of Canada in the *BCE* case, *supra* n. 500, where the importance of looking to reasonable expectations was noted (para. 56) referring to the *Ebrahimi* case (paras 60–61) and where the court added that:

> Factors that emerge from the case law that are useful in determining whether a reasonable expectation exists include: general commercial practice; the nature of the corporation; the relationship between the parties; past practice; steps the claimant could have taken to protect itself; representations and agreements; and the fair resolution of conflicting interests between corporate stakeholders.

absence of good faith to succeed under the oppression remedy,[520] others have held that it is not.[521] The latter now appears to be the dominant view.

8. Application of the Oppression Remedy to Public Companies

229. The oppression remedy applies to both public and private companies. Despite this, and the fact that there are cases involving public companies in which relief has been granted,[522] the vast majority of cases arising under the oppression remedy have involved private companies. This reflects the fact that in private companies, the mutual expectations and entitlements of the parties are less likely to be reduced to the four corners of the legal documents setting out their relationship. This creates a much larger role for the courts in interpreting or extrapolating from the strict legal relationship. Indeed, while the courts have repeatedly drawn on the 'expectations' principle[523] in resolving disputes involving private corporations, it is not at all clear that the expectations principle applies to public companies. Some courts have held that it does,[524] while other courts have held that it does not.[525] It remains to be seen whether the oppression remedy will be used any more frequently in relation to public companies in the future.

9. Meaning of 'Affiliates'

230. Parent and subsidiary corporations are affiliated corporations where the parent holds a majority of the votes attached to the shares of the subsidiary.[526] The term 'affiliated corporation' also includes subsidiaries under the control of a common parent corporation, companies controlled by the same person, and companies with common affiliates.[527] There is some ambiguity about whether legal or majority control is necessary for this purpose, or whether 'de facto' control will suffice. The statutory definition suggests that legal control is necessary,[528] but at least one court has held otherwise.[529]

520. *See*, for example, *Gillespie v. Overs; Tesari Holdings Ltd. v. Pizza Pizza Ltd.*, unreported, 14 Aug. 1989, Ont. H.C., summarized (1987), 5 A.C.W.S. (3rd) 430.
521. *See*, for example, *Brant Investments v. KeepRite Inc.* (1991), 3 O.R.(3rd) 289 (C.A.); *Sidaplex-Plastic Suppliers Inc. v. Elta Group Inc.* (1998), 40 O.R. (3rd) 563 (C.A.); and *Krynen v. Bugg* (2003), 64 O.R. (3rd) 393 (Ont. S.C.J.).
522. *See*, for example, *Sparling v. Southam Inc.* (1989), 66 O.R. (2nd) 225 (H.C.).
523. *See infra* para. 339.
524. *See*, for example, 820099 *Ontario Inc. v. Harold E. Ballard Ltd.* (1992), 3 B.L.R. (2nd) 113 (Ont. Div. Ct.), aff'd (1992), 3 B.L.R. (2nd) 123 (Ont. C.A.); *Westfair Foods Ltd. v. Watt* (1989), 48 B.L.R. 43 (Alta. Q.B.), aff'd (1991), 79 D.L.R. (4th) 48 (Alta. C.A.).
525. *See*, for example, *Goldstream Resources Ltd.* (1986), 2 B.C.L.R. 244 (S.C.).
526. CBCA ss 2(1)–2(5).
527. *Ibid.*
528. CBCA s. 2(3).
529. *See Sparling v. Javelin International Ltd. (No. 1)*, [1986] R.J.Q. 1073 (Que. Sup. C.).

10. Oppression Remedy Applies to Omissions As Well As Isolated Acts

231. As will be clear from paragraph 222, the oppression remedy applies both to corporate acts *and* to omissions. In addition, it applies to isolated acts; there is no need under the Canadian legislation to establish a continuing course of oppressive conduct.[530]

11. Inter-shareholder Disputes over Business Policy

232. The oppression remedy has no application to disputes between shareholders over the management of the company.[531] So long as all proper corporate decision-making procedures are observed and the expectations of the complainant have not been violated, the courts have shied away from deciding matters of pure business policy.[532]

12. Mismanagement

233. In general, the courts have held that mismanagement of the company does not fall within the purview of the oppression remedy.[533] Where, however, there is oppressive conduct falling within the oppression remedy, the fact that there is also mismanagement may be an added factor in a court's decision to grant relief.[534]

13. Threats That Oppressive Conduct Will Occur in the Future

234. The federal legislation does not specifically make threatened oppression actionable.[535] For this reason, some courts have held that threatened or anticipated oppression is not actionable under the CBCA.[536] Other courts have held, however, that threatened conduct is actionable.[537]

530. *See,* for example, *Miller v. F. Mendel Holdings Ltd* (1984), 26 B.L.R. 85 (Sask. Q.B.).
531. *See,* for example, *Bernard v. Montgomery* (1987), 36 B.L.R. 257 (Sask. Q.B.); *Re Five Minute Car Wash Service Ltd.*, [1966] 1 All E.R. 242 (Ch.).
532. *See,* for example, *Buchan v. East Island Developments Inc.*, unreported, 31 Mar. 1974, B.C.S.C.
533. *See,* for example, *Re Five Minute Car Wash Service Ltd.*, [1966] 1 All E.R. 242 (Ch.).
534. *See,* for example, *Re Van-Tel TV Ltd.* (1974), 44 D.L.R. (2nd) 136 (B.C.S.C.); *Credit Foncier Franco-Canadien v. C.S.W. Enterprises Ltd.* (1986), 54 Sask. R. 97 (Q.B.).
535. Some of the provincial incorporation statutes specifically make threatened conduct actionable. *See,* for example, OBCA s. 248(2). In B.C., the courts have arrived at a similar result. *See,* for example, *Re Peterson and Kanata Investments Ltd.* (1975), 60 D.L.R. (3rd) 527 (B.S.S.C.). *See also* now BCBCA s. 227(2)(b).
536. *See,* for example, *Bank of Montreal v. Dome Petroleum Ltd.* (1987), 54 Alta. L.R. (2nd) 289 (Q.B.); *Bowater Canadian Ltd. v. R.L. Crain Inc.*, summarized at (1987), 3 A.C.W.S. (3rd) 380, aff'd (1988), 62 O.R. (2nd) 752 (C.A.).
537. *See,* for example, 820099 *Ontario Inc. v. Harold E. Ballard Ltd.* (1992), 3 B.L.R. (2nd) 113 (Ont. Div. Ct.), aff'd (1992), 3 B.L.R. (2nd) 123 (C.A.).

14. Powers of Court in Connection with an Oppression Application

235. Under the federal legislation, the statute gives the following powers to the court:[538]

> Powers of court – In connection with an application under this section, the court may make any interim or final order it thinks fit including, without limiting the generality of the foregoing,

(a) an order restraining the conduct complained of,
(b) an order appointing a receiver or receiver-manager;
(c) an order to regulate a corporation's affairs by amending the articles or bylaws or creating or amending a unanimous shareholder agreement;
(d) an order directing an issue or exchange of securities;
(e) an order appointing directors in place of or in addition to all or any of the directors then in office;
(f) an order directing a corporation, subject to subsection (6), or any other person, to purchase securities of a security holder;
(g) an order directing a corporation, subject to subsection (6), or any other person, to pay to a security holder any part of the moneys paid by him for securities;
(h) an order varying or setting aside a transaction or contract to which a corporation is a party and compensating the corporation or any other party to the transaction or contract;
(i) an order requiring a corporation, within a time specified by the court, to produce to the court or an interested person financial statements in the form required by section 155 or an accounting in such other form as the court may determine;
(j) an order compensating an aggrieved person;
(k) an order directing rectification of the registers or other records of a corporation under section 243;
(l) an order liquidating and dissolving the corporation;
(m) an order directing an investigation under Part XIX to be made;
(n) an order requiring the trial of any issue.

15. Buyout Orders

236. Although virtually all of the above powers have been exercised by the courts at one time or another, the most common form of order under the oppression remedy is an order that the corporation[539] or the controlling shareholder(s)[540] buy the shares of the complainant at a judicially appraised 'fair value'. Where this is done, the

538. CBCA s. 241(3).
539. CBCA s. 241(3)(f). *See,* for example, *Diligenti v. RWMD Operations (Kelowna) Ltd. (No. 2)* (1977), 4 B.C.L.R. 134 (S.C.).
540. CBCA s. 241(3)(f). *See,* for example, *Tilley v. Hails* (1992), 7 O.R. (3rd) 257 (Ont. Gen. Div.); *Millar v. McNally* (1991), 3 B.L.R. (2nd) 102.

shares of the complainant are valued as if the oppression had not occurred,[541] and the 'fair value' is determined in a manner similar to a fair value determination under the appraisal right.[542] The most common valuation date is the date upon which the application alleging oppression was filed,[543] although the courts have sometimes chosen other dates, such as the date of the order requiring the buyout.[544]

16. Procedures

237. One of the advantages of the oppression remedy is that it allows a complainant to proceed by way of 'application' rather than 'action'.[545] An application is a simplified procedure with no pleadings or discoveries and the leading of affidavit evidence only, greatly reducing the cost of the proceeding and allowing for much quicker relief. If there are complex issues of fact or law to be tried, however, the courts will typically order the trial of one or more issues, with the benefit of pleadings, discoveries, and other rules of procedure applicable to actions.[546]

17. Costs

238. As in respect of derivative actions, the complainant is not required to give security for costs.[547] Moreover, the court may also award interim costs to the complainant, although these may have to be repaid should the complainant lose the action.[548] It is not entirely clear if an indemnification for costs can be awarded against the corporation.[549] In general, the usual rule that 'costs follow the event' governs the disposition of costs at the conclusion of the proceeding (i.e., the successful party is given an award of costs).

---

541. *See,* for example, *Scottish Co-operative Wholesale Society Ltd. v. Meyer*, [1958] 3 All E.R. 66 (H.L.); *Miller v. F. Mendel Holdings Ltd.* (1984), 26 B.L.R. 85 (Sask. Q.B.).
542. *See,* for example, *Re Abraham and Inter Wide Investments Ltd.* (1985), 20 D.L.R. (4th) 267 (Ont. H.C.); *Nystad v. Harcrest Apartments Ltd.* (1986), 3 B.C.L.R. (2nd) 39 (S.C.); and *see* §3.I.E below.
543. *See,* for example, *Scottish Co-operative Wholesale Society Ltd. v. Meyer*, [1958] 3 All E.R. 66 (H.L.); *Re National Building Maintenance Ltd.*, [1971] 1 W.W.R. 8 (B.C.S.C.).
544. *See,* for example, *Millar v. McNally* (1991), 3 B.L.R. (2nd) 102 (Ont. Ct.J.).
545. CBCA s. 248.
546. CBCA s. 241(3)(n). *See,* for example, *Journet v. Superchef Industries Ltd.* (1984), 29 B.L.R. 206 (Que. Sup. Ct.).
547. CBCA s. 242(3).
548. CBCA s. 242(4). *See,* for example, *Re Television Antenna & Service Co. Limited* et al.; *Alles v. Maurice* et al., *unreported*, 23 Jan. 1992, Ont. Ct. J. (arising under the Ontario legislation).
549. Cf. CBCA s. 240(d) (allowing for the awarding of an indemnification in relation to a derivative action).

D. Duty of Majority Shareholders to Minority Shareholders

1. At Common Law, Shareholders Owe No Fiduciary Duties

239. At common law, neither controlling nor majority shareholders owe any fiduciary duty, either to the company, or to other shareholders. The absence of a fiduciary duty has been expressed in a number of functionally equivalent ways. Some courts have simply stated that shareholders owe no fiduciary duties.[550] Others have stated that the courts will not interfere in the internal affairs of a company – indeed, that they have no jurisdiction to do so.[551] Yet other courts have enunciated the 'rule of selfish ownership', which is that shareholders may exercise their votes in any way they choose, 'whatever their motives for such exercise'.[552] The absence of a shareholder fiduciary duty is illustrated by a famous case that went to the Privy Council, in which ratification of the sale of a steamship to the company by a director was allowed to stand, even though the director's own votes were instrumental in securing the ratification.[553]

2. Common Law Exceptions to the Principle That Shareholders Owe No Fiduciary Duties

240. Despite the traditional dogma that holds that shareholders owe no fiduciary duties, it is possible to find instances in which the courts have held that conduct of the majority is actionable at the instance of the minority. At common law, for example, one exception to the rule that shareholders could not commence a derivative action for a wrong done to the company was where the majority committed a 'fraud on the minority', although the meaning of fraud on the minority was essentially limited to stealing of corporate assets or the appropriation of corporate opportunities.[554] In a number of cases involving discriminatory amendments to the company's charter, the courts also held that the majority had a duty to act 'bona fide (i.e., in good faith) for the benefit of the company as a whole'.[555] This good faith duty was severely circumscribed, however, given that only overwhelming evidence of bad faith would displace the presumption that the majority was acting in good faith.[556] Moreover, as long as all shareholders were treated in a formally identical manner, the courts would not find bad faith.

---

550. *See,* for example, *Phillips v. Manufacturer's Securities Limited* (1917), 116 L.T. 290 (C.A.).
551. *See,* for example, *Burland v. Earle*, [1902] A.C. 73 (P.C.).
552. *Pender v. Lushington* (1877), 6 Ch. D. 70, at 75 (C.A.).
553. *Northwest Transportation Co. v. Beatty* (1877), 12 App. Cas. 589 (P.C.).
554. *See,* for example, *Menier v. Hooper's Telegraph Works* (1874), L.R. 9 Ch. App. 350, 43 L.J. Ch. 330 (C.A.); *Cook v. Deeks*, [1916] 1 A.C. 554 (P.C.).
555. *See,* for example, *Allen v. Gold Reefs of West Africa Ltd.*, [1900] 1 Ch. 656 (C.A.); *Brown v. British Abrasive Wheel Company Ltd.*, [1919] 1 Ch. 290 (Ch. D.).
556. *See,* for example, *Shuttleworth v. Cox Brothers and Company (Maidenhead) Ltd.*, [1927] 2 K.B. 9, [1926] All E.R. Rep. 498 (C.A.).

3. Duty of 'Fairness'

241. In other cases, the courts have held that there is a duty of fairness on the part of the majority. Thus, for example, the Ontario Court of Appeal has held that the majority has a 'burden of fair dealing',[557] and that 'the majority must act fairly and honestly',[558] failing which the court will draw upon its equitable jurisdiction to intervene.

4. The Majority of the Minority Principle

242. Rather than finding that the majority has a fiduciary duty to the company or to the minority, some courts have taken into account shareholder conflicts of interest by excluding majority or controlling shareholders from voting where there is a conflict of interest.[559] Others have shifted an onus of proof to the majority to uphold the fairness of the transaction where it has not been approved by a majority of disinterested shareholders[560] or have given a majority of the minority approval evidentiary weight in deciding the fairness of a transaction.[561] The issue of majority of the minority approval is dealt with further in §3.I.A.[562]

5. Shareholder Fiduciary Duties under the Oppression Remedy

243. While the courts have steadfastly clung to the notion that shareholders owe no fiduciary duties, they have arguably imposed fiduciary duties on shareholders under the statutory oppression remedy (dealt with in §3.I.C above). The oppression remedy only deals with conduct of the corporation or any of its affiliates, or of the directors.[563] A parent company holding de jure control will, however, be an 'affiliate'.[564] Thus, parent company shareholders are drawn directly under the purview of the oppression remedy. Further, where shareholders pass a resolution with a view to initiating corporate or directorial conduct, the resulting corporate or directorial conduct fall directly within the oppression remedy. In addition, once the court has found that the corporation has acted oppressively, it may make an order against a majority or controlling shareholder (e.g., an order that the controller buy the shares of the complainant).[565] In this manner,

557. *Re R.J. Jowsey Mining Co. Ltd.* (1969), 6 D.L.R. (3rd) 97 (Ont. C.A.).
558. *Goldex Mines Ltd. v. Revill* (1975), 7 O.R. (2nd) 216, 54 D.L.R. (3rd) 672 (C.A.).
559. *See*, for example, *Re Hellenic & General Trust Ltd.*, [1976] 1 W.L.R. 123, [1975] 3 All E.R. 382; *Hansen v. The Canada Trust Company and Bondholders Reorganization Committee*, [1951] S.C.R. 366 (S.C.C.).
560. *See*, for example, *Re Bugle Press*, [1960] 1 All E.R. 768 (Ch.), aff'd [1961] 1 Ch. 270 (C.A.); *Imperial Trust Co. and Taylor Assets (Dominion) Ltd. v. Canbra Foods Ltd.* (1987), 50 Alta.L.R. (2nd) 375 (Alta.Q.B.).
561. *See*, for example, *Rights and Issues Investments Trust Ltd. v. Stylo Shoes Ltd.*, [1965] 1 Ch. 251 (Ch.); *Triad Oil Holdings Ltd. v. Provincial Secretary for Manitoba* (1967), 59 W.W.R. 1 (Man.C.A.).
562. Paragraphs 195–197.
563. CBCA s. 241(2).
564. *See* §3.I.C, para. 230.
565. *See*, for example, *Miller v. F. Mendel Holdings Ltd.*, [1984] 2 W.W.R. 683, 26 B.L.R. 85 (Q.B.); *Re National Building Maintenance Ltd.*, [1971] 1 W.W.R. 8 (B.C.S.C.).

most shareholder conduct can be drawn into the oppression remedy. Indeed, in some cases, the courts have essentially identified controlling shareholder conduct as conduct of the corporation, thus bringing controlling shareholders even more directly under the purview of the oppression remedy.[566] As indicated in §3.I.C above, the general standard of conduct under the oppression remedy is one of 'fairness'.[567] Thus, whether or not one identifies the fairness standard as 'fiduciary' in nature,[568] it now seems clear that majority and controlling shareholders must act fairly towards the minority, not only in using their voting powers, but also in acting in other ways that might impact on the company.[569]

E. Appraisal Remedies

1. Generally

a. Purpose of the Appraisal Remedy

244. In general, the appraisal right was designed to be of central importance in protecting minority shareholders on the occurrence of a variety of fundamental corporate transactions. When a triggering event occurs, the appraisal remedy enables a shareholder to sell his shares to the corporation at a court appraised 'fair value'. In theory, the appraised fair value is designed to protect the dissenting shareholder against any fall in market price that might occur following the announcement of the transaction.[570] It is also designed to protect shareholders against the consequences of transactions that discriminate against the interests of a class, or of a minority of shareholders. In respect of the latter, the existence of an appraisal right is meant to supply the shareholder with an effective remedy that is cheaper than alternative means of redress – like suing for breach of fiduciary duty or claiming under the oppression remedy. The appraisal remedy was also thought to have the virtue of providing relief for a minority, while allowing a majority of shareholders to proceed with the transaction in question.[571]

566. *See*, for example, *Re H.R. Harmer Ltd.*, [1958] 3 All E.R. 689, [1959] 1 W.L.R. 62 (C.A.); *Re Jermyn Street Baths Ltd.*, [1971] 3 All E.R. 184 (C.A.); *Re Ferguson and Imax Systems Corp.* (1983), 43 O.R. (2nd) 128, 150 D.L.R. (3rd) 718 (C.A.).

567. *See* §3.I.D.3, para. 241.

568. In *Brant Investments Ltd. v. KeepRite Inc.* (1991), 3 O.R. (3rd) 289 (C.A.), the court declined to find that shareholders owed any fiduciary duty. However, it noted that '[b]ecause the [oppression remedy] is so broadly formulated, the evidence necessary to establish a breach of fiduciary duty would be subsumed in the broader range of evidence which would be appropriately adduced on an application under the section'. This suggests that the court was of the view that the duty of fairness imposed under the oppression remedy is a fiduciary duty in substance, if not in name.

569. *See*, for example, *Scottish Co-operative Wholesale Society v. Meyer*, [1959] A.C. 324, [1958] 3 All E.R. 66 (H.L.).

570. If there is no fall in market value, then clearly the existence of a public market for the corporation's securities will be an adequate protection for shareholders.

571. *See* R. Dickerson et al., *Proposals for a New Business Corporations Law for Canada*, vol. 1 (Ottawa: Ministry of Supply and Services Canada, 1971) at Part 14.00.

b. Triggering Events

245. There are a number of situations in which an appraisal proceeding may occur:

- in connection with particular types of corporate transactions, such as amalgamations and changes in the articles of incorporation;
- in connection with a 'compulsory acquisition' of shares by an acquiring bidder;
- under the CBCA and the OBCA, where one person owns 90% or more of the shares of the corporation (a 'reverse compulsory acquisition'); and
- as a remedial device in connection with an oppression proceeding.

These are considered in turn.

2. Where the Appraisal Remedy Is Triggered by a Corporate Transaction

a. Triggering Corporate Transactions

246. Under the corporate legislation, transactions that trigger the appraisal remedy include an amendment of the articles to add, change, or remove any provisions restricting the issue, transfer, or ownership of shares of the class; amendment to the articles to change or remove any restriction on the business or businesses that the corporation may carry on; amalgamation, continuance (reincorporation) in another jurisdiction; and sale, lease, or exchange of all or substantially all of the property of the corporation.[572] Where a class of shares is entitled to a class vote on a resolution to amend the articles, a holder of shares of that class may also dissent and claim the remedy.[573] In connection with any of these transactions, a holder of shares of any class may dissent and claim the appraisal remedy.[574] In addition, if the court permits, the remedy may be claimed in connection with an arrangement.[575] Under the Ontario legislation, a 'going private transaction' in which participating shareholders are forcibly evicted from the corporation also triggers an appraisal remedy.[576]

b. Procedures

247. Where the appraisal remedy is triggered by a particular corporate event (like an amalgamation), the remedy does not arise until the body of shareholders has approved a resolution adopting the transaction and the transaction has become effective.[577] In order to claim the remedy, a dissenting shareholder must send a written objection

572. CBCA s. 190(1).
573. CBCA s. 190(2).
574. In Ontario, only a holder of shares of any class entitled to vote on the resolution may dissent [OBCA s. 185(2)].
575. CBCA ss 190(1), 192(4)(d).
576. OBCA s. 190.
577. CBCA s. 190(3).

to the resolution being voted on before the shareholder vote approving the transaction,[578] and must not vote in favour of the transaction.[579] Once the resolution is adopted, and the shareholder makes a demand for payment, all of the shareholder's rights (including the right to vote and to receive dividends) are suspended, and the shareholder acquires the right to be paid the fair value of the shares.[580] The company and shareholders will attempt to bargain toward a fair value.[581] Should this fail, then either the company or the shareholder may require the court to determine a fair value for the shares,[582] and all shareholders whose shares have not been purchased by the corporation will be joined together in one appraisal proceeding.[583] Some courts have converted the appraisal proceeding into an 'action', in which the 'plaintiff' is the corporation and the 'defendant' is the shareholder, in order that an onus of proof be cast upon the corporation to prove fair value.[584] Other courts, however, have held that there is no onus of proof in the appraisal proceeding, and that both parties should assist the court in determining fair value.[585] Nonetheless (and despite the fact that the court is empowered to appoint one or more appraisers to assist it in determining fair value[586]), most appraisal hearings proceed in an 'adversarial' manner, with each side calling its own expert witnesses and making submissions as to fair value.

3. Compulsory Acquisitions

a. Meaning of Compulsory Acquisition

248. When a bidder makes a general offer to purchase shares of the company and 90% of the shares are tendered to the bidder (not counting any shares initially held by the bidder), the legislation allows the bidder to force the remaining shareholders out of the company.[587] Shareholders forced out pursuant to this 'compulsory acquisition' procedure are, however, given an election. They may either tender their shares to the bidder at the initial bid price, or they may elect to demand payment of the fair value of their shares.[588]

b. Procedures in Connection with Compulsory Acquisitions

249. Where a bidder has secured 90% tender into a takeover bid, and wishes to cash out the remaining shareholders, it may do so by sending timely notice to the

578. CBCA s. 190(5).
579. CBCA s. 190(6).
580. CBCA s. 190(11).
581. CBCA s. 190(12), 190(13).
582. CBCA s. 190(15), 190(16).
583. CBCA s. 190(19).
584. *See*, for example, *Neonex International Ltd. v. Kolasa* (1978), 84 D.L.R. (3rd) 446 (B.C.S.C.).
585. *See*, for example, *Les Investissements Mont-Soleil Inc. v. National Drug Ltd.* (1982), 22 B.L.R. 139 (Que. Sup. Ct.).
586. CBCA s. 190(21).
587. CBCA s. 206.
588. CBCA s. 206(3)(c).

shareholders who did not tender into the bid.[589] The dissenting shareholder is entitled to elect to accept the consideration that was offered in the takeover bid, or to demand payment of the fair value of the shares.[590] The shareholder's share certificates are cancelled, and an equivalent number of shares issued to the bidder by the offeree corporation.[591] If either the corporation or the dissenting shareholder requests it to do so, a court will determine the fair value of the shares,[592] and the claims of all shareholders who have not been paid by the corporation are joined together in one proceeding.[593] Although the court may appoint one or more appraisers to assist it in determining fair value, most appraisal hearings have proceeded in an adversarial fashion, with each side calling witnesses and adducing evidence to support its claim as to fair value.

c. Reverse Compulsory Acquisition

250. Under the CBCA and the OBCA, where 90% or more of a class of shares is acquired by one person (or a group of persons acting jointly), then a minority shareholder may force the corporation to purchase her shares at a fair value.[594] This provision is designed to avoid an 'illiquidity lock-in', where a shareholder is trapped in an enterprise with an illiquid market and few opportunities to sell the shares.

d. Procedures in Connection with a Reverse Compulsory Acquisition

251. The reverse compulsory acquisition is triggered when a person becomes the owner of 90% or more of a class of securities.[595] When this happens, the corporation must notify every shareholder of her right to have her shares purchased, and make an offer at a specific price.[596] A shareholder may elect to accept the offer or have a court determine the fair value of the shares.[597] Otherwise, the procedures are substantially the same as in connection with a compulsory acquisition.

4. Oppression: Appraisal of Fair Value as a Remedy for Oppressive Conduct

252. Where the courts have found oppressive conduct, one of the remedies most frequently resorted to is an order for one shareholder (or the corporation) to buy the shares of another shareholder (usually the complainant). The oppression remedy

589. CBCA s. 206(3).
590. *Ibid.* Under CBCA s. 206(5.1) a shareholder who fails to make an election is deemed to have elected to accept the offer that was made under the takeover bid.
591. CBCA s. 206(8).
592. CBCA s. 206(9), 206(10).
593. CBCA s. 206(14).
594. *See* CBCA s. 206.1 and OBCA s. 189.
595. OBCA s. 189(1).
596. OBCA s. 189(2), (3).
597. OBCA s. 189(4).

authorizes the court to require the trial of any issue,[598] and the courts have frequently ordered a trial to determine the 'fair value' of the shares to be cashed out.

5. Determination of 'Fair Value'

a. Generally

253. There are four different methods which the courts have used to determine the fair value of shares. These are:

(1) market value;
(2) net asset value;
(3) the earnings or investment value approach; and
(4) a combined approach.

These are discussed in turn.

b. Market Value

254. Market value has been used as the exclusive indicia of value only where the company's shares trade in liquid markets with substantial public floats.[599] In general, market value has been used sparingly, since the shares of many Canadian issuers trade in thin markets.[600] Even in thinly traded markets market value can, however, have some evidentiary value.[601]

c. Net Asset Value

255. The net asset value of the firm is the market value of all assets after deducting all liabilities. Once the firm's net asset value is determined, the value of the shares is derivatively determined. This method is used only in the case of non-operating companies (i.e., holding companies), or companies that have essentially no 'going concern' value.[602]

d. Earnings or Investment Value

256. The theory that motivates the earnings or investment value approach is that the value of a business (and, derivatively, the value of a share) is determined by what it will earn in the future. In general, there are two methods that the courts have used to determine the value of shares on this basis. The first is the 'discounted cash

598. CBCA s. 241(3) (n).
599. *See,* for example, *Montgomery v. Shell Canada Ltd.* (1980), 11 D.L.R. (3rd) 116 (Sask. Q.B.); *Lough v. Canadian Natural Resources Ltd.* (1983), 45 B.C.L.R. 335 (S.C.).
600. *See,* for example, *Re Whitehorse Copper Mines Ltd.; Hudson Bay Mining & Smelting Co. v. Lueck* (1980), 10 B.L.R. 113 (B.C.S.C.).
601. *See,* for example, *Brant Investments Ltd. v. KeepRite Inc.* (1991), 3 O.R. (3rd) 289 (C.A.).
602. *See,* for example, *Re Domglas Inc.* (1980), 13 B.L.R. 135 (Que. Sup. Ct.).

flow' technique, whereby an estimate is made of future cash flows and a capitalized value of these cash flows is computed using a discount rate that reflects both the financial and business risk faced by the shareholders.[603] In determining the latter, factors that are relevant will include the quality of management, future growth prospects, both for the industry and the particular firm, and the degree of leverage. The second is the earnings multiple approach, which takes current earnings (or some weighted average of the past few years' earnings) and multiplies them by a price/earnings ratio. The price/earnings ratio is determined using both the firm's historical price/earnings ratio and price/earnings ratios for comparable firms, as well as other risk factors. In general, because of the difficulty of making estimates of future cash flows, Canadian courts have relied more heavily on the second technique than the first.[604]

e. The Combined Approach

257. In a small number of cases, the courts have combined the above approaches. In one case, for example, the court used the asset value approach in relation to the firm's redundant assets, while using the earnings approach for leased properties.[605] In another, the court considered both the net asset value of the firm and the earnings value in fixing a fair value.[606] In general, however, the Canadian courts have *not* used a weighted approach in calculating fair value.

f. The Valuation Date

258. Where the appraisal remedy is triggered by the occurrence of any of the transactions noted above, the valuation date is 'the close of business on the day before the resolution was adopted or the order was made'.[607] Where the trigger is a compulsory acquisition, the statute does not indicate a valuation date. Some courts have, however, chosen the date on which the shareholder elects an appraisal of fair value as the valuation date.[608]

g. The Use of 'Hindsight' Information, or Information Acquired after the Valuation Date

259. As a matter of theory, the courts have accepted the proposition that information acquired after the valuation date may not be used in valuing shares. The courts have, however, carved out a number of exceptions to this rule. For example, it

603. *See*, for example, *Brant Investments v. KeepRite Inc.* (1987), 37 B.L.R. 65 (Ont. H.C.), aff'd (1991), 3 O.R. (3rd) 289 (C.A.).
604. *See*, for example, *Re Whitehorse Copper Mines Ltd.; Hudson Bay Mining & Smelting Co. v. Lueck* (1980), 10 B.L.R. 113 (B.C.S.C.); *Re Brant Investments and KeepRite Inc.* (1988), 60 O.R. (2nd) 737 (H.C.).
605. *See Re VCS Holdings Ltd. and Helliwell* (1978), 5 B.L.R. 265 (B.C.S.C.).
606. *Cyprus Anvil Mining Corp. v. Dickson* (1986), 8 B.C.L.R. (2nd) 145 (C.A.).
607. CBCA s. 190(3).
608. *See*, for example, *Re Whitehorse Copper Mines Ltd.; Hudson Bay Mining & Smelting Co. v. Lueck* (1980), 10 B.L.R. 113 (B.C.S.C.).

has been held that after-acquired information may be admitted into evidence to test the reasonableness of the valuers' assumptions where the proffered valuations are in conflict,[609] or to shed light on a state of affairs that has not varied since the valuation date (like the quantity of ore in the ground). In practice, these exceptions swallow the rule, particularly given that the valuations proffered by the different parties will always be in conflict. Thus, however inappropriate, it is more accurate to state that after-acquired information is admissible in an appraisal proceeding.

h. Minority Discounts

260. In the usual case, a control block of shares will trade in the market at a premium to a pro rata share of enterprise value. In like fashion, minority interests will often trade at a discount from their pro rata share of enterprise value. Since the usual procedure in valuing shares is to first value the enterprise as a whole, and then derive the value of a share, this raises the question of whether a 'minority discount' should be subtracted from the pro rata share of enterprise value represented by a minority share on an appraisal. In almost every case, the courts have declined to make a minority discount, even where the dissenting shareholder purchased his shares in the public market at a price that reflected a minority discount.[610] Where the courts have awarded the market price of the shares, however, they have implicitly made a minority discount, since the publicly posted price will reflect a minority discount.[611]

i. Expropriation Premium

261. Where shareholders are claiming the appraisal remedy as a result of being forced out of the corporation, a number of courts have added an 'expropriation premium' to the pro rata value of the dissenter's shares.[612]

j. Transaction Synergies

262. In some cases, the transaction dissented from will yield synergistic benefits, raising the question of whether these benefits should be added to the appraised fair value. In general, the courts will not add transaction synergies to the award except in situations in which the dissenting shareholder is being forced out of the corporation

609. *See*, for example, *Cyprus Anvil Mining Corp. v. Dickson* (1982), 40 B.C.L.R. 180 (S.C.), rev'd on other grounds (1986), 8 B.C.L.R. (2nd) 145 (C.A.).

610. *See generally* Dennis H. Peterson & D.H. Cumming, *Shareholder Remedies in Canada*, 2d ed. (LexisNexis Canada, 2009).

611. *See*, for example, *Montgomery v. Shell Canada Ltd.* (1980), 11 D.L.R. (3rd) 116 (Sask. Q.B.); *Lough v. Canadian Natural Resources Ltd.* (1983), 45 B.C.L.R. 335 (S.C.).

612. *See*, for example, *Re Domglas Inc.* (1980), 13 B.L.R. 135 (Que. Sup. Ct.) (20% premium); *Les Investissements Mont-Soleil Inc. v. National Drug Ltd.* (1982), 22 B.L.R. 139 (Que. Sup. Ct.) (20% premium). The B.C. Court of Appeal, however, has held that the court does not have jurisdiction to award an expropriation premium. *See Manning v. Harris Steel Group Inc.* (1989), 44 B.L.R. 225 (B.C.C.A.).

and, therefore, is unable to elect to stay in the corporation and participate in the synergistic benefits.[613]

k. Costs

263. Costs can be very significant in an appraisal proceeding, particularly given that each side in the dispute will hire expert witnesses to establish its version of 'fair value'. The usual rule in appraisal proceedings is that 'costs follow the event', meaning that costs are awarded to the party whose submissions as to 'fair value' are closest to those ultimately chosen by the court.[614]

l. The Appraisal Remedy Is Non-exclusive

264. The appraisal remedy can be claimed simultaneously with other means of redress, such as the oppression remedy.[615]

F. Right to Corporate Information, Including Annual Financial Statements

1. Financial Disclosure Requirements

a. Corporate Law Requirements to Place Financial Statements Before Shareholders

265. At every annual meeting of shareholders, the directors must place before the shareholders financial statements relating to the previous financial year (and any subsequently completed six-month period).[616] These financial statements must also be sent to shareholders at least twenty-one days in advance of the annual meeting.[617] All public companies must also place a copy of the financial statements in the public file.[618] In addition to receiving the financial statements, the shareholders are entitled to receive the report of the auditor,[619] and any further financial information required by the articles, by-laws, and any unanimous shareholder agreement.[620]

---

613. *See*, for example, *Smeenk v. Dexleigh Corp.* (1991), 74 O.R. (2nd) 385 (H.C.); *Brant Investments v. KeepRite Inc.* (1991), 3 O.R. (3rd) 289 (C.A.).
614. *See*, for example, *Fraser v. Aitken* (1988), 41 B.L.R. 87 (Ont. H.C.).
615. *See*, for example, *Re Brant Investments Ltd. and KeepRite Inc.* (1983), 24 B.L.R. 201 (Ont. H.C.).
616. CBCA s. 155(1).
617. CBCA s. 159(1).
618. CBCA s. 160(1)(a).
619. CBCA s. 155(1)(b).
620. CBCA s. 155(1)(c).

b. Similar Requirements in Securities Law

266. Securities law also requires any 'reporting issuer' (public company) to assemble and distribute quarterly and audited year-end financial statements and to distribute these to all holders of equity securities.[621]

2. Material Change Reports

267. Securities laws also require that a public corporation immediately disclose any 'material change' relating to the corporation.[622] A 'material change' is a change in the business, operations, or capital of an issuer of securities that would reasonably be expected to have a significant effect on the price or value of any of the securities of the reporting issuer.[623] The TSX extends the reporting obligation to 'material information' for issuers with securities listed on the exchange. The TSX defines 'material information' as 'any information relating to the business and affairs of a company that results in or would reasonably be expected to result in a significant change in the market price or value of any of the company's listed securities'.[624]

3. Disclosure in Connection with Specific Transactions

268. Upon the undertaking of specific transactions, additional disclosure obligations come into play. For example, the raising of capital in public markets requires the filing of a prospectus, which will contain detailed financial (and other) information about the company.[625] The undertaking of a corporate fundamental change, like an amalgamation, will also require management to assemble a management proxy circular, which may contain financial information.[626]

4. Other Disclosure: Information to Which Shareholders and Creditors Have Access

269. The corporation is required to maintain records containing the articles, by-laws, and any unanimous shareholder agreement; minutes of shareholders' meetings

621. *See,* National Instrument 51-102, Part 4.
622. *See,* National Instrument 51-102, para. 7.1.
623. ASA s. 1(ff); BCSA s. 1(1) 'material change'; NBSA s. 1(1) 'material change'; NSA s. 2(1)(w); NSSA s. 2(1)(v); OSA s. 1(1) 'material change'; SSA s. 2(1)(y). *See also* QSA s. 5.3.
624. *See* TSX Company Manual ss 407–411.
625. *See,* for example, OSA s. 53. On the prospectus requirements *see* Canadian Securities Administrators National Instrument 41-101.
626. *See,* for example, CBCA s. 149. Canadian Securities Administrators National Instrument 51-102, Part 8 requires a 'business acquisition report' disclosing specified information concerning a significant business acquisition by a 'reporting issuer' (which, in very general terms, is an issuer of securities (such as a corporation) that has made a public distribution of securities). There are particular disclosure requirements, including requirements for disclosure of a 'formal valuation', were the proposed transaction involves an insider bid, an issuer bid, a business combination, or a related party transaction. *See* Multilateral Instrument 61-101 adopted by the securities regulators in the provinces of Ontario and Quebec.

and resolutions passed thereat; a listing of the directors of the corporation; and a register of security holders.[627] Any creditor or shareholder may have access to these records.[628] In addition, any member of the public may obtain a copy of the securities register upon signing an affidavit that the list will be used only in an effort to influence the voting of shareholders, an offer to acquire shares, or any other matter relating to the affairs of the corporation.[629] Neither shareholders nor creditors are entitled to see the accounting records of the corporation, nor the minutes of directors' meetings or directors' resolutions.

G. *Profits and Dividends*

1. Debt Holders Have First Priority over the Earnings Stream

270. In general, profits are distributed to security holders in accordance with the terms upon which the securities were issued. The highest priority to the earnings stream is held by the holders of debt securities, who will typically hold a contractual entitlement to payment of the interest owing on their debt obligations before any dividend may be declared in favour of equity holders (i.e., those holding share interests). In addition, the corporate statutes forbid a corporation from declaring or paying a dividend if there are reasonable grounds for believing that either the corporation would, after the payment, be unable to pay its liabilities as they become due, or the realizable value of the corporation's assets would, after payment of the dividend, be less than the aggregate of its liabilities and stated capital of all classes of shares.[630] This limitation on the payment of dividends protects the interests of all fixed claimants, and not merely bondholders, by requiring that there be adequate resources to meet fixed claims before dividends are declared.

2. The Shareholder's Entitlement to Receive Any Declared Dividend

271. Shareholders are not automatically entitled to receive dividends. The corporation's articles will be the most important determinant of the entitlement to dividends. Modern corporation statutes do not greatly restrict the types of securities that may be created. Where a corporation has only one class of shares, however, that class must be entitled to receive any dividend declared by the corporation.[631] Where there is more than one class of shares, then at least one class must be entitled to receive any dividend declared by the corporation.[632] Aside from these restrictions, the articles will indicate the relative priorities to payment of dividends for various classes of shareholder.

627. CBCA s. 20(1).
628. CBCA s. 21.
629. CBCA s. 21(3), 21(9).
630. CBCA s. 42.
631. CBCA s. 24(3)(b).
632. CBCA s. 24(4).

3. Priorities to Receipt of Dividends

272. It is not uncommon in Canadian corporations to have 'preferred shares', which are entitled to receive a preferential dividend before other classes of shareholders are paid any dividend. Indeed, there may be several classes of preferred shares, with the relative priority over dividends set out in the articles. It is commonplace to have at least one class of voting common shares which are entitled to receive any dividend declared by the directors, after the payment of a dividend on any preferred shares. It is also not uncommon in many Canadian public corporations to have non-voting common shares, which are usually entitled to receive a small preferential dividend (after payment of any dividend due to the preferred shareholders) and then to share equally with the common shareholders in the declaration of any further dividend.

4. Residual and Non-residual Share Claims

273. In general, preferred shares are fixed claims. That is, the articles will only give them the entitlement to receive their fixed dividend (which may be a stated dollar amount, a percentage of stated capital, among others) after which their claim over the earnings of the corporation will be exhausted. By contrast common shares are typically 'residual' claims in that the directors may pay out as dividends to common shareholders all of the profits remaining after fixed claimants and preferred shareholders have been paid. Despite this important distinction, however, both preferred and common shares are referred to as 'equity' claims. More importantly, it should be borne in mind that the terms 'preferred' or 'preference' and 'common' shares are not legal terms of art, but rather are defined by commercial usage.[633] It is possible to create many intermediate types of securities, with varying entitlements over the earnings stream. It is thus legally possible, for example, to create a 'preferred' share that has a preferential dividend and in addition an entitlement to share equally with the common shareholders in any additional dividend. These so-called participating preferred shares have a residual claim, despite being called a preferred share.

5. The Directors' Discretion to Pay Dividends

274. Shareholders are not entitled to receive dividends. They are paid dividends only insofar as the directors choose to pay dividends in any particular quarter or year.[634] The discretion of directors to pay dividends is simply part of their mandate to manage the business and affairs of the corporation.[635] If they choose to retain corporate earnings for other purposes, then, absent bad faith or some improper ulterior motive,[636] shareholders may not challenge the decision not to pay a dividend, even if ample earnings are available out of which a dividend might be paid. If directors decide to pay dividends,

633. *See supra* , para. 131.
634. *See,* for example, *Burland v. Earle*, [1902] A.C. 83 (P.C.).
635. *M.N.R. v. McClurg*, [1991] 1 C.T.C. 169 (S.C.C.).
636. *See,* for example, *Re Ferguson and Imax Systems Corp.* (1983), 150 D.L.R. (3rd) 718 (Ont. C.A.).

they must of course do so with regard to the priorities set out in the articles of the company.

6. Cumulative Dividends

275. The dividends that are required to be paid to a particular class may be cumulative or non-cumulative. If a cumulative dividend is not paid to a class of shareholders with a preferential dividend in a particular period (e.g., a year), shareholders have no entitlement to sue the directors for payment. The amount of the unpaid dividend is, however, thereafter 'in arrears'. This means that, before the directors can declare a dividend in any subsequent period in favour of an inferior class of shares, they must not only pay the amount of the preferred dividend for that period, but also all accumulated arrears as well. If, in the same situation, the dividends are non-cumulative, then the decision not to pay a dividend in any given period has no effect at all on subsequent periods: in any period that follows, the directors need only pay the preferred dividend for that period before they may pay a dividend to an inferior class of shares. If the articles of the company are silent, there is a presumption that the dividend rights of any class of preferred shares are cumulative.

7. The Record Date

276. When directors decide to declare a dividend, they must declare a 'record date'.[637] Only those persons who are shareholders as of the record date are entitled to receive the dividend. Shareholders who purchase shares in the secondary market after this date buy their shares 'ex dividend', or without the benefit of the dividend, and the price is adjusted accordingly.

8. Declared Dividends Become a Debt of the Corporation

277. Once a dividend has been declared, it becomes an ordinary debt of the corporation.[638] Thus, after declaration, a shareholder can sue for payment of the dividend as she would sue to collect any other unpaid debt.

II. Directors, Officers, and the Management of the Corporation

A. Appointment Requirements, Remuneration, Dismissal

1. Directors' Power to Manage

278. Under the CBCA directors of the corporation have the legal power and duty to manage the corporation subject to the terms of a unanimous shareholder

637. CBCA s. 134(1)(a).

638. *See*, for example, *Re Severn & Wye & Severn Bridge Railway Co.*, [1896] 1 Ch. 559 (Ch.).

agreement.[639] The CBCA provides that 'director' means a person occupying the position of director by whatever name called.[640] The directors' power to manage may be delegated to some extent to the administrative group known as the officers. These are often the president, vice president, secretary, and treasurer.

2. Appointment of Directors

279. Under the CBCA first directors of a corporation are named at the time of incorporation and they act as directors until the first shareholders' meeting.[641] Thereafter,[642] directors are elected by ordinary resolution.[643] Normally one vote is taken for each director, so that the majority of shares elects each director.[644] A vacancy may be filled by the directors between elections, subject to alternate provisions in the articles.[645]

3. Cumulative and Class Voting for Directors

280. Two exceptions to the simple majority vote for directors are cumulative voting and class voting. Cumulative voting[646] is a method by which minority shareholders can elect a representative minority of directors by concentrating their votes in the election of a small number of directors. The CBCA provisions are permissive and, therefore, if cumulative voting is desired, it must be provided for in the articles.[647] Class voting is a method by which a director's position is filled by a vote of the members

---

639. CBCA s. 102(1). In British Columbia, the directors have the duty to manage the affairs of the corporation, but subject to the legislation and the company's articles [BCBCA s. 136(1)]. In New Brunswick, the directors' duty to manage is subject to the articles, the by-laws or a unanimous shareholder agreement [NBBCA s. 60(1)]. In Prince Edward Island, the directors' duty to manage is not qualified [PEICA s. 21(1)].
640. CBCA s. 2(1).
641. CBCA s. 106(1) and (2).
642. CBCA s. 106(3).
643. A resolution passed by a majority of the votes cast by the shareholders who voted [CBCA s. 2(1)].
644. A proposed amendment adding s. 106(3.4) to the CBCA would make this procedure for electing directors mandatory for a 'distributing corporation' (basically a public corporation – *see supra* n. 168) and allow shareholders to vote for or against the election of each nominated director. *See* Bill C-25, s. 13, for the first session of the forty-second Parliament, which, as of 14 Dec. 2017 had been passed by the House of Commons and was being considered by the Senate. This amendment would bring an end to slate voting on an election of directors for distributing corporations. Slate voting calls for one vote by shareholders for an entire proposed slate of directors that would fill all the available directorship positions and the vote would either be in favour or withheld rather than a vote for or against.
645. CBCA s. 111. In memorandum jurisdictions, directors are elected in accordance with the company's articles and in some cases, additional directors may be appointed by the elected directors. *See,* for example, BCBCA s. 122.
646. *See* CBCA s. 107.
647. CBCA s. 137(4). In those jurisdictions which have no statutory provisions, cumulative voting may still be provided for in the constitutional documents. In New Brunswick, cumulative voting is mandatory [NBBCA s. 65].

of a specified class. While this method is recognized in the CBCA,[648] the provisions for class voting must be contained in the articles. Normally directors are nominated by management, however, under the CBCA shareholders holding at least 5% of the voting shares[649] may make a proposal containing a nomination for the election of directors. If the nomination is submitted to the corporation at least ninety days before the anniversary date of the previous annual meeting of shareholders, it must be included in the management proxy circular, with a statement of not more than 500 words supporting the proposal. Shareholders may also nominate directors at a shareholders' meeting,[650] although this is usually ineffective, as in most widely held corporations management controls a majority of the votes to be cast through proxy solicitation.

4. Term of Office

281. The directors who are named in the notice of directors filed with the incorporating documents hold office until the first meeting of shareholders.[651] Thereafter directors' appointments are usually for a term of one year, although directors may be elected for different terms up to a maximum of three years.[652] All directors need not be elected for the same term, and this allows for staggered terms. If the term of office is not specified, the director ceases to hold office at the close of the first annual meeting of shareholders after his election.[653] Notwithstanding a director's original term of office, if succeeding directors are not duly elected at a shareholders' meeting, the incumbent directors remain in office until their successors are elected.[654]

648. CBCA s. 109(2).
649. CBCA s. 137(4). There is no similar provision in Quebec. In New Brunswick, shareholders who nominate directors must have at least 10% of the voting shares [NBBCA s. 89(4)].
650. CBCA s. 137(4).
651. CBCA s. 106(2).
652. CBCA s. 106(3), (4) and (5). There is a proposed amendment to the CBCA that would add s. 106(3.1) which would provide that for a 'distributing corporation' (basically a public corporation – *see supra* n. 168) a director's term would be limited to one year (*see* the first session of the forty-second Parliament, Bill C-25, s. 13, which, as of 14 Dec. 2017 had been passed by the House of Commons and was being considered by the Senate). This would eliminate the potential for staggered boards in distributing corporations and would be consistent with Toronto Stock Exchange requirements for corporations with shares listed on the Toronto Stock Exchange. In New Brunswick and Prince Edward Island, a director holds office for a one-year term [NBBCA s. 65(5); PEICA s. 24 and s. 25(a)]. In Nova Scotia and British Columbia, this matter is dealt with only in the corporate articles and not in the act.
653. CBCA s. 106(5).
654. CBCA s. 106(6).

5. Qualifications

282. The following persons are disqualified from acting as directors:[655] anyone who is less than 18 years of age,[656] anyone who has been found by a court to be of unsound mind, a person who is not an individual, or a person who is a bankrupt.[657] A body corporate, therefore, may not act as a director. A director is not required to hold shares of the corporation unless required by the articles of the corporation.[658] One quarter of the directors must be resident Canadians.[659] Where, however, the CBCA prescribes, or an act of Parliament requires, with respect to a particular business sector, that there be a specified level of Canadian ownership or control then a majority of the directors must be resident Canadians.[660] Where there is a requirement for a majority of Canadian directors in a particular business sector, there is an exception for a holding corporation that earns in Canada directly or through its subsidiaries less than 5% of its total gross revenues in Canada. In that situation only one-third of the directors need be resident Canadians.[661]

6. Number of Directors

283. A corporation must have one or more directors, but where the corporation has outstanding issued securities which are or were part of a distribution to the public and are held by more than one person, there must be at least three directors, at least

655. CBCA s. 105(1). In those provincial jurisdictions which do not provide for directors' qualifications, such provisions are often contained in the corporation's constitution.
656. In New Brunswick and Newfoundland, directors must be at least 19 years old [NBBCA s. 63(1); NCA s. 172(a)].
657. BCBCA s. 124(2)(d) provides for an additional disqualification where a person has been convicted of an offence in connection with the promotion, formation or management of a corporation or involving fraud, for a period of five years following suspension of sentence or imposition of a fine or the end of imprisonment. The court may exempt a person from this disqualification and it ceases if a pardon is granted. There is a similar provision in New Brunswick, however it applies only for a three-year term [NBBCA s. 63(1)(e)].
658. CBCA s. 105(2).
659. CBCA s. 105(3). A 'resident Canadian' is defined in s. 2(1) to mean an individual who is (a) a Canadian citizen ordinarily resident in Canada, (b) a Canadian citizen not ordinarily resident in Canada who is a member of a prescribed class of persons (s. 13 of the Regulations), or (c) a permanent resident within the meaning of the *Immigration and Refugee Protection Act* and ordinarily resident in Canada, except a permanent resident who has been ordinarily resident in Canada for more than one year after the time when he first became eligible to apply for Canadian citizenship. Likewise, one quarter of the directors of a Saskatchewan corporation must reside in Saskatchewan [SBCA s. 100(3)]. In Quebec, Nova Scotia, and New Brunswick, none of the directors need be Canadian citizens or residents of the province.
660. CBCA s. 105(3.1).
661. CBCA s. 105(4).

two of whom are not officers or employees of the corporation or its affiliates.[662] The actual number of directors is set out in the articles, which may provide for a fixed number or a range, except that where the articles provide for cumulative voting, a fixed number of directors must be specified.[663] The shareholders can amend the articles by special resolution[664] to increase or decrease the number or minimum or maximum number of directors, but no decrease can shorten a director's term of office and no decrease is permitted where cumulative voting is provided for in the articles and there are a sufficient number of votes opposing the decrease to elect a director.[665]

7. Remuneration of Directors

284. Directors do not have an inherent right to receive remuneration for their services.[666] Subject to the articles, the by-laws or a unanimous shareholder agreement, directors' compensation is established by the directors themselves[667] and there are no specific statutory provisions governing the procedure for doing so, other than the directors' duty to act honestly and in good faith with a view to the best interests of the corporation.[668] There are, however, corporate governance guidelines for 'reporting issuers' (i.e., public companies) issued by the Canadian Securities Administrators that address the issue of compensation. The corporate governance guidelines and required corporate governance disclosure are discussed in paragraphs 293–296.

8. Ceasing to Hold Office or Removal from Office

285. A director ceases to hold office when he dies or resigns, is removed from office, or becomes disqualified from acting (*see* §3.II.A.4 and 5 above – paragraphs

662. CBCA s. 102(2). In Ontario only one-third of the directors of an offering corporation must not be officers or employees of the corporation or any of its affiliates. *See* OBCA s. 115(3). In British Columbia a public company must have an audit committee that consists of at least three members of the board of directors and a majority of the audit committee must not be officers or employees of the company or of an affiliate of the company [BCBCA s. 224]. There is no similar outsider provision in Prince Edward Island or Quebec. In New Brunswick, subject to the articles, the number of directors is specified in the by-laws and is not set out in the act [NBBCA s. 60(2)]. The NSCA provides for a minimum of one director [NSCA s. 93].
663. CBCA s. 107(a).
664. A 'special resolution' is defined in the CBCA as a resolution passed by a majority of not less than two-thirds of the votes cast by the shareholders who voted or signed by all the shareholders entitled to vote on that resolution [CBCA s. 2(l)].
665. CBCA ss 112, 173(l)(m).
666. *Roray v. Howe Sound Mills & Logging Co.* (1915), 22 D.L.R. 855, 21 B.C.R. 406, 31 W.L.R. 409 (C.A.).
667. CBCA s. 125.
668. CBCA s. 122(1)(a). In British Columbia however the articles of the company may provide for the establishment of compensation.

281 and 282).[669] A director may be removed by ordinary resolution[670] at a special meeting held for that purpose.[671] There are special rules where cumulative voting or class voting provisions are in effect. Problems may arise when an individual has a contractual arrangement with a corporation, for example, as a managing director, and is both an employed manager and a director. If he is removed from his position as a director and as a result can no longer act as manager, he may have a claim for breach of contract. A director who resigns, or learns of the calling of a meeting for the purpose of removing or replacing him, is entitled to attend and be heard at the meeting and may submit a written statement giving reasons for his resignation or opposing the corporation's proposed action, a copy of which must be sent by the corporation to the shareholders and the Director.[672]

9. Appointment of Officers and Delegation of Powers

286. Subject to the articles, the by-laws, or a unanimous shareholder agreement, the directors designate the offices of the corporation, appoint as officers persons of full capacity, specify their duties, and delegate to them powers to manage the business and affairs of the corporation.[673] The directors may not delegate the powers specifically reserved to the directors by CBCA section 115(3). A director may also be appointed an officer and two or more offices of the corporation may be held by the same person.[674] The offices of the corporation and duties of senior officers may be specified in the corporation's by-laws.

10. Remuneration of Officers

287. Officers, as employees of the corporation, are likely entitled to receive reasonable remuneration for their services. Subject to the articles, the by-laws, or a unanimous shareholder agreement, compensation for officers is established from time to time by the board of directors.[675] There are no specific statutory provisions governing the procedure for doing so, other than the directors' duty to act honestly and in good

669. CBCA s. 108. In Ontario, a director named in the articles (a first director) may not resign unless at the time his resignation takes effect a successor is elected or appointed [OBCA s. 119(2)]. There are no provisions in the NSCA or PEICA dealing with this matter, however the articles or by-laws of the company may provide for directors' ceasing to hold office.
670. An 'ordinary resolution' is defined in the CBCA as a resolution passed by a majority of the votes cast by the shareholders who voted [CBCA s. 2(1)].
671. CBCA s. 109. In British Columbia, directors may be removed in accordance with the memorandum or articles, but by BCBCA s. 128(3), a company may remove a director by special resolution (a resolution passed by three quarters of the votes cast). A replacement director may then be appointed by ordinary resolution.
672. CBCA s. 110. There is no similar provision in many of the provincial statutes.
673. CBCA s. 121(a). This matter is not dealt with in the NSCA, but the articles of the company may provide for appointment of officers.
674. CBCA s. 121(b) and (c).
675. CBCA s. 125. In British Columbia, Nova Scotia, and Prince Edward Island, there are no statutory provisions relating to remuneration of officers. The articles or by-laws of the company may, however, provide for the establishment of compensation.

faith with a view to the best interests of the corporation.[676] *See,* however, the discussion of the corporate governance guidelines in paragraphs 293–296.

11. Removal of Officers

288. The board of directors may remove an officer from his position, subject to the officer's contractual rights, if any. There are no provisions in the act relating to the removal of officers.

B. Powers of Management and Representation

1. Scope of the Directors' Power to Manage

289. Directors generally have the formal legal power to manage the business and affairs of the corporation.[677] This power is exercised directly, for example, through long range corporate planning, and indirectly through employees and agents of the corporation. The directors' power to manage is subject to the provisions of a unanimous shareholder agreement, which may restrict it in whole or in part.[678] Under most corporate statutes in Canada directors' management powers are not subject to the articles or by-laws.[679] Directors may make, amend, or repeal by-laws, subject to subsequent approval by ordinary resolution[680] of the shareholders at the next shareholders' meeting.[681] Directors are answerable to the shareholders for the general performance of the corporation. Specific decisions made by the directors acting within their authority are, however, not reviewable by the shareholders. Matters over which directors have authority cannot validly be dealt with by the shareholders unless a unanimous shareholder agreement removes a power or powers normally held by the directors and gives it, or them, to the shareholders.

---

676. CBCA s. 122(1)(a).
677. CBCA s. 102(1).
678. CBCA s. 146(2). In Prince Edward Island, the directors' power to manage is not qualified [PEICA s. 21(1)]. Unanimous shareholder agreements are discussed *infra* para. 432.
679. In British Columbia, however, BCBCA s. 136 provides that the directors shall manage or supervise the management of the affairs and business of the company, but this provision is subject to the BCBCA and the company's articles. As a result, the directors' powers to manage can be limited in the articles, but by BCBCA s. 136(2), such a limitation is not effective against a person who does not have knowledge of it. In Saskatchewan, although the directors' power to manage as set out in SBCA s. 97(1) is subject only to a unanimous shareholder agreement, s. 97(3) provides that where the articles restrict the powers of the directors, the shareholders assume the rights, powers, and duties of the directors to that extent. The NCA is the same [NCA ss 167 and 169]. In New Brunswick, the directors' duty to manage is subject to the articles, the by-laws and a unanimous shareholder agreement [NBBCA s. 60(1)]. There are no provisions in the NSCA dealing with this matter, but the articles of the company may provide for directors' powers.
680. An 'ordinary resolution' is defined as a resolution passed by a majority of the votes cast by the shareholders who voted in respect of the resolution [CBCA s. 2(1)].
681. CBCA s. 103. There is no similar provision in the BCBCA, although changes to the articles are generally initiated by management and put before the shareholders for approval.

2. The Application of Principles of Agency Law

290. A corporation must carry out its business through agents and is bound by the acts of its agents in accordance with the principles of agency law. These principles may become complicated because corporations often have many individuals who purport to act as agents, some of whom may be exceeding their authority in doing so. In the past, the courts have held that special agency rules apply to corporations. One of these rules, the constructive notice doctrine, held that third parties were deemed to have knowledge of the contents of a corporation's constating documents and any other documents filed at the public registry. If a provision of such a document limited the actual authority of an agent of the corporation, including its board of directors or managers, so that the agent was prohibited from carrying out an act, the third party, even though he had no actual knowledge of such a prohibition, could not claim that the agent had apparent authority based on the agent's title or position.[682] The constructive notice doctrine was, however, qualified by the indoor management rule,[683] whereby the third party was deemed to have knowledge only of publicly available documents and was not obliged to ensure that all internal regulations of the corporation had been complied with. The constructive notice doctrine has now been abolished under general statutes of incorporation in Canada,[684] so that no person is affected by or is deemed to have knowledge of the contents of a corporate document merely because it is filed or available for inspection at the corporation's offices. The CBCA also provides that neither the corporation nor any guarantor of an obligation of the corporation may assert against a person dealing with the corporation that the articles, by-laws, or a unanimous shareholder agreement have not been complied with, the persons named in the most recent notice of directors are not the directors, a person held out by a corporation as a director, officer, or agent has not been duly appointed or has no authority to perform customary duties, a document issued by a director, officer or, agent of a corporation with actual or usual authority to issue the document is not valid or genuine or certain specified types of transactions were not authorized, except where the person has or ought to have knowledge to the contrary by virtue of his position or relationship with the corporation.[685]

3. Procedure for the Exercise of the Powers of the Directors

291. Individual directors have no inherent authority to bind the corporation. Their authority is collective. They usually act by a majority vote at formally held meetings of which proper notice has been given. The notice requirements, procedure, quorum, and location[686] for directors' meetings may be set out in the articles or by-

682. *Ernest v. Nicholls* (1857), 6 H.L. Cas. 401, 10 E.R. 1351.

683. Developed in *Royal British Bank v. Turquand* (1856), 6 E.&B. 327, 119 E.R. 886.

684. *See,* for example, CBCA s. 17.

685. CBCA s. 18. There is no similar provision in British Columbia or Prince Edward Island.

686. In Ontario and New Brunswick, except where the by-laws otherwise provide, directors' meetings must be held at the corporation's registered office, and in Ontario, except where the articles or by-laws otherwise provide, the majority of directors' meetings in any financial year of the corporation, must be held in Canada [OBCA s. 126(1) and (2); NBBCA s. 72(l) and (2)].

laws. If not otherwise set out, the CBCA[687] provides that the quorum is a majority of directors or minimum number of directors provided for by the articles.[688] One quarter of the directors present at a directors' meeting must be resident Canadians or the resident Canadian director(s) unable to be present must approve of the business transacted at the meeting, in writing or by telecommunication.[689] The exception to this is a corporation which does not require a majority of resident Canadian directors as described in §3.II.A.5 (paragraph 282) above. Subject to the by-laws, if all the directors of the corporation consent, a director may participate in a meeting by telephone or other communication facilities.[690] A resolution signed by all the directors entitled to vote is as valid as if it had been passed at a meeting of directors or committee of directors.[691] The CBCA provides that an act of a director or officer is valid notwithstanding an irregularity in his election or appointment or a defect in his qualification.[692]

4. The Delegation of the Powers of the Directors

292. The directors, subject to contrary provisions in the articles, by-laws, or a unanimous shareholder agreement, may delegate to the officers,[693] a managing director, or a committee of the directors,[694] the power to manage the corporation. However, there are statutory restrictions on delegation[695] which prohibit the delegation of fundamental powers. Accordingly, the directors cannot delegate their power to:

- submit to the shareholders any question or matter requiring shareholder approval;
- fill a vacancy among the directors or in the office of the auditor;
- issue securities except in the manner and on the terms authorized by the directors;
- declare dividends;
- purchase, redeem, or otherwise acquire shares issued by the corporation;
- pay a commission in connection with a purchase of shares;
- approve a management proxy circular;
- approve a takeover bid circular or directors' circular;
- approve financial statements; or
- adopt, amend, or repeal by-laws.

---

687. CBCA s. 114(2).
688. In Ontario, the quorum cannot be less than two-fifths of the number of directors, or minimum number of directors, as the case may be. Where a corporation has less than three directors, all directors must be present to constitute a quorum [OBCA s. 126(3) and (4)].
689. CBCA s. 114(3) and (4). There are no similar provisions in jurisdictions which do not have residency requirements for directors. (*See* §3.II.A.5).
690. CBCA s. 114(9). Not all jurisdictions permit telephone meetings.
691. CBCA s. 116. There is no similar provision in Prince Edward Island.
692. CBCA s. 116.
693. CBCA s. 121.
694. CBCA s. 115(1).
695. CBCA s. 115(3).

5. Corporate Governance Guidelines

293. In 1994 the Dey Report, commissioned by the Toronto Stock Exchange (TSX), recommended that a majority of directors of corporations listed on the TSX be 'independent' directors. The Dey Report recommended other corporate governance guidelines. Corporations would not be required to follow the guidelines but if they did not follow the 'guidelines' they would be required to disclose this in their annual reports and explain why the guidelines were not followed. The TSX adopted the Dey Report recommendations in 1995.

294. The TSX guidelines have since been replaced by National Instrument 58-101 (NI 58-101) issued by the Canadian Securities Administrators. NI 58-101 became effective on 30 June 2005.[696] It applies to all persons who distribute securities to the public. It requires that when an issuer that has distributed securities to the public solicits a proxy from its securities holders for the purpose of electing directors (or persons in equivalent positions), its management information circular must include certain specified disclosure concerning its corporate governance. If the issuer is not, in a particular year, soliciting a proxy from security holders for the purpose of electing directors, it must nonetheless include the required corporate governance disclosure in its annual information form disclosure (a type of disclosure document that must be provided under securities laws if a person has issued securities to the public).

Corporate governance disclosure requires disclosure of the identity of directors who are independent and the identity of directors who are not independent. For the directors that are identified as not being independent the disclosure must identify the basis for the determination that they are not independent. A director is not 'independent' if the director has a relationship with the corporation that could 'in the view of the issuer's board of directors, be reasonably expected to interfere with the exercise of a member's independent judgment'. Persons who would not be considered 'independent' include an individual who is, or has been within the last three years, an employee or executive officer of the issuer, an individual one of whose immediate family members is, or has been within the last three years, an executive officer of the issuer, or an individual who is, or was within the last three years, a partner or employee of a firm that is the issuer's internal or external auditor.

The corporate governance disclosure must also note whether a majority of the board of directors is independent. If a majority is not independent the corporate disclosure must indicate what the board does to facilitate independent judgment in carrying out its responsibilities. It must also disclose other directorship positions held by the directors. It must further disclose whether or not the chair of the board is an independent director and whether or not the independent directors hold regularly

696. There were proposed amendments to National Instrument 58-101 in 2008 (*see* 'Request for Comment – Proposed Repeal and Replacement of National Policy 58-201 and National Instrument 58-101' (2008) 31 OSCB 12158 available at http://www.osc.gov.on.ca/documents/en/Securities-Category5/rule_20081219_58-201_rfc.pdf) but comments on the proposed amendments suggested it was not an appropriate time to introduce significant changes to the corporate governance regime in Canada and the Canadian Securities Administrators chose not to implement the proposed amendments. *See* Canadian Securities Administrators Staff Notice 58-305, 13 Nov. 2009 (2009) 32 OSCB 9347 (available at http://www.osc.gov.on.ca/en/26274.htm).

scheduled meetings at which non-independent directors and members of management are not present.

The corporate governance disclosure must disclose the attendance record of each director for all board meetings in the year. It must include the written mandate of the board if it has one and whether or not the board has a written code of ethics for directors, officers, and employees. The disclosure must also describe the process by which the board determines the compensation for the issuer's directors and officers and must disclose whether or not the board has a compensation committee composed entirely of independent directors.

295. Form 58-101F1 dealing with corporate governance disclosure was amended effective on 31 December 2014 for Manitoba, Newfoundland and Labrador, Northwest Territories, Nova Scotia, Nunavut, Ontario, Quebec, and Saskatchewan to require disclosure of whether the issuer has adopted a written policy relating to the identification and nomination of women directors. It also requires that if the issuer has not adopted such a policy it must disclose why it has not done so. The amended form also requires disclosure of whether the issuer has adopted a written policy for the identification and nomination of women directors and if it has not done so to explain why not. The form further requires disclosure of whether the board considers the level of representation of women on the board in identifying and nominating candidates for election or re-election to the board. If no such consideration is given, the issuer must disclose the reasons for not doing so. Disclosure is also required of whether the issuer considers the level of representation of women in executive officer positions when making executive officer appointments or to explain why it does not do so. Disclosure of targets for representation of women on the board and in executive positions is required and an explanation is required if the issuer has not adopted targets. Finally, disclosure is required of the number and percentage of women on the board and among executive officer positions.[697]

NI 58–101 does not require a public corporation to have an independent board of directors or that it have a written code of ethics or an independent compensation committee. It simply requires corporations that have distributed securities to the public in Canada to provide disclosure to investors about these aspects of their corporate governance. The corporation could thus choose to have a largely management-controlled board (subject to, for instance, a CBCA requirement to have two independent directors). It would, however, have to disclose to investors that it did not have a majority of independent directors.

296. In addition to NI 58-101 the Canadian Securities Administrators have issued National Policy 58-201 (NP 58-201) that provides guidelines on corporate governance.[698] It addresses issues such as the composition of the board, meetings of

697. There is a proposed amendment to the CBCA that would add s. 172.1 requiring directors of prescribed corporations to disclose to shareholders at the annual meeting certain information concerning diversity among the directors and members of the senior management of the corporation. *See* Bill C-25, s. 24, for the first session of the forty-second Parliament, which, as of 14 Dec. 2017 had been passed by the House of Commons and was being considered by the Senate.

698. There were proposals in 2008 to amend National Policy 58-101 but these proposals were not adopted. *See supra* n. 696.

independent directors, the mandate of the board, the orientation, and continuing education of directors, codes of conduct and ethics, the nomination of directors, and compensation policies. NP 58-201 sets out guidelines that, according to the policy, are not intended to be prescriptive. NP 58-201 says that the Canadian Securities Administrators 'encourage issuers to consider the guidelines in developing their own corporate governance practices'.

NP 58-201 recommends that the board should consist of a majority of independent directors. It recommends that the chair of the board be an independent director. It adds that the independent directors should hold regularly scheduled meetings at which non-independent directors and members of management are not in attendance.

NP 58-201 recommends that boards adopt a written mandate explicitly acknowledging responsibility for stewardship of the corporation, including satisfying itself as to the integrity of the chief executive officer and other executive officers, and that the CEO and other executive officers create a culture of integrity throughout the organization. The mandate, it is recommended, should adopt a strategic planning process and approve, on at least an annual basis, a strategic plan. The mandate should identify the principal risks of the business and ensure the implementation of systems to manage the risks. The mandate should address succession planning, adopting a communication policy, internal control and management information systems, and develop the corporation's approach to corporate governance. In addition, the mandate should set out measures for receiving feedback from stakeholders, perhaps, for instance, permitting stakeholders to contact independent directors directly. It should set out as well the expectations and responsibilities of directors, including basic duties and responsibilities with respect to attendance at board meetings and advance review of meeting materials.

NP 58-201 recommends that the board ensures that all new directors receive a comprehensive orientation, understand the nature and operation of the corporation's business, and provide continuing education for all directors.

The board should, according to NP 58-201, adopt a written code of business conduct and ethics. The code should provide written standards that are reasonably designed to promote integrity and deter wrongdoing. It should address conflicts of interest, the protection, and proper use of corporate assets and opportunities, confidentiality of corporate information, fair dealing with the issuer's security holders, customers, suppliers, competitors, and employees, compliance with laws, rules and regulations, and reporting of any illegal or unethical behaviour. The board should be responsible for monitoring compliance with the code and is required to publicly disclose any material departure from the code.

According to NP 58-201, the board should appoint a nominating committee composed entirely of independent directors. The nominating committee should have a written charter that clearly establishes the committee's purpose, responsibilities, member qualifications, member appointment and removal, structure and operations, and manner of reporting to the board. The nominating committee should consider what competencies and skills the board, as a whole, should possess, assess what competencies and skills each existing director possesses, and the competencies and skills each new nominee would bring to the boardroom.

NP 58-201 further recommends that the board appoint a compensation committee composed entirely of independent directors. The compensation committee should have a written charter that establishes its purpose, responsibilities, member qualifications, member appointment and removal, structure and operations, and manner of reporting to the board. The compensation committee should be given authority to engage any outside advisor that it determines to be necessary to permit it to carry out its duties.

NP 58-201 also recommends regular board assessments in which each director's effectiveness and contribution is assessed and the mandate of the board is reviewed.

As the Canadian Securities Administrators indicate in the Policy, it is not intended to be prescriptive. Concern is expressed that the guidelines in the policy might not be appropriate for some corporations, particularly so-called controlled corporations.

C. Duties of Directors and Officers to the Corporation, Shareholders, and Third Parties

1. Fiduciary Duties Generally

297. The obligation of directors and officers to manage the corporation is regulated by standards of care and skill in carrying out those management duties. In addition, because directors and officers manage and control assets of the corporation, fiduciary duties are imposed on them. The standard of care and extent of fiduciary duties were first developed by the courts and were subsequently codified by legislation. The legislation has also imposed specific statutory duties, prohibitions, and liabilities regulating the activities of directors and officers.[699]

2. Duty of Care and Other Statutory Obligations

a. Duty of Care

298. At common law,[700] the standard of care and skill established for directors is partly objective and partly subjective. A director need not exhibit in the performance of his duties a greater degree of skill than may reasonably be expected from a person of his knowledge and experience.[701] Statutory provisions were introduced in an attempt to upgrade this common law standard. The CBCA[702] provides that every director and officer in exercising his powers and discharging his duties must exercise the care, diligence, and skill that a reasonably prudent person would exercise in comparable circumstances. They cannot be relieved from their statutory liabilities except to the extent that shareholders assume the directors' responsibilities in a unanimous shareholder

699. There are no such statutory provisions in the NSCA or the PEICA.
700. In Quebec, the courts have described the role of a director as that of a mandatory, as described in the Civil Code. The obligations of a mandatory to the mandator (the company) and to third parties are set out in the Civil Code. The mandatory must exercise the reasonable skill and care of a prudent administrator.
701. *Re City Equitable Fire Insurance Co. Ltd.*, [1925] 1 Ch. 407, aff'd [1925] 1 Ch. 500 (C.A.).
702. CBCA s. 122(1)(b). The NSCA and PEICA do not set out a standard of care and skill and, therefore, the common law governs.

agreement,[703] and therefore, they cannot contract out of liability. At common law, a director is not bound to give continuous attention to the affairs of the corporation and is not required to attend all meetings.[704] A director who is absent from a meeting may, however, be deemed to have consented to a resolution which was passed or action taken at the meeting unless he has expressly dissented within seven days after he became aware of the resolution.[705] A director may rely on officials of the corporation to whom a matter has been properly delegated unless there are grounds for suspicion[706] and is not liable for breach of duty if he relies in good faith on properly presented financial statements or a report of a professional.[707]

In *Peoples Department Store v. Wise*[708] the Supreme Court of Canada considered the duty of care in the context of section 122(1)(b) of the CBCA. The Court held that if there is a breach of the standard of care creditors may be able to succeed in an action against the directors where they also show damages and causation. The Court also discussed the scope of the statutory standard. It noted that the phrase 'in comparable circumstances' 'modifies the statutory standard by requiring the context in which a given decision was made to be taken into account'. The Court (at paragraph 63) described the standard as an objective standard saying:

> To say that the standard is objective makes it clear that the factual aspects of the circumstances surrounding the actions of the director or officer are important in the case of the section 122(1)(b) duty of care, as opposed to the subjective motivation of the director or officer, which is the central focus of the statutory fiduciary duty of section 122(1)(a) of the CBCA.

The Court noted (at paragraph 67):

> Directors and officers will not be held in breach of the duty of care under section 122(1)(b) of the CBCA if they act prudently and on a reasonably informed basis. The decisions they make must be reasonable business decisions in light of all the circumstances about which the directors or officers knew or ought to have known.

The Court also noted the causation requirement stating that 'in order for a plaintiff to succeed in challenging a business decision he or she has to establish that the directors acted (i) in breach of the duty of care, and (ii) in a way that caused injury to the plaintiff'.

703. CBCA s. 122(3).
704. *Re City Equitable Fire Insurance Co. Ltd., supra* n. 701.
705. CBCA s. 123(3). There is no provision in the ABCA or NBBCA dealing with absent-directors.
706. *Re City Equitable Fire Insurance Co. Ltd., supra* n. 701.
707. CBCA s. 123(4). In *Peoples Department Store* (2002), 244 D.L.R. (4th) 564 (S.C.C.) the Supreme Court of Canada said that the word 'profession' in this provision in the CBCA suggests someone 'subject to the regulatory overview of [a] professional organization and [having] independent insurance coverage'.
708. (2002), 244 D.L.R. (4th) 564 (S.C.C.).

The *Peoples Department Store* case also spoke of what has been referred to in US cases as the 'business judgment rule'. The Supreme Court of Canada stated:

> In determining whether directors have acted in a manner that breached the duty of care, it is worth repeating that perfection is not demanded. Courts are ill-suited and should be reluctant to second-guess the application of business expertise to the considerations that are involved in corporate decision making, but they are capable, on the facts of any case, of determining whether an appropriate degree of prudence and diligence was brought to bear in reaching what is claimed to be a reasonable business decision at the time it was made.[709]

While the Court referred to the US terminology of the 'business judgment rule' it did not thereby import the US law associated with that term. The Court used the expression in noting the principle that a court will not second-guess management decisions. It did not, however, import the notion of the US business judgment rule that operates as a presumption that the directors' decisions have been made honestly and in good faith by a disinterested board of directors exercising due care. The Court noted that 'directors and officers will not be held in breach of the duty of care under section 122(1)(b) of the CBCA if they act prudently and on a reasonably informed basis'. The Court has not expressly adopted a presumption in favour of the directors and officers and they are thus protected by the 'business judgment rule', as it applies in Canada, only if they acted honestly, prudently, in good faith, and on reasonable grounds.

Another important case addressing the duty of care was *UPM-Kymmene Inc. v. UPM-Kymmene Miramichi Corp.*[710] The trial court held that the directors have a duty to proceed cautiously (particularly on a non-urgent matter) and to educate themselves thoroughly. The Court added that they should obtain the views of management and of experts on executive compensation. The Court further noted that the business judgment rule only protects directors who 'are scrupulous in their deliberations and demonstrate diligence in arriving at decisions'.

b. Other Statutory Obligations

299. In addition to the general duty of care, diligence, and skill, the CBCA imposes specific statutory duties and liabilities on directors and officers.[711] The CBCA requires that directors and officers comply with the act, regulations, articles, by-laws,

709. In the *BCE* case, *supra* n. 500, at para. 99, the Supreme Court of Canada noted that, 'under the business judgment rule, deference should be accorded to business decisions of directors taken in good faith and in the performance of the functions they were elected to perform by the shareholders'.
710. (2002), 214 D.L.R. (4th) 496 (Ont. Sup. Ct.), affirmed (2004), 250 D.L.R. (4th) 256 (Ont. C.A.) (known in Canada simply as the *Repap* case since the corporation involved was Repap Enterprises Inc.).
711. The NSCA does not provide statutory duties or liabilities. Directors' statutory liability in Prince Edward Island is limited to a declaration and payment of a dividend in insolvent circumstances [PEICA s. 65].

and a unanimous shareholder agreement.[712] This duty is enforceable by obtaining a compliance or restraining order.[713] In addition, non-compliance without reasonable cause is an offence.[714]

300. Most of the other statutory duties and liabilities are specific and often relate to maintaining the solvency of the corporation. Directors are jointly and severally liable to the corporation to make good its loss in the following circumstances:

- issuance of a share for which the consideration other than money is less than full value;[715]
- purchase, redemption, or acquisition of shares in insolvent circumstances;[716]
- payment of an improper commission on an issuance of shares;[717]
- payment of a dividend in insolvent circumstances;[718]
- payment of an indemnity to an officer or director of a corporation in circumstances where indemnification is not permitted under the act;[719] and
- payment to a dissenting shareholder or pursuant to an oppression claim in insolvent circumstances.[720]

Directors are jointly and severally liable to employees for all corporate debts not exceeding six months' wages, payable to each such employee for services performed for the corporation, while they were directors.[721] The act contains certain procedural limitations to a successful claim.

301. The CBCA also contains provisions regulating the obligations of directors and officers as insiders of the corporation.[722] A director or officer who purchases or sells a security of the corporation with knowledge of confidential information that, if generally known, might reasonably be expected to affect materially the value of any of the securities of the corporation is liable to compensate the seller or purchaser for any damages suffered by the seller or purchaser as a result of the purchase or sale.[723] Provincial securities legislation also deals with reporting and trading requirements for

712. CBCA s. 122(2).
713. CBCA s. 247.
714. CBCA s. 251.
715. CBCA ss 25 and 118; however, by s. 118(6), a director is not liable if he proves that he did not know and could not reasonably have known that the share was issued for less than full value.
716. CBCA ss 34, 35, 36, and 118.
717. CBCA ss 41 and 118.
718. CBCA ss 42 and 118.
719. CBCA ss 118 and 124.
720. CBCA ss 118, 190, and 241.
721. CBCA s. 119. In Saskatchewan, there is no time limitation on the amount of wages [SBCA s. 114]. There is no provision in the BCBCA, NBBCA, NSCA or NCA making directors liable for employees' wages, however liability for employees' wages may be provided for in other provincial statutes.
722. CBCA ss 126–130.
723. CBCA s. 131(4). *See also supra* paras 161–165.

insiders of federal corporations.[724] Legislation, both provincial and federal, provides for directors' liability in respect of a variety of other matters.

c. Indemnification and Insurance

302. A director or officer may be indemnified by the corporation for liability incurred in breaching his duty of care and skill and for other statutory liabilities, provided that he has acted honestly and in good faith with a view to the best interests of the corporation.[725] In the case of a criminal or administrative action or proceeding punished by a monetary penalty, the director or officer must have had reasonable grounds for believing that his conduct was lawful. Approval of the court is required where the corporation is to indemnify an officer or director for costs, charges, or expenses reasonably incurred in connection with an action by the corporation itself. Amounts paid in settlement of an action by a third party may be indemnified. Where the action is brought by the corporation, the director or officer may be indemnified against all costs, charges, and expenses reasonably incurred. This does not appear to extend to an amount paid to settle an action or satisfy a judgment. In addition to those situations in which a corporation may provide an indemnity, the corporation must indemnify a director or officer who has been substantially successful in defending an action or proceeding to which he has been made a party because of his position as an officer or director.[726] A corporation may purchase and maintain liability insurance for the benefit of officers and directors against any liability incurred.[727]

3. Duty to Act in the Best Interests of the Corporation

303. Directors and officers owe fiduciary duties to the corporation they serve. They must act honestly and in good faith with a view to the best interests of the corporation.[728] The case law in the area of directors' and officers' fiduciary duties is extensive and is marked by an ongoing expansion of these duties. A director who acts for two corporations owes a fiduciary duty to both of them. Some cases have extended the duty beyond the corporation and have held that directors owe a fiduciary duty to

724. In some provincial jurisdictions, insider trading and reporting requirements for provincial corporations are dealt with only in the securities legislation and not the corporate legislation. *See supra* §2.III.E, paras 155–165.

725. CBCA s. 124. There are no statutory indemnification provisions in the NSCA. In Prince Edward Island, there is a general indemnification provision in favour of directors subject to shareholder approval [PEICA s. 64].

726. In Quebec a corporation must indemnify a director or officer of the corporation or a former director or officer of the corporation against all costs, charges, and expenses reasonably incurred in the exercise of their functions, including an amount paid to settle an action or satisfy a judgment, or arising from investigative or other proceeding in which the person is involved, if the person acted with honesty and loyalty in the interest of the corporation and the person had reasonable grounds for believing that his or her conduct was lawful. *See* QBCA s. 159.

727. CBCA s. 124(6).

728. CBCA s. 122(1)(a). In Quebec, an obligation similar to a fiduciary one is imposed by the courts by reference to the obligations of a mandatory to the mandator (the company).

shareholders, particularly minority shareholders,[729] and other directors.[730] The categories of situations in which a fiduciary duty may be found are not closed and it may be that courts will find that directors owe a fiduciary duty to third parties such as creditors.

304. It is sometimes difficult to determine what is in the best interests of the corporation. The courts will not generally second-guess a decision of the directors of a corporation where the directors honestly believed they acted in the corporation's best interests.[731] The courts have established however, that directors' decisions must be motivated by a desire to maximize corporate profits and not simply to benefit a group of shareholders, employees, customers, or society as a whole.[732] Directors, as noted, must act in the best interests of the 'corporation'. The interests of the corporation may be broader than just the interests of shareholders. In *Peoples Department Store v. Wise*[733] it was said:

> We accept as an accurate statement of law that in determining whether [the directors] are acting with a view to the best interests of the corporation, it may be legitimate, given all the circumstances of a given case, for the board of directors to consider, inter alia, the interests of shareholders, employees, suppliers, creditors, consumers, governments and the environment.

Directors do not, in their capacity as directors, owe duties to individual shareholders.[734]

Since directors owe a duty to 'act in the best interests of the *corporation*' and since that includes not just the interests of shareholders but also the interests of employees, suppliers, creditors, consumers, governments, and the environment, the directors 'may find themselves in a situation where it is impossible to please all stakeholders'.[735] Where this is the case it is not sufficient for a complainant to show there was an alternative transaction that would have been more beneficial to the complainant. The complainant must show that a particular alternative was definitely

---

729. *See*, for example, *Dusik v. Newton* (1985), 62 B.C.L.R. 1; but *see Brant Investments Ltd. v. Keeprite Inc.* (1991), 3 O.R. (3rd) 289, 80 D.L.R. (4th) 161, affirming (1987), 60 O.R. (2nd) 737, 42 D.L.R. (4th) 15 (H.C.), additional reasons at (1987), 61 O.R. (2nd) 469, 43 D.L.R. (4th) 141 (H.Q.). *See also supra* §3.I.D, paras 239–43.
730. *See*, for example, *Beamish v. Solnick* (1980), 10 B.L.R. 224.
731. *See* the discussion of *Peoples Department Store v. Wise supra* para. 298 concerning the application of the 'business judgment rule' in Canada.
732. *Parke v. Daily News Ltd.*, [1962] 1 Ch. 927; 2 All E.R. 929 (Ch.D.). In Alberta, however, a director who has been elected or appointed by the holders of a class or series of shares or by employees or creditors or a class of employees or creditors, may give special, but not exclusive consideration to the interests of those who elected or appointed him [ABCA s. 117(4)].
733. [2004] 3 S.C.R. 461, 244 D.L.R. (4th) 564 (at para. 42). This statement in the *Peoples* case was referred to with approval in 2008 in the unanimous judgment of the Supreme Court of Canada in the *BCE* case, *supra* n. 500, at paras 39–40. On the potential liability of directors to employees of the corporation *see Nielsen Estate v. Epton* (2006), 13 B.L.R. (4th) 209 (Alta. Q.B.), paras 565–574.
734. *See*, for example, *Percival v. Wright*, [1902] 2 Ch. 421; *Weiss v. Schad* (1999), [1999] O.J. No. 4356 (S.C.J.), aff'd 161 O.A.S. 137 (Ont. C.A.).
735. *BCE* case, *supra* n. 500, at para. 83.

available and that it was clearly more beneficial to the company than the chosen transaction.[736]

305. The question of whether directors or officers have acted in good faith in the best interests of the corporation has arisen most often in the context of takeover bids. Some cases have expanded on the best interests approach in the takeover bid context. In *Teck Corporation v. Millar*[737] the Court said that if directors have acted in what they honestly believe to be the best interests of the corporation, and if they have reasonable grounds for that belief, then they will have acted for a proper purpose.[738]

Later, in *347883 Alberta Ltd. v. Producers Pipelines Inc.*[739] the Saskatchewan Court of Appeal considered the adoption of a poison rights plan and an issuer bid by Producers Pipelines Inc. The majority held that the test developed in *Teck Corporation v. Millar* did not go far enough in giving principles for determining whether or not the defensive strategy was reasonable in relation to the threat posed. The court referred to several US cases and concluded that when a corporation is faced with susceptibility to a takeover bid or an actual takeover bid, the directors must exercise their powers in accordance with their overriding duty to act bona fide and in the best interests of the corporation even though they may find themselves, through no fault of their own, in a conflict of interest situation. If, after investigation, they determine that action is necessary to advance the best interests of the company, they may act, but the onus will be on them to show that their acts were reasonable in relation to the threat posed and were directed to the benefit of the corporation and its shareholders as a whole, and not for an improper purpose such as entrenchment of the directors.

The majority of the court also noted that defensive actions should, wherever possible, be put to the shareholders for approval. Since the shareholders have the right to decide to whom and at what price they will sell their shares, defensive action must interfere as little as possible with that right. Accordingly, any defensive action should be put to the shareholders for prior approval where possible, or for subsequent ratification if not possible. Further, the court noted that '[d]efensive tactics that result in shareholders

736. In the *BCE* case, *supra* n. 500, the Supreme Court of Canada adopted the following statement from *Pente Investment Management Ltd. v. Schneider Corp.* (1998), 113 O.A.C. 253, (sub nom. *Maple Leaf Foods Inc. v. Schneider Corp.*) 42 O.R. (3d) 177, 1998 CarswellOnt 4035, 44 B.L.R. (2d) 115 (Ont. C.A.): 'the fact that alternative transactions were rejected by the directors is irrelevant unless it can be shown that a particular alternative was definitely available and clearly more beneficial to the company than the chosen transaction'.

737. [1973] 2 W.W.R. 385 (B.C.S.C.).

738. For a more recent case dealing with whether directors had acted on reasonable grounds in the best interests of the corporation *see Icahn Partners LP v. Lions Gate Entertainment Corp.* (2011), 17 B.C.L.R. (5th) 391 (B.C.C.A.). In that case the directors altered conversion rights on debentures allowing conversion of the debenture into shares sooner than they otherwise could have been converted. This had the effect of diluting the interest of a major shareholder who owned 37.9% of the shares but did not hold any of the debentures. One of the directors of the board held a significant interest in a company that held the debentures. The British Columbia Court of Appeal decided not to interfere with the decision of the trial judge who had found that the directors had made their decision in the best interests of the company based on reasonable grounds and after making a reasonable investigation.

739. [1991] 4 W.W.R. 577 (Sask. C.A.).

being deprived of the ability to respond to a takeover bid or to a competing bid are unacceptable'.

The *Producers Pipelines* case has been applied in a number of subsequent cases. In the 1998 decision in *CW Shareholding Inc. v. WIC Western International Communications Ltd.*[740] it was, however, held that the *Producers Pipelines* case went too far to the extent that it put the onus on the directors of the target to justify their actions. It was held that the directors of the target should be protected by the business judgment rule. If the *CW Shareholding* approach were followed the onus would be on complainants to show that the directors of the target acted in a way that was not reasonable in relation to the threat posed. In 2004, however, the Supreme Court of Canada held in *Peoples Department Store v. Wise* that the business judgment rule in Canada does not operate as a presumption in favour of the directors.[741]

Whether the directors bear an initial burden of proof in the context of a takeover bid before the business judgment rule will be applied was discussed in the Ontario Court of Appeal decision in *Pente Investment Management Ltd. v. Schneider Corp.*[742] The court did not appear to take a clear position on whether the directors bear an initial burden of proof. It did, however, suggest, in language similar to that in the US case of *Paramount Communications Inc. v. QVC Network Inc.*[743] (which was referred to by the court) that, '[p]rovided the decision taken is within a range of reasonableness, the court ought not to substitute its opinion for that of the board even though subsequent events may have cast doubt on the board's determination'. The *Schneider* case also considered whether the directors of a target owe a duty to conduct an auction upon a sale of control. The court said that the US case of *Revlon Inc.*, in which it was held that on a sale of control the duty of the directors is to get the maximum value for the shareholders, 'is not the law in Ontario' and that in Ontario 'an auction need not be held every time there is a change in control of a company'.

4. Duty with Respect to Conflicts of Interest

306. At common law, a director or officer was precluded from entering into a transaction where his duty to the corporation and personal interest or duty to a third person would conflict. Accordingly, a director could not cause the corporation to enter into transactions with himself or in which he otherwise had a personal interest conflicting with the interests of the corporation. The rule was strictly applied and it was irrelevant whether the transaction was fair.[744] The strict rule would not be applied if the corporate constitution allowed the transaction[745] or the shareholders consented.[746] Legislation

740. (1998) 39 O.R. (3rd) 755, 160 D.L.R. (4th) 131 (Ont. Ct. J.).

741. *See* the discussion *supra* para. 298.

742. (1998) 42 O.R. (3rd) 177, 113 O.A.C. 253, 44 B.L.R. (2nd) 115 (Ont. C.A.).

743. 637 A.2nd 34 (Del. 1994).

744. *See*, for example, *Aberdeen Railway Co. v. Blaikie Bros.*, [1843–60] All E.R. Rep. 249, 2 Eq. Rep. 1281 (H.L.).

745. *See*, for example, *The Liquidators of the Imperial Mercantile Credit Association v. Edward John Coleman and John Watson Knight*, [1873] L.R. 7; E&I App 189.

746. *See*, for example, *North-West Transportation Company Limited v. Beatty* (1887), 12 App. Cas. 589 (P.C.).

has been introduced for two purposes: first, to allow corporations to take advantage of beneficial contracts with interested directors and officers, and second, to regulate disclosure requirements for directors and officers. The CBCA[747] provides that a director or officer[748] who is a party to a material or proposed material contract with the corporation or who is a director or officer or has a material interest in an entity who is such a party, must disclose in writing or enter in the directors' minutes, the nature and extent of his interest. The director or officer may give a general notice declaring that he is a director or officer or has a material interest in an entity and, therefore, has a continuous material interest in that entity. A director or officer must also make a similar disclosure where the contract is one not normally requiring approval by the directors or shareholders. A contract in which a director or officer is interested is not void or voidable if the director or officer disclosed his interest in accordance with the act, the contract was approved by the directors or by a special resolution of the shareholders and the contract was fair and reasonable to the corporation at the time it was approved.[749]

5. Duty Not to Usurp Corporate Opportunities

307. A director or officer may not take, or make a personal profit from, a business opportunity which comes to him because of his position. The courts have held that a director or officer who has made a profit through taking advantage of an opportunity that belongs to the corporation, or for which it is negotiating, must account to the corporation for that profit.[750] The requirement to account does not depend on proof of *mala fides*. It is sometimes difficult to determine whether a particular opportunity belongs to the corporation. The recent cases have not set out strict guidelines and it is difficult to formulate a set of rules. The courts have the flexibility to look at the particular facts and determine whether it is fair to allow a director or officer to retain his profit from a transaction.[751] The court will look at all the relevant factors, including the position or office held, the nature of the opportunity, its ripeness, its specificness, and the degree of knowledge possessed by the fiduciary. It does not matter that the third party refused to deal with the corporation and that the corporation could not itself have

747. CBCA s. 120.
748. Under the BCBCA the disclosure requirements apply only to directors and senior officers (*See*, BCBCA s. 147).
749. There is considerable variation in the conflict of interest provisions in the general statutes of incorporation of the provinces and territories. For instance, in Saskatchewan, by SBCA s. 115(9), shareholders may by unanimous shareholder agreement, exclude the disclosure requirements of s. 115 or set forth other disclosure requirements, or both. By s. 115(10), where the shareholders have by unanimous shareholder agreement, excluded the provisions of s. 115 from application to the corporation, the rules of common law and equity do not apply to disclosure of interests in material contracts by directors. There are also significant differences in the general statutes of incorporation in New Brunswick and Nova Scotia. There are no provisions in the PEICA requiring that directors and officers disclose their interest, however it is advisable for directors and officers to do so.
750. This doctrine was established in *Regal (Hastings), Ltd. v. Gulliver*, [1942] 1 All E.R. 378 (H.L.).
751. *Canadian Aero Services Ltd. v. O'Malley*, [1974] S.C.R. 592, 62 D.L.R. (3rd) 635.

profited from the transaction.[752] If there is any doubt as to whether an opportunity rightfully belongs to the corporation, the director or officer can protect himself by fully informing the corporation of the circumstances and abiding by its independent decision.

6. Duty to Act for a Proper Purpose

308. Directors must exercise their powers only for the purpose for which they were granted. In cases where the directors have exercised their powers for an improper purpose, the transactions were held void and the directors made liable.[753] This doctrine applies whether the scope of the power is stated expressly in the statute or articles, or by implication. In many cases however, the purpose for which a particular power has been given to the directors is not clear. While it has been suggested that the courts should fall back upon the general obligation of directors to exercise their powers in the best interests of the corporation, they do not uniformly do so. Many of the cases deal with the issuance of shares by the directors to change the balance of power. A special rule arose in these cases suggesting that even if the directors used their power to issue shares in what they genuinely believed to be the best interests of the corporation, issuing shares for the purpose of defeating a majority interest was an improper purpose. In those cases where a purpose for the power to issue shares was not stated, the courts inferred a limited purpose, the raising of capital.[754] This approach has not been consistently followed. In *Teck Corporation v. Millar*,[755] the British Columbia Supreme Court held that the power to issue shares was no different than any other power given to the directors and should be limited only by constraints contained in the governing legislation and corporate articles. The judge held that where no such constraints could be found, the court should not imply a constraint. The only limitation was that the directors must have conducted themselves in the honest belief that they were acting in the best interests of the corporation. There must have been reasonable grounds for this belief. The decision apparently influenced a subsequent decision of the English House of Lords,[756] however that court still attempted to imply a purpose where one was not apparent. The law in Canada in this area is not clear. It appears, however, that the exercise by directors of a power will be held invalid if it is exercised for an improper purpose. A purpose is improper if it conflicts with the purpose which is stated in the legislation or the corporation's constating documents. If no purpose is stated, the court may infer a purpose or if that is not possible, may fall back on the general equitable obligation to exercise the power honestly in the best interests of the corporation.

It should be noted that securities administrators in Canada can exercise various powers where directors have engaged in defensive tactics in response to a takeover bid or an anticipated takeover bid.[757] Securities administrators in Canada have indicated

752. *Abbey Glen Property Corp. v. Stumborg* (1976), 65 D.L.R. (3rd) 325, aff'd 85 D.L.R. (3rd) 35 (Alta. C.A.).
753. *See,* for example, *Re Smith and Fawcett, Ltd.*, [1942] Ch. 304, [1942] 1 All E.R. 542 (C.A.).
754. *See,* for example, *Hogg v. Cramphorn Ltd.*, [1967] Ch. 254, [1966] 3 All E.R. 420 (Ch. D.).
755. 33 D.L.R. (3rd) 288; [1973] 2 W.W.R. 385 (B.C.S.C.).
756. *Howard Smith Ltd. v. Ampol Petroleums Ltd.*, [1974] 1 All E.R. 1126, [1974] A.C. 821 (H.L.).
757. *See* National Policy 62-202 issued by the Canadian Securities Administrators.

that they may, for instance, issue a cease trade order with respect shares issued as a defensive tactic to dilute the interests of a takeover bidder or prospective takeover bidder. For example, in 2017, in *Re Eco Oro Minerals Corp.*,[758] the Ontario Securities Commission issued a cease trade order with respect to the issuance of new shares to persons who supported incumbent management in the context of a proxy contest. In the view of the Ontario Securities Commission the timing of the issuance was designed to influence the outcome of the vote at a shareholder meeting where a dissident group proposed the election of a slate of directors other than the incumbent directors. The Ontario Securities Commission did not accept the alleged purpose of the new share issuance as being to raise equity capital to pay down debt – the rushed timing of the new share issuance to complete it before the shareholder meeting for which there was a proxy contest was such that there was an ulterior motive of influencing the outcome of the vote at the meeting. Also, in 2016, in *Re Hecla Mining Co.*[759] the Ontario and British Columbia securities commissions set out considerations they would take into account in assessing whether a cease trade order should be issued with respect to a dilutive private placement share issuance. Their joint decision said that the first question is whether the evidence clearly established that the private placement is not, in fact, a defensive tactic designed, in whole or in part, to alter the dynamics of the bid process. In answering that question they said that a non-exhaustive list of considerations is:

(i) whether the target has a serious and immediate need for the financing;
(j) whether there is evidence of a bona fide, non-defensive, business strategy adopted by the target; and
(k) whether the private placement has been planned or modified in response to, or in anticipation of, a bid.[760]

If the private placement is, or may be, a defensive tactic, the question then is whether the private placement should be interfered with. The two securities commissions set out the following non-exhaustive list of considerations in assessing this question:

(i) would the private placement otherwise be to the benefit of shareholders by, for example, allowing the target to continue its operations through the term of the bid or in allowing the board to engage in an auction process without unduly impairing the bid?
(ii) to what extent does the private placement alter the pre-existing bid dynamics, for example by depriving shareholders of the ability to tender to the bid?
(iii) are the investors in the private placement related parties to the target or is there other evidence that some or all of them will act in such a way as to enable the target's board to 'just say no' to the bid or a competing bid?
(iv) is there any information available that indicates the views of the target shareholders with respect to the takeover bid and/or the private placement?
(v) where a bid is underway as the private placement is being implemented, did the target's board appropriately consider the interplay between the private

758. 2017 ONSEC 23.
759. 39 O.S.C.B. 8927.
760. *Ibid.*, para. 97.

placement and the bid, including the effect of the resulting dilution of the bid and the need for financing?[761]

7. Ratification of Breaches of Fiduciary Duties

309. At common law, in some cases shareholders have been allowed to ratify an act of a director or directors that is a breach of the directors' fiduciary duty.[762] The cases have been inconsistent. It appears, however, that at common law shareholders may be allowed to validate a breach of fiduciary duty where a director has acted bona fide in the best interests of the corporation, even if he makes an incidental profit in the transaction. The CBCA[763] provides that no provision in a contract, the articles, the by-laws, or a resolution relieves a director or officer from liability for a breach of the act. Accordingly, shareholder ratification will not relieve a director or officer from the penalties provided for under the act for breach of duty. It is not clear whether shareholder ratification can relieve a director or officer from civil liability. An application under the CBCA to enforce an alleged breach of a right or duty owed to a corporation is not stayed or dismissed by reason only of shareholder approval, but evidence of such approval may be taken into account by the court.[764] Shareholder ratification, while not conclusively relieving a director or officer from liability for breach of fiduciary duty, may carry some weight.

8. Liability to Third Parties

310. Although the corporation is treated as a separate legal entity, a court may, in some circumstances, disregard the separate personality of the corporation and impose liability on shareholders, directors, or officers of the corporation. It has been said that courts may disregard the separate corporate entity where not to do so would be 'too flagrantly opposed to justice'.[765] It has also been said that the decisions in which courts disregard the corporate entity 'follow no consistent principle'.[766] Directors and officers may also, in some circumstances, be liable for torts committed by them while acting in their capacities as directors and officers.[767]

761. *Ibid.*, para. 100.
762. *See*, for example, *North-West Transportation Company, Limited v. Beatty* (1887), 12 App. Cas. 589 (P.C.); *Bamford v. Bamford*, [1970] Ch. 212 (C.A.).
763. CBCA s. 122(3).
764. CBCA s. 242(1).
765. *See Kosmopolous v. Constitution Insurance Co. of Canada* [1987] 1 S.C.R. 2.
766. *Ibid.*
767. *See ADGA Systems International Ltd. v. Valcom Ltd.* (1999), 43 O.R. (3rd) 101.

III. Auditor

A. Appointment Requirements, Remuneration, and Dismissal

311. The auditor of the corporation is an independent party, chosen by the shareholders to review and comment on the financial information provided by the corporation. The auditor reports to the shareholders the results of his review, and helps to ensure that the financial information fairly and accurately portrays the corporation's financial situation. The methods by which the auditor is appointed and removed, his competency assured and the safeguards for maintaining the auditor's independence from management are, therefore, of importance.

312. At their first organizational meeting after the incorporation of a corporation, the directors appoint an auditor to hold office until the first annual meeting of shareholders.[768] Thereafter, the shareholders of the corporation must appoint an auditor by ordinary resolution[769] at each annual meeting,[770] subject to the exception discussed under the heading 'Closed Corporations'.[771] The auditor holds office until the next annual meeting or until a successor is appointed.[772] The directors of the corporation fill vacancies unless the articles provide that a vacancy may only be filled by the shareholders.[773] If there is no quorum of directors, the vacancy is filled at a special shareholders' meeting.[774] If a corporation does not have an auditor, the court may appoint one on application by a shareholder or the Director, unless the shareholders have properly resolved not to appoint an auditor.[775]

313. A person is disqualified from being an auditor of a corporation if he is not independent from the corporation, any of its affiliates or the directors or officers of any of them. Independence is a question of fact; however, the act sets out some deeming provisions.[776] On application by an interested person, a court may declare that an auditor is disqualified[777] or may exempt an auditor from disqualification.[778] An auditor who becomes disqualified while acting as auditor for a corporation must resign.[779]

---

768. CBCA s. 104(1)(e).
769. An 'ordinary resolution' is a resolution passed by a majority of the votes cast by the shareholders who voted in respect of the resolution [CBCA s. 2(1)].
770. CBCA s. 162(1).
771. *See infra* para. 430.
772. CBCA s. 162(1) and (3).
773. CBCA s. 166(1) and (3).
774. CBCA s. 166(2).
775. CBCA s. 167. There is no provision in the NSCA for a court appointed auditor.
776. CBCA s. 161. In British Columbia, BCBCA s. 204 provides that an auditor must be a member in good standing of the Canadian Institute of Chartered Accountants or the Certified General Accountants' Association of British Columbia, or must be certified by the Auditor Certification Board established under the BCBCA.
777. CBCA s. 161(4).
778. CBCA s. 161(5). In Manitoba, the shareholders may resolve on an annual basis to appoint an auditor who would otherwise be disqualified under the act, if the resolution is consented to by all the voting and non-voting shareholders [MCA s. 155(6) and (7)].
779. CBCA s. 161(3).

314. The auditor's remuneration is fixed by an ordinary resolution[780] of the shareholders, or if not fixed by them, may be fixed by the directors.[781] When a court appoints an auditor, it also fixes the auditor's remuneration.[782]

315. An auditor ceases to hold office when he dies or resigns or when he is removed by ordinary resolution[783] at a special meeting of the shareholders.[784] A court appointed auditor cannot be so removed.[785] An auditor who has resigned or learns of a meeting being called to remove or replace him may submit a written statement to the corporation giving reasons for his resignation or why he opposes the proposed action. A copy of the statement must be sent by the corporation to every shareholder entitled to notice of a shareholders' meeting and to the Director.[786] A replacement auditor holds office for the unexpired term of his predecessor.[787] An auditor who is replacing a previous auditor must request and receive a written statement of the circumstances for the replacement.[788]

B. Auditor's Powers and Duties

316. At common law, it was held that the auditor must see that the financial statements of the corporation do not contain errors of computation, omission or commission, or untruth. He must approach the task with an inquiring mind, not suspicious of dishonesty, but suspicious of errors.[789] The auditor owes his fiduciary duty to the corporation, but may be held liable to shareholders and others who the auditor could reasonably foresee might rely on the financial statements.[790] The CBCA provides that an auditor must make the examination that in his opinion is necessary to enable him to report to the shareholders on the financial statements in accordance with the Regulations.[791] The auditor of a holding corporation may reasonably rely on the report of the auditor on the financial statements of the subsidiary.[792] If an auditor becomes aware of an error or misstatement in a financial statement on which he has

780. An 'ordinary resolution' is a resolution passed by a majority of the votes cast by the shareholders who voted in respect of the resolution [CBCA s. 2(1)].
781. CBCA s. 162(4).
782. CBCA s. 167(1).
783. An 'ordinary resolution' is a resolution passed by a majority of the votes cast by the shareholders who voted in respect of the resolution [CBCA s. 2(1)].
784. CBCA ss 164 and 165(1).
785. CBCA s. 165(1).
786. CBCA s. 168(5) and (6).
787. CBCA s. 166(4).
788. CBCA s. 168(7).
789. *Re Kingston Cotton Mill Company (No. 2)*, [1896] 2 Ch. 279 (C.A.); *Formento (Sterling Area) Ltd. v. Selsdon Fountain Pen Co. Ltd.*, [1958] 1 W.L.R. 45 (H.L.).
790. *Nocton v. Ashburton*, [1914] A.C. 932 at 971; *Turner v. C.P. Limited* (1979), 107 D.L.R. (3rd) 142 (Ont H.C.); *Haig v. Bamford*, [1977] 1 S.C.R. 466.
791. CBCA s. 169(1). By Regulations 71 and 71.1, with some exceptions, the financial statements and auditor's report must be prepared in accordance with the standards of the Canadian Institute of Chartered Accountants.
792. CBCA s. 169(2) and (3).

reported which in his opinion is material, he must inform each director.[793] An auditor or former auditor must attend a shareholders' meeting on ten days' notice from a director or shareholder of the corporation.[794]

317. The auditor is entitled to receive on demand from present and former directors, officers, employees, and agents of the corporation, information and explanations and access to records and documents which the auditor considers necessary.[795] The auditor has the right to receive notice of and to attend and be heard at shareholders' meetings.[796] Any oral or written statement or report of an auditor made under the CBCA has qualified privilege.[797]

C. The Audit Committee

318. A corporation, any of the issued securities of which are or were part of a distribution to the public and which remain outstanding and are held by more than one person, must have an audit committee composed of at least three directors, a majority of whom are not officers or employees of the corporation or any of its affiliates.[798] Other corporations may also appoint an audit committee. The Director under the CBCA may exempt a corporation from the requirement to have an audit committee where he is satisfied that the shareholders will not be prejudiced.[799] The audit committee reviews the financial statements and reports on them to the directors.[800] The auditor is entitled to attend all audit committee meetings and must attend if so requested by the audit committee.[801] The auditor may call a meeting of the audit committee. The duties of the audit committee are not precisely prescribed in the act and, therefore, may be established by the corporation either in the by-laws or in a unanimous shareholder agreement.

D. Auditor Oversight

319. The Canadian Securities Administrators have issued National Instrument 52-108 (NI 58-108) requiring that the auditor of a 'reporting issuer' (i.e., a person that has issued securities to the public such as a public corporation) be a public accounting firm that has entered into a written agreement with the Canadian Public Accountability Board. The auditor must be in compliance with any restrictions or sanctions imposed by the Canadian Public Accountability Board.

---

793. CBCA s. 171(7).
794. CBCA s. 168(2).
795. CBCA s. 170.
796. CBCA s. 168(1).
797. CBCA s. 172.
798. CBCA s. 171(1). There is no provision in the NBBCA or the NSCA requiring that an audit committee be appointed.
799. CBCA s. 171(2).
800. CBCA s. 171(3).
801. CBCA s. 171(4).

E. Financial Statement Certification

320. National Instrument 52-109 issued by the Canadian Securities Administrators provides that annual and interim financial statements must be certified by the chief financial officer and chief executive officer of the reporting issuer.

IV. Worker Participation

321. The CBCA does not contain provisions allowing corporations to give employees (or any group other than shareholders) the right to elect a director. Such a provision could however be included in a unanimous shareholder agreement.

There are legislative provisions in some provincial jurisdictions which do contemplate special interest group appointments. The Alberta Business Corporations Act (ABCA) provides that the articles or a unanimous shareholder agreement may provide for the election or appointment of directors by creditors or employees of the corporation or by a class or classes of creditors or employees. In determining whether a transaction is in the best interests of the corporation, such a director may give special but not exclusive consideration to the interests of those who elected him.[802] The Saskatchewan Business Corporations Act (SBCA) simply states that the articles may provide for election or appointment of directors by creditors or employees of the corporation or by a class or classes of creditors or employees.[803] In memorandum jurisdictions (British Columbia and Nova Scotia), it would be possible for the articles to specifically provide that employees be entitled to elect directors. Notwithstanding some legislative provisions and the ability in other jurisdictions to provide for employee representation on boards of directors, this has not become a common practice in Canada.

§4. Liquidation of the Corporation

I. Grounds for Liquidation and Dissolution

A. Generally

1. Application of Federal and Provincial Corporate Legislation to Solvent Corporations

322. The provisions of the federal and provincial corporate statutes dealing with liquidation and dissolution only apply to solvent corporations.[804] The federal government has jurisdiction over bankruptcy,[805] and thus insolvencies are dealt with under the

802. ABCA ss 106(9) and 122(4).
803. SBCA s. 101(8).
804. *See,* for example, CBCA s. 208(1).
805. *Constitution Act*, 1867, *supra* n. 11, s. 91, para. 21.

federal *Bankruptcy and Insolvency Act*.[806] If a liquidation and dissolution is begun under the corporate legislation, and the corporation is subsequently found to be insolvent, then all proceedings under the corporate legislation are stayed and all proceedings transferred to the federal domain.[807] Thus, no question of priorities of creditors arises under the corporate legislation applying to liquidation and dissolution, since the fundamental assumption is that all creditors can be paid. If the corporation is insolvent, then the *Bankruptcy and Insolvency Act* specifies a comprehensive listing of priorities among creditors.

2. Meaning of 'Liquidation' and 'Dissolution'

323. The term 'liquidation' refers to the disposal of any assets of the corporation preparatory to dissolution. The term 'dissolution' refers to the termination of the corporation's existence.

B. Liquidation and Dissolution of Inactive Corporations

1. Grounds for Dissolution

324. The 'Director', under both federal and most provincial legislation is the term, used to refer to the administrative official charged with the task of overseeing the application of the corporation statute. The Director may issue a certificate of dissolution where the corporation has not commenced business within three years of incorporation, has not carried on business for three years, or is in default for a period of one year in sending the Director any fee, notice, or document required by the act.[808]

2. Director May Apply to a Court for an Order Dissolving the Corporation

325. If it is necessary to liquidate assets of the corporation, it may not be practicable to simply issue a certificate of dissolution. In this case, the Director may apply to a court for appropriate orders to facilitate the liquidation of the corporation prior to dissolution.[809]

---

806. R.S.C. 1985, c. B-3. A solvent federally incorporated company may in some circumstances also be wound up under the federal *Winding-Up and Restructuring Act*, R.S.C. 1985, c. W-11, which is not dealt with further here.

807. CBCA s. 208(2).

808. CBCA s. 212(1).

809. CBCA s. 212.

C. Liquidation and Dissolution of Corporations in Default of Certain Requirements of the Act

1. Grounds for Dissolution

326. The Director or an 'interested person' (e.g., a shareholder) may apply to a court for an order dissolving a corporation if the corporation has failed for two or more consecutive years to hold annual shareholder meetings in compliance with the act, carried on business or exercised powers in a manner contrary to the articles, denied shareholders or creditors statutory rights to information, failed to send shareholders financial statements and the auditor's report, failed to make financial statements available for inspection by shareholders, or procured any certificate under the act by misrepresentation.[810]

2. Powers of Court

327. In connection with such an application, the court has very broad powers to make orders to facilitate the liquidation and dissolution of the corporation. These include an order appointing a liquidator, giving notice to any person, determining the validity of a claim of any person, governing the conduct of the directors of the corporation, determining the liability of any director, officer, or shareholder to the corporation, making a distribution to shareholders.[811]

D. Voluntary Liquidation and Dissolution

328. The shareholders may resolve by special resolution to liquidate and dissolve the corporation.[812] The special resolution may authorize the directors to distribute any property of the corporation.[813] Once the resolution is passed, the corporation must take appropriate steps to notify its creditors of its intent to dissolve, discharge its liabilities, and distribute the remaining property to its shareholders.[814]

329. The Director or an interested person may apply to a court at any time during the liquidation of the corporation for an order that the liquidation be carried out under the supervision of the court.[815] In such a case, the court may make any order it thinks fit, including those orders referred to in paragraph 327.

810. CBCA s. 213(1).
811. CBCA ss 213(3), 217.
812. CBCA ss 210, 211. The resolution may be put before the shareholders by the directors, or by means of a shareholder proposal [CBCA s. 211(1)].
813. CBCA s. 210(3).
814. CBCA s. 211(7).
815. CBCA s. 211(8).

E. *Involuntary Judicial Liquidation and Dissolution for Corporate Misconduct or Other Reasons*

1. Generally

330. A shareholder may apply to a court for an order liquidating and dissolving a corporation, or any of its affiliated corporations, where any of the grounds of misconduct enumerated in paragraph 326 are made out. Parent and subsidiary corporations are affiliated corporations where the parent holds a majority of the votes attached to the shares of the subsidiary. The term 'affiliated corporation' also includes subsidiaries under the control of a common parent corporation, companies controlled by the same person and companies with common affiliates.[816] When filing an application for a liquidation and dissolution, the shareholder must also file an affidavit stating the reasons why the corporation should be liquidated and dissolved.[817]

2. Powers of Court

331. The court may require the corporation or any person having an interest in or claim against the corporation to show cause why the corporation should not be liquidated and dissolved.[818] The court may also order the directors and officers of the corporation to furnish the court with all material information known or reasonably ascertainable by them, including financial statements and the names of all shareholders and creditors or other claimants of the corporation.[819] The court may make any other order it thinks fit, including those orders indicated in paragraph 327 and any order that would be available in connection with an oppression application.[820] The ability to make remedial orders other than those sought by the applicant gives the court great freedom to remedy instances of wrongdoing while stopping short of the severe sanction of liquidation and dissolution. Thus, for example, the fact that a company is being run at a profit will militate against an order of liquidation and dissolution and in favour of some lesser remedy.[821]

3. Shareholder Approval of Alleged Wrong Not Dispositive

332. The act provides that a court shall not dismiss or stay an application for a liquidation and dissolution only because the shareholders have approved the alleged wrong that forms the foundation of the application.[822] However, such approval may be taken into account by the court in making any order.[823]

816. CBCA s. 2(1) and (2).
817. CBCA s. 216(1).
818. CBCA s. 216(2).
819. CBCA s. 216(3).
820. CBCA s. 214(2).
821. *See*, for example, *Re Sharon Golf and Country Club Ltd.* (1975), 20 C.B.R. (N.S.) 159 (Ont. H.C.).
822. CBCA ss 242, 214(3).
823. *Ibid.*

4. First Ground for Application: Oppression

333. The first substantive ground upon which a liquidation and dissolution application may be maintained is that the business and affairs of the corporation or any of its affiliates have been conducted in a manner, or the powers of the directors have been exercised in a manner that is oppressive, unfairly prejudicial to, or that unfairly disregards the interests of any security holder, creditor, director, or officer. This ground is identical to the grounds for relief under the oppression remedy.[824]

5. Second Ground for Application: Failure to Observe a Unanimous Shareholder Agreement

334. A shareholder may apply for a liquidation and dissolution where a unanimous shareholder agreement entitled a complaining shareholder to demand dissolution of the corporation after the occurrence of a specified event and that event has occurred.[825] This ground will be of no relevance for public companies, since such companies never have unanimous shareholder agreements.

6. Third Ground for Application: The Just and Equitable Ground

335. The just and equitable ground for a liquidation and dissolution has a long common law lineage, and has been imported into the statutes as a ground for securing a court-ordered liquidation and dissolution.[826] Despite the fact that the oppression ground poses a lower threshold for securing a liquidation and dissolution (arguably making the just and equitable ground redundant) the just and equitable ground was 'retained so that a useful fund of case law [would not be] discarded'.[827] In general, there are four different grounds upon which a court would order a just and equitable liquidation and dissolution:

(1) 'loss of substratum';
(2) 'justifiable lack of confidence';
(3) 'deadlock'; and
(4) 'the partnership analogy'.

These are dealt with in turn below.

a. Loss of Substratum

336. The courts will find a loss of substratum where the object for which the corporation was formed has failed or is impossible of fulfilment, or it is impossible for the corporation to carry on business except at a loss. Where, for example, a company

824. *See supra* §3.I.C paras 222–238, especially para. 224.
825. CBCA s. 214(1)(b)(i).
826. CBCA s. 214(1)(b)(ii).
827. R. Dickerson et al., *Proposals for a New Business Corporations Law for Canada*, vol. 1 (Ottawa: Ministry of Supply and Services Canada, 1971) para. 455.

was incorporated to obtain a German patent to manufacture 'date coffee', but was unable to obtain the patent, the court declared that there was a loss of substratum and ordered a liquidation and dissolution.[828] Another example of loss of substratum occurred where a company was incorporated to purchase certain oil fields, but the oil fields were nationalized.[829] In general, loss of substratum cases are rare,[830] and this ground for liquidation and dissolution is not likely to be a concern for public companies.

b. Justifiable Lack of Confidence

337. A justifiable lack of confidence will be held to occur where corporate management, or controlling shareholders, have conducted themselves in such a manner as to justifiably lose the confidence of shareholders. For example, in a leading case,[831] the majority shareholder of the company ran the company as if it were entirely his own. He failed to call shareholder meetings, keep books of account, appoint auditors (in violation of the relevant company law), or pay dividends. He had also doubled his remuneration and transferred a valuable asset to his own account as 'deferred salary', and presented a derisory offer to the minority to purchase their shares. In these circumstances, the Privy Council found that there was a justifiable lack of confidence and ordered a liquidation and dissolution. Other cases finding a justifiable lack of confidence tend to involve similar behaviour.[832] Like the loss of substratum ground, this ground for a liquidation and dissolution is unlikely to be applied to public companies. Cases of this sort would now more likely be dealt with under the oppression remedy.[833]

c. Deadlock

338. The deadlock ground for liquidation and dissolution typically involves a private company in which the principals (i.e., shareholders/directors) are unable, because of philosophical differences or personality conflicts, to make important, or even day-to-day, decisions in the life of the corporation.[834]

---

828. *Re German Date Coffee* Co. (1882), 20 Ch.D. 169 (C.A.). The liquidation and dissolution was ordered despite the fact that the company was able to obtain a Swedish patent which was apparently just as good.

829. *Re Baku Consolidated Oil Fields Ltd.*, [1944] 1 All E.R. 24 (Ch.). *See* generally Dennis H. Peterson & D.H. Cumming, *Shareholder Remedies in Canada*, 2d ed. (LexisNexis Canada, 2009) at 20.37.

830. Indeed, because Canadian corporations now have the powers and capacity of a natural person (*See*, for example, CBCA s. 15(1)) and are thus able to engage in any business except insofar as restricted from doing so in the articles of the company, it is expected that such cases will become even rarer.

831. *Loch v. John Blackwood Ltd.*, [1924] A.C. 783 (P.C.).

832. *See*, for example, *Sound Advice Inc. v. 358074 Ontario Ltd. and Burt* (1983), 5 O.A.C. 288 (Div. Ct.).

833. *See* paras 222–238 above.

834. *See*, for example, *In re Yenidje Tobacco Co. Ltd.*, [1916] 2 Ch. 426 (C.A.).

d. The Partnership Analogy

339. A court will order a liquidation and dissolution under the partnership analogy if the fundamental expectations of shareholders in a private corporation have been violated by directors or other shareholders.[835] Thus, the partnership analogy applies only in the case of private companies.

II. The Effect of Liquidation and Dissolution

A. Liquidation

340. As indicated in paragraph 323, 'liquidation' refers to the orderly disposal of any assets of the corporation. While the corporation is in liquidation, it continues to exist as a corporate entity. However, it ceases to carry on business except to the extent necessary to effect the liquidation.[836]

B. Powers of Court Appointed Liquidator

341. If a liquidator is appointed by a court to effect the liquidation, then the powers of the directors and shareholders cease and vest in the liquidator,[837] although the liquidator may delegate any of his powers to the directors or shareholders.[838] In general, the liquidator is given broad powers to effect the liquidation of the corporate assets, including the power to retain lawyers or other professionals, bring or defend any civil, criminal, or administrative suit, sell the assets of the corporation, settle or compromise any claim against the corporation, and do all other things necessary for the liquidation of the corporation and distribution of its property.[839]

C. Dissolution

342. As indicated in paragraph 323, 'dissolution' refers to the termination of the corporation's existence. Dissolution is effected by the issuance of a 'Certificate of Dissolution' either by the Director[840] or by a court, and the dissolution takes effect on the date specified in the Certificate of Dissolution.[841]

835. *See Ebrahimi v. Westbourne Galleries Ltd.*, [1972] 2 All E.R. 492 (H.L.).
836. *See*, for example, CBCA ss 211(6) (voluntary dissolution); ss 219(1) (court ordered liquidation).
837. CBCA s. 219(1)(b).
838. CBCA s. 219(2). Further, the court may appoint any person, including a director, officer or shareholder, to serve as liquidator [CBCA s. 220(1)].
839. CBCA s. 222(1).
840. *See*, for example, CBCA s. 210(5), (6) and s. 212(3), (4).
841. *See*, for example, CBCA ss 210(6), 211(16), 212(4).

D. Revival

343. After a corporation has been dissolved, any interested person may apply to the Director to have the corporate existence 'revived'. The Director may revive the corporation by issuing a certificate of revival, and the corporation is revived as of the date shown in the certificate.[842] After revival, the corporation has the same status as if it had never been dissolved.[843]

§5. Mergers and Takeovers

I. Introduction: Business Combinations

344. There is no legal definition of the term 'merger' in Canadian statutes of incorporation (although, as noted in paragraph 380 below, the term 'merger' is defined in the *Competition Act*). There are several techniques for combining the assets of two or more separate business entities and these transactions might more conveniently be described as business combinations. The techniques for combining businesses include the purchase by one corporation of the assets of another corporation, the purchase by one corporation of the shares of another corporation, or the combination of two or more corporations by a statutorily prescribed process of 'amalgamation'.[844]

The process and effect of amalgamation and inter-jurisdictional aspects of amalgamations are briefly set out in § II below. The corporate law requirements with respect to a sale of assets are then briefly noted in § III. The purchase of shares by way of a 'takeover bid' is discussed in § IV and competition law, foreign investment, and other constraints on business combinations are briefly noted in § V.

II. Amalgamations ('Mergers')

A. Process

345. Statutes of incorporation in Canada typically provide that two or more corporations, including holding and subsidiary corporations, may amalgamate and continue as one corporation.[845] Each corporation proposing to amalgamate must enter

842. CBCA s. 209(3), (3.1), and (4).
843. CBCA s. 209(4).
844. *See*, for example, the discussion in *Legislative Assembly Select Committee on Company Law: Report on Mergers, Amalgamations and Certain Related Matters* (the 'Hodgson Report') (Toronto: Queen's Printer, 1973).
845. *See*, for example, CBCA s. 181. *See also* ABCA s. 181; BCBCA s. 269; MCA s. 175(1); NBBCA s. 120; NCA s. 288; NWTBCA s. 183; NSCA s. 134(1); OBCA s. 174; PEICA s. 77(1); QBCA s. 276; SBCA s. 175; YBCA s. 183.

into an agreement (typically referred to as an 'amalgamation agreement') setting out such matters as:[846]

- the manner in which the shares of each amalgamating corporation are to be converted into shares of other securities of the amalgamated corporation;
- if any shares of an amalgamating corporation are not to be converted into securities of the amalgamated corporation, the amount of money or securities of anybody corporate that the holders of such shares are to receive in addition to or instead of securities of the amalgamated corporation;
- the manner of payment of money instead of the issue of fractional shares of the amalgamated corporation or of any other body corporate the securities of which are to be received in the amalgamation;
- details of any arrangements necessary to perfect the amalgamation and to provide for the subsequent management and operation of the amalgamated corporation.

If shares of one of the amalgamating corporations are held by or on behalf of one of the amalgamating corporations the amalgamation agreement must provide for the cancellation of such shares without any provision for repayment of capital in respect of the shares, and without any provisions for the conversion of such shares into shares of the amalgamated corporation.[847]

346. The amalgamation agreement must be submitted for approval to the shareholders of each of the amalgamating corporations. The shareholder approvals required for a statutory amalgamation vary somewhat from province to province. Under the CBCA an amalgamation requires a special resolution (two-thirds of the votes cast) of all shareholders including the holders of classes or series of shares that do not otherwise carry the right to vote.[848] Also, under the CBCA, each class or series of shares is entitled to vote separately as a class if the amalgamation agreement contains a provision which, if contained in a proposed amendment to the articles, would entitle

846. CBCA s. 182(1); ABCA s. 182(1); MCA s. 176(1); NBBCA s. 121(1); NCA s. 289(1); NWTBCA s. 184(1); OBCA s. 175(1); QBCA s. 277; SBCA s. 176(1); YBCA s. 184(1). There is a similar but somewhat different approach in BCBCA s. 270; NWTCA s. 148(2), (3); NSCA s. 134(2), (3); PEICA s. 77(2).

847. CBCA s. 182(2). *See also* ABCA s. 182(2); BCBCA s. 270(3); MCA s. 176(2); NBBCA s. 121(2); NCA s. 289(2); NWTBCA s. 184(2); OBCA s. 175(2); QBCA s. 277(6); SBCA s. 176(2); YBCA s. 184(2).

848. CBCA s. 183(1), (3), (5). *See also*, for example, ABCA s. 183(1), (3), (5); BCBCA s. 271; MCA s. 177(1), (3), (5); NBBCA s. 122(1), (3), (5); NCA s. 290(1), (4); NSCA s. 134(4); OBCA s. 176(1), (4); PEICA s. 77(3); QBCA s. 279 and s. 191; SBCA s. 177(1), (3), (5). *See* the definition of 'special resolution' in CBCA s. 2(1); ABCA s. 1(ii); MCA s. 1(1); NBBCA s. 1(1); OBCA s. 1(1); SBCA s. 2(1)(ff). For the NSCA and PEICA a special resolution requires 3/4ths of the votes cast or consent by every person entitled to vote. The BCBCA s. 1(1) definitions 'special resolution' and 'special majority' require a vote of 2/3rds unless the articles require a greater majority (up to 3/4ths). The NCA and OBCA don't say all shares are entitled to vote whether or not they otherwise carry the right to vote but allow class or series voting where the interests of the class or series are affected as provided under s. 280.

the holders of the class or series to vote separately as a class or series.[849] Generally speaking, provisions which prejudicially affect the rights of a class or series would entitle the class or series to vote separately as a class or series. In such circumstances, special resolutions of the prejudicially affected class or series would be required.

347. Once the amalgamation has been approved by the shareholders of the amalgamating corporations, articles of amalgamation can be forwarded to the Registrar or Director together with other required documents.[850] Upon receipt of the required documents the Director is required to issue a certificate of amalgamation.[851]

348. In the interests of protecting creditors, the articles of amalgamation must have attached to them a statutory declaration of a director or officer of each amalgamating corporation that establishes to the satisfaction of the Director that there are reasonable grounds for believing that:[852]

- each amalgamating corporation is able to pay its liabilities as they become due;
- the amalgamated corporation will be able to pay its liabilities as they become due;
- the realizable value of the amalgamated corporation's assets will not be less than the aggregate of its liabilities and the stated capital of all classes of shares; and
- no creditor will be prejudiced by the amalgamation or adequate notice has been given to all known creditors of the amalgamated corporations and no creditor objects to the amalgamation otherwise than on grounds that are frivolous and vexatious.

Adequate notice is considered to have been given to creditors if a notice in writing is sent to each known creditor having a claim against the corporation that exceeds CAD 1,000, a notice is published once in a newspaper published or distributed in the place where the corporation has its registered office and reasonable notice thereof is given in each province in Canada where the corporation carries on its business, and each notice states that the corporation intends to amalgamate with one or more specified

---

849. CBCA s. 183(4). *See also* ABCA s. 183(4); MCA s. 177(4); NBBCA s. 122(4); NCA s. 290(3); NWTBCA s. 185(4); OBCA s. 176(4); QBCA s. 191; SBCA s. 177(4); YBCA s. 185(4). BCBCA s. 271(6)(h) requires a class vote in all cases and a series vote if the rights of the series are prejudicially affected or interfered with.

850. CBCA s. 185(1). *See also* ABCA s. 185(1); BCBCA s. 275; MCA s. 179(1); NBBCA s. 124(1); NCA s. 293(1); NSCA s. 134(9); NWTBCA s. 187(1); OBCA s. 178(1); PEICA s. 77(4); QBCA ss 283 and 285; SBCA s. 179(1); YBCA s. 187(1).

851. CBCA s. 185(4). *See also* ABCA s. 185(4); BCBCA s. 281; MCA s. 179(4); NBBCA s. 124(4); NCA s. 294(1); NSCA s. 134(10); NWTBCA s. 187(4); OBCA s. 178(4); PEICA s. 77(4); QBCA s. 286; SBCA s. 179(4); YBCA s. 187(4). Under the PEICA the application is for a letters patent and the grant of the letters patent is in the discretion of the Director.

852. CBCA s. 185(2). *See also* ABCA s. 185(2); BCBCA s. 277; MCA s. 179(2); NBBCA s. 124(2); NCA s. 293(2); NWTBCA s. 187(2); OBCA s. 178(2) (the OBCA requires some additional statements); SBCA s. 179(2); YBCA s. 187(2). *See also* NWTCA s. 148(5)–(8) and NSCA s. 134(5)–(8). The protection of creditors under the PEICA would presumably be through the discretion of the Director in granting the letters patent with respect to the amalgamation.

corporations unless a creditor of the corporation objects to the amalgamation within thirty days from the date of the notice.[853]

B. Effect

349. When a certificate of amalgamation is granted the effect is that:[854]

- the amalgamation of the amalgamating corporations and their continuance as one corporation becomes effective;
- the property of each amalgamating corporation is considered to be the property of the amalgamated corporation;[855]
- the amalgamated corporation continues to be liable for the debts of each of the amalgamating corporations;
- existing causes of action, claims, or liability to prosecution is unaffected;
- civil, criminal, or administrative actions or proceedings pending by or against an amalgamating corporation may continue to be prosecuted by or against the amalgamated corporation; and
- convictions against, or rulings, orders, or judgments in favour of or against an amalgamating corporation can be enforced by or against the amalgamated corporation.

The amalgamation does not result in the creation of a new corporation with the discontinuance of the amalgamating corporations. Instead, it is considered to be a continuance of the amalgamating corporations as one corporation.[856]

C. Appraisal Rights and Oppression Remedy

350. Shareholders can exercise appraisal rights with respect to an amalgamation by sending a written objection to the amalgamation resolution at or before the meeting

853. CBCA s. 185(3). *See also* ABCA s. 185(3); BCBCA s. 278; MCA s. 179(3); NBBCA s. 124(3); NCA s. 293(3); NWTBCA s. 187(3) (claims over CAD 2,000); OBCA s. 178(3) (the OBCA requires notice to creditors with claims over CAD 2,500); SBCA s. 179(3); YBCA s. 187(3).

854. CBCA s. 186. *See also* ABCA s. 186; MCA s. 180; NBBCA s. 125; NCA s. 294(2); NWTBCA s. 188; OBCA s. 179; SBCA s. 180; YBCA s. 188. There is a provision to similar effect in BCBCA s. 282; NSCA s. 134(11)–(13); and PEICA s. 77(4).

855. Thus, it is not necessary to convey the property by deed and consequently the amalgamation provisions provide a convenient technique for combining business entities. Also where there is a lease which cannot be assigned without the landlord's consent, it has been held that an amalgamation does not constitute an assignment of the lease (*see Rossi v. MacDonald's Restaurants of Canada Ltd.*, 25 A.C. W S. (3rd) 639; *Loeb Inc. v. Cooper*, 5 O.R. (3rd) 259).

856. *See R. v. Black & Decker*, [1975] 1 S.C.R. 411; *Witco Chemical Co. Canada Ltd. v. Corporation of Oakville*, [1975] 1 S.C.R. 273; *R. v. Armco Canada Ltd. (No. 2)*, [1975] 8 O.R. (2nd) 573; *Re Seaboard Life Insurance Co. and Attorney General of British Columbia* (1986), 30 D.L.R. (4th) 264.

at which the amalgamation resolution is to be voted on.[857] The notice of the meeting must be accompanied by a copy or summary of the amalgamation agreement and must state that the dissenting shareholder is entitled to be paid the fair market value of her or his shares.[858] Failure to state that the dissenting shareholder is entitled to be paid fair value for her or his shares does not invalidate the transaction.[859] However, if the corporation fails to give notice of such a right a shareholder may not be bound by the strict procedural requirements with respect to the application of the appraisal remedy. For instance, where the corporation has failed to give notice of the right the shareholder may not be precluded from exercising an appraisal right where the shareholder failed to send a written objection to the amalgamation at or before the meeting at which the resolution approving the amalgamation is to be voted on.[860]

351. The availability of appraisal rights does not preclude a subsequent oppression application.[861] Thus a subsequent oppression application may arise where the amalgamation is oppressive, unfairly prejudicial, or unfairly disregards the interests of any security holder, creditor, director, or officer.[862]

D. Short-Form Amalgamations

352. A simpler amalgamation approval procedure is available where a parent, or holding corporation, amalgamates with a wholly owned subsidiary corporation. This is referred to as a 'vertical short-form amalgamation'. A vertical short-form amalgamation can proceed without shareholder approval and without the application of shareholder appraisal rights.[863] It can proceed if it is approved by a resolution of the directors of each amalgamating corporation and the resolutions provide that:[864]

857. CBCA s. 190(1)(c), (5). *See also* ABCA s. 191(1)(c), (5); BCBCA s. 238(1)(c); MCA s. 184(1)(c), (5); NBBCA s. 131(l)(d), (5); NCA s. 304(1)(c), (6); NWTBCA s. 193(1)(c), (5); OBCA s. 185(l)(c), (6); SBCA s. 184(1)(c), (5); YBCA s. 193(1)(c), (5). For a general discussion of the appraisal remedy *see supra* §3.I.E, paras 244–264.
858. CBCA s. 183(2). *See also* ABCA s. 183(2); MCA s. 177(2); NBBCA s. 122(2); NCA s. 290(2); NWTBCA s. 185(2); OBCA s. 176(2); SBCA s. 177(2); YBCA s. 185(2).
859. CBCA s. 183(2). *See also* ABCA s. 183(2); MCA s. 177(2); NBBCA s. 122(2); NCA s. 290(2); NWTBCA s. 185(2); OBCA s. 176(2); SBCA s. 177(2); YBCA s. 185(2).
860. *See*, for example, CBCA s. 190(5), 183(2); ABCA s. 191(5), 183(2); MCA s. 184(5), 177(2); NBBCA ss 131(5), 122(2); NCA ss 304(6), 290(2); NWTBCA ss 193(5), 185(2); OBCA ss 185(6), 176(2); SBCA ss 184(5), 177(2); YBCA ss 193(5), 185(2). *See also Fitch v. Churchill Corp.* (1990), 66 D.L.R. (4th) 569, 105 A.R. 25, 72 Alta. L.R. (2nd) 343, [1990] 4 W.W.R. 256 (C.A.).
861. *See Re Brant Investments Ltd. and KeepRite Inc.* (1983), 24 B.L.R. 201 (Ont. H.C.). With respect to the appraisal remedy generally *see supra* §3.I.E, paras 244–264.
862. With respect to the oppression remedy *see supra* §3.I.C paras 222–238.
863. CBCA s. 184(1) and s. 190(1)(c). *See also* ABCA ss 184(1), 191(1)(c); BCBCA s. 273(1)(c); MCA s. 178(1), s. 184(1)(c); NBBCA ss 123(1), 131(1)(d); NCA ss 291, 304(1)(c); NWTBCA ss 186(1), 193(1)(c); OBCA ss 177(1), 185(1)(c); QBCA s. 282; SBCA ss 178(1), 184(1)(c); YBCA ss 186(1), 193(1)(c).
864. CBCA s. 184(1). *See also* ABCA s. 184(1); BCBCA s. 273(1); MCA s. 178(1); NBBCA s. 123(1); NCA s. 291; NWTBCA s. 186(1); OBCA s. 177(1); QBCA s. 282; SBCA s. 178(1); YBCA s. 186(1).

- the shares of each amalgamating subsidiary are to be cancelled without any repayment of capital in respect of the amalgamation;
- the articles of the amalgamated corporation are the same as the articles of the parent corporation; and
- no securities are issued by the amalgamated corporation in connection with the amalgamation and the stated capital of the amalgamated corporation is to be the same as the stated capital of the amalgamating parent corporation.

353. A simpler amalgamation procedure is also available where two or more wholly owned subsidiary corporations of the same parent, or holding corporation, amalgamate and continue as one corporation. This is referred to as a 'horizontal short-form amalgamation'. A horizontal short-form amalgamation can also proceed without shareholder approval and without the application of shareholder appraisal rights.[865] It can proceed if it is approved by a resolution of the directors of each amalgamating corporation and the resolutions provide that:[866]

- the shares of all but one of the amalgamating subsidiary corporations are to be cancelled without any repayment of capital in respect of the amalgamation;
- the articles of amalgamation are to be the same as the articles of incorporation of the amalgamating subsidiary whose shares are not cancelled; and
- the stated capital of the amalgamating subsidiary whose shares are cancelled will be added to the stated capital of the amalgamating subsidiary corporation whose shares are not cancelled.

E. Cross-Border or Inter-jurisdictional Amalgamations

354. The provisions with respect to amalgamation in general incorporation statutes usually provide that the amalgamating corporations must both be incorporated under the particular statute.[867] Thus if the two corporations are incorporated under different statutes it may be necessary to first cause one of the amalgamating corporations

865. CBCA ss 184(2), 190(1)(c). *See also* ABCA ss 184(2), 191(1)(c); BCBCA s. 274; MCA s. 178(2), s. 184(1)(c); NBBCA ss 123(2), 131(1)(d); NCA ss 292, 304(l)(c); NWTBCA ss 186(2), 193(1)(c); OBCA ss 177(2), 185(1)(c); QBCA s. 281; SBCA ss 178(2), 184(1)(c); YBCA ss 186(2), 193(1)(c).

866. CBCA s. 184(2). *See also* ABCA s. 184(2); MCA s. 178(2); NBBCA s. 123(2); NCA s. 292; NWTBCA s. 186(2); OBCA s. 177(2); QBCA s. 281; SBCA s. 178(2); YBCA s. 186(2).

867. For instance, CBCA s. 181 says that 'two or more corporations may amalgamate and continue as one corporation'. Section 2(1) of the CBCA defines 'corporation' as 'a body corporate incorporated or continued under this Act' (i.e., a 'corporation' is a corporation incorporated or continued under the CBCA itself). *See also* ABCA s. 1(l), s. 175; MCA s. 1(1) 'corporation', s. 175(1); NBBCA s. 1(1) 'corporation', s. 120; NCA s. 2(i), s. 288; NWTCA s. 2(7), s. 148(1); NSCA s. 134(20); OBCA s. 1(1) 'corporation', s. 174; SBCA s. 2(1)(j); YBCA s. 1 'corporation', s. 183. ABCA s. 180.1 (and YBCA s. 189) allow for an amalgamation of a corporation incorporated under the ABCA (or the YBCA in the case of an amalgamation under the YBCA) to amalgamate with an extra-provincially (or extraterritorially) registered corporation which is authorized to amalgamate by the laws of the jurisdiction in which the extra-provincially incorporated corporation is incorporated and if one of the corporations is the wholly owned subsidiary of the other.

to be continued under the statute of the other amalgamating corporation.[868] The BCBCA allows for amalgamations with a foreign corporation to form an amalgamated BCBCA company.[869] The BCBCA also allows a BCBCA company to amalgamate with a foreign corporation to form an amalgamated foreign corporation subject to specified restrictions.[870]

F. Arrangements

355. A business combination may, in some instances, be effected through an 'arrangement'. Under the CBCA the court is given the power to make an order approving an arrangement where it is not practicable for a corporation that is not insolvent to effect a fundamental change in the nature of an arrangement under any other provision of the act.[871] Similar powers are granted to courts under other general incorporation statutes in Canada.[872]

356. An 'arrangement' is defined to include an amalgamation of two or more corporations, a transfer of all or substantially all the property of a corporation to another body corporate in exchange for property, money, or securities of the other body corporate, and an exchange of securities of a corporation held by security holders for property, money, or securities of another body corporate (other than by way of a takeover bid).[873] An arrangement has been held to involve some degree of mutual accommodation or compromise[874] and courts have viewed their role as one of assessing whether the proposed arrangement is fair and reasonable.[875]

III. Sale of Assets

357. A sale, lease, or exchange of all or substantially all the property of a corporation, other than in the ordinary course of business of the corporation, requires the approval of the shareholders of the corporation.[876] Under the CBCA each share of the corporation carries the right to vote.[877] The holders of shares of a class or series

868. With respect to the process of continuance *see supra* , the General Introduction, Ch. 5, §2, paras 60–64.
869. BCBCA s. 269. *See also* NWTBCA s. 189 and YBCA s. 189.
870. BCBCA s. 284 and s. 285.
871. CBCA s. 192.
872. ABCA s. 193; BCCA s. 276; MCA s. 185; NBBCA s. 128; NCA s. 315; NSCA ss 130, 131; NWTBCA s. 195; OBCA s. 182; QBCA s. 414; YBCA s. 195.
873. CBCA s. 192(1). *See also* ABCA s. 193(1); MCA s. 185(1); NBBCA s. 128(1); NCA s. 315(1); NWTBCA s. 195(1); OBCA s. 182(1); YBCA s. 195(1).
874. *Re N.F.U. Development Trust Ltd.*, [1973] 1 All E.R. 135.
875. *See*, for example, *Re Canadian Pacific Ltd.* (1990), 73 O.R. (2nd) 212; 70 D.L.R. (4th) 349 and the cases cited therein.
876. CBCA s. 189(3). *See also* ABCA s. 190(1); BCBCA s. 301(1); MCA s. 183(3); NBBCA s. 130(1); NCA s. 303(1); NWTBCA s. 192(1); OBCA s. 184(3); SBCA s. 183(2); YBCA s. 192(1).
877. CBCA s. 189(6). *See also* ABCA s. 190(4); MCA s. 183(6); NBBCA s. 130(4); NWTBCA s. 192(4); SBCA s. 183(5); YBCA s. 192(4). Some statutes do not specifically provide, with respect to a sale or lease of all or substantially all the assets, that shares carry the right to vote whether or not they otherwise carry the fight to vote – *see* BCBCA s. 301; NCA s. 303; OBCA s. 184.

are entitled to vote separately as a class or series if the particular class or series is affected in a manner different from the shares of another class or series.[878] The sale, lease, or exchange is approved when the holders of the shares of each class or series entitled to vote on the matter have approved the transaction by a special resolution.[879]

358. The notice of the meeting at which the sale, lease, or exchange is to be voted on must include or be accompanied by a copy or summary of the agreement of sale, lease, or exchange and must state that a dissenting shareholder is entitled to be paid the fair value of her or his shares.[880] Failure to state that the dissenting shareholder is entitled to be paid fair value for her or his shares does not invalidate the transaction.[881] If, however, the corporation fails to give notice of such a right a shareholder may not be bound by the strict procedural requirements with respect to the application of the appraisal remedy. For instance, where the corporation fails to give notice of the right the shareholder may not be precluded from exercising an appraisal right where the shareholder failed to send a written objection to the sale, lease or, exchange of assets at or before the meeting at which the resolution approving the sale, lease, or exchange of assets is to be voted on.[882] The availability of appraisal rights does not preclude a subsequent oppression application.[883] Thus a subsequent oppression application may arise where the sale, lease, or exchange of assets is oppressive, unfairly prejudicial, or unfairly disregards the interests of any security holder, creditor, director, or officer.[884]

IV. Takeover Bids

359. A change in control of a corporation may occur through a 'takeover bid' in which the bidder acquires sufficient voting securities to allow it to elect a majority of the directors of the offeree corporation and, therefore, gain control over the offeree

878. CBCA s. 189(7). *See also* ABCA s. 190(5); NBBCA s. 130(5); NCA s. 303(4); NWTBCA s. 192(5); OBCA s. 184(6); SBCA s. 183(6); YBCA s. 192(5). BCBCA s. 301 and MCA s. 183 do not specifically confer a class voting right.
879. CBCA s. 189(8). *See also* ABCA s. 190(6); BCBCA s. 301; MCA s. 183(7); NBBCA s. 130(6); NCA s. 303(5); NWTBCA s. 192(6); OBCA s. 184(7); SBCA s. 183(7); YBCA s. 192(6).
880. CBCA s. 189(4). *See also* ABCA s. 190(2); MCA s. 183(4); NBBCA s. 130(2); NCA s. 303(2); NWTBCA s. 192(2); OBCA s. 184(4); SBCA s. 183(3); YBCA s. 192(2). Under s. 301(5) of the BCBCA any shareholder of the company may dissent and have their shares acquired by the company for a fair value.
881. CBCA s. 189(4). ABCA s. 190(2); MCA s. 183(4); NBBCA s. 130(2); NCA s. 303(2); NWTBCA s. 192(2); OBCA s. 184(4); SBCA s. 183(3); YBCA s. 192(2).
882. *See*, for example, CBCA ss 190(5), 189(4); ABCA ss 191(5), 190(2); MCA ss 184(5), 183(4); NBBCA ss 131(5), 130(2); NCA ss 304(6), 303(2); NWTBCA ss 193(5), 192(2); OBCA ss 185(6), 184(4); SBCA ss 184(5), 183(3); YBCA ss 193(5), 192(2). *See also Fitch v. Churchill Corp.* (1990), 66 D.L.R. (4th) 569, 105 A.R. 25, 72 Alta. L.R. (2nd) 343, [1990] 4 W.W.R. 256 (C.A.). Failure to give notice of a right to dissent might constitute grounds for an oppression claim where there has been prejudice to the shareholder (*see Re Soft Tracks Enterprises Ltd.* (2004), 43 B.L.R. (3rd) 236 (B.C.S.C.)).
883. *See Re Brant Investments Ltd. and KeepRite Inc.* (1983), 24 B.L.R. 201 (Ont. H.C.) with respect to the appraisal remedy generally *see supra* §3.I.E, paras 244–264.
884. With respect to the oppression remedy *see supra* §3.I.C paras 222–238.

corporation. Acquisition of control over a corporation in this manner is subject to regulation under provincial securities acts.

A. Takeover Bid Requirements

1. Disclosure

360. The laws governing takeover bids subject takeover bids to several requirements. Disclosure with respect to the bid must be provided in the form of a takeover bid circular.[885] The takeover bid circular must be sent to the offeree shareholders and the offeree issuer, and must be filed with the securities commissions in the provinces where there are holders of the shares sought.[886]

The directors of the offeree corporation must send a directors' circular to the offeree shareholders within fifteen days of the day on which the takeover bid is made.[887] The directors must give reasons for either making a recommendation to accept or reject the bid, or not making a recommendation.[888]

Offeree shareholders have a statutory civil right of action for misstatement in either a takeover bid circular or a directors' circular.[889]

2. Minimum Bid Period, Minimum Tender, Pro Rata Take-Up, and Withdrawal Rights

361. The takeover bid must remain open for a period of 105 days unless the target board states in a news release an acceptable shorter deposit period of not less than 35 days.[890] If there is a variation of the bid then the bid period must not expire until 10 days after notice of the variation has been given.[891] Shares cannot be taken up under the bid until the requisite bid period has expired, the terms and conditions of the bid have been complied with or waived, and more than 50% of the outstanding securities of the class subject to the bid (excluding securities beneficially owned or controlled by the offeror or a person acting jointly or in concert with the offeror) have been deposited under the bid and not withdrawn.[892]

Where there is a bid for less than all the shares of a particular class, a first-come first-served bid could defeat the purpose of the minimum bid period by putting pressure on offeree shareholders to tender early in the bid period. Consequently, first-come

---

885. *See* National Instrument 62-104 (hereinafter 'NI 62-104') issued by the Canadian Securities Administrators, s. 2.10(1) and Form 62-104F1 (Take Over Bid Circular). As of 9 May 2016 National Instrument 62-104 has been adopted in all Canadian jurisdictions.
886. NI 62-104, s. 2.10(2).
887. NI 62-104, s. 2.17(1). *See also* Form 62-104F3 (Directors' Circular).
888. NI 62-104, s. 2.17(2).
889. *See*, for example, ASA s. 205; BCSA s. 132; NBSA s. 153; NSA s. 131; NSSA s. 139; OSA s. 131; QSA ss 222–225; SSA s. 139.
890. NI 62-104, s. 2.28.
891. NI 62-104, s. 2.12(3).
892. NI 62-104, s. 2.29.1.

first-served bids where there is an offer for less than all the shares of a class are precluded by a requirement that the bidder takes up the shares on a pro rata basis.[893]

For shareholders who do tender early in the bid period their shares could be 'locked up' and thus be unavailable for tender under subsequent competing bids. To prevent such a lock-up of offeree shares the bidder cannot take up shares until the end of the minimum bid period and the offeree shareholder is entitled to withdraw shares deposited under the bid at any time prior to the time when the bidder takes up the shares.[894] The shares can be withdrawn after being taken up if the bidder has failed to pay for the shares within three days of taking them up.[895] A variation in the bid extends the withdrawal right by ten days unless the variation is just a waiver of a condition on a cash bid, is an increase in the consideration offered under the bid, or the shares have already been taken up.[896]

3. Equal Treatment

362. One of the principles governing the takeover bid requirements is that where a bid is made all holders of the shares subject to the bid must be treated equally. Thus the bid must be made to all holders of the shares sought in the province.[897] The offeror must also offer identical consideration to all holders of the shares sought.[898]

Where the bid price is increased, the increased price must be paid on all shares tendered whether they are tendered before or after the increase in the bid price.[899] Further, the bidder is not to enter into collateral agreements with shareholders with the result that one or more shareholders would receive a greater consideration than other shareholders would receive.[900]

4. Formal Valuation

363. If, after a successful bid, the target corporation enters into an amalgamation, arrangement, or consolidation, makes an amendment to the terms of a class of equity securities, or engages in any other transaction in which the interest of a holder of an equity security of the target may be terminated without the holder's consent, the target corporation will have to call a meeting of the holders of the affected securities and provide a circular that includes a formal valuation of the affected securities.[901] The 'formal valuation' is to be done by an independent valuer as of a date that is not more than 120 days before the date of the takeover bid.[902] An exemption from the formal valuation requirement is provided for a 'second step business combination' where the

893. NI 62-104, s. 2.26(1).
894. NI 62-104, s. 2.29 and s. 2.30.
895. NI 62-104, s. 2.30(1)(c).
896. NI 62-104, s. 2.30(1)(b) and (2).
897. NI 62-104, s. 2.8.
898. NI 62-104, s. 2.23(1).
899. NI 62-104, s. 2.23(3).
900. NI 62-104, s. 2.24.
901. Multilateral Instrument 61-101, part 4 (adopted in Ontario and Quebec).
902. Multilateral Instrument 61-101, part 6.

equity securities being acquired were the subject of an earlier bid, the transaction is completed within 120 days of the date of the expiry of the bid, and the consideration provided to remaining holders of the equity securities is at least equal in value to and in the same form as the consideration that the tendering equity security holders received under the bid.[903]

5. Adequate Financing and the Taking Up of and Payment for Shares

364. The bidder must also be able to demonstrate that it has made adequate arrangements prior to the bid to finance full payment for all the shares it has offered to acquire for cash or partly in cash.[904] Shares deposited under the bid must be taken up within ten days of the expiry of the bid.[905] Shares taken up under the bid must be paid for within three days after they are taken up.[906]

6. Purchases and Sales of Shares During the Bid Period

365. To prevent the bidder from significantly altering the success of the bid, unbeknownst to offeree shareholders, there are restrictions on open market purchases by the bidder. Such purchases are limited to 5% of the outstanding offeree shares subject to the bid. The intention to make such purchases must be announced in the takeover bid circular, or, if the intention to make such purchases arises after the bid is made, the intention to make such purchases is announced in a press release issued at least one business day before purchases are made. The purchases must be made on a published market and a press release must be made at the close of business of the exchange on each day that purchases have been made.[907] Such purchases cannot commence until three days after the date of the bid.[908] During the bid period bidders are restricted from selling, except under an issuer bid or a competing takeover bid, securities of the class subject to the bid.[909]

---

903. Multilateral Instrument 61-101, s. 4.4(1)(d).
904. NI 62-104, s. 2.27.
905. NI 62-104, s. 2.32(1). If the offeror is obligated pursuant to NI 62-104, s. 2.32 to take up securities deposited under a takeover bid, the offeror must extend the period during which securities may be deposited for a further period of at least ten days and must promptly issue and file a press release disclosing that the minimum 50% tender requirement has been satisfied, the number of securities deposited and not withdrawn as at the expiry of the initial bid period, that the period for deposit of securities has been extended for ten days and that the shares will paid for as soon as possible and not later than three business days after the securities are taken up. *See* NI 62-104, s. 2.31.1.
906. NI 62-104, s. 2.32(2).
907. NI 62-104, s. 2.2.
908. NI 62-104, s. 2.2(3).
909. NI 62-104, s. 2.7.

B. When the Takeover Bid Requirements Apply

366. The takeover bid requirements apply when there is a 'takeover bid'. Under provincial securities acts a 'takeover bid' is defined to mean an 'offer to acquire'[910] voting or equity securities that are held by a person in the province where the acquisition will result in the bidder ending up with more than 20% of the outstanding shares of a class of voting or equity securities.[911]

C. Exemptions from the Takeover Bid Requirements

1. The Stock Exchange Exemption

367. There are several exceptions to the application of the takeover bid requirements on the test noted above. Bids made through the facilities of a stock exchange were, in the past, exempted from the takeover bid requirements of provincial securities legislation if they complied with the requirements of the stock exchange. Stock exchange mergers in Canada left the Toronto Stock Exchange as the only relevant accepted exchange for this exemption. In 2005 the Toronto Stock Exchange repealed its takeover bid rules and now simply provides that takeover bids follow the takeover bid requirements under provincial securities laws.

2. 'Normal Course' Purchase Exemption

368. An exception to the takeover bid requirements is provided for so-called normal course purchases. Once one owns or controls 20% or more of the shares of a class a purchase of a single additional share would, under the definition of 'takeover bid', trigger the takeover bid requirements. The normal course purchase exemption allows for the purchase of up to 5% of the outstanding securities of a class in any twelve-month period without triggering the takeover bid requirements as long as the consideration paid for the securities is not in excess of the market price plus reasonable brokerage fees or commissions actually paid.[912]

3. 'Control Block' or 'Private Agreement' Exemption

369. There is also an exemption for an acquisition of a controlling block of shares from one or a few shareholders. The takeover bid requirements will not apply

910. 'Offer to acquire' is defined to include an offer to purchase securities, a solicitation of an offer to sell securities or an acceptance of an offer to sell securities – *see* NI 62–104, s. 1.1.

911. NI 62-104, s. 1.1. 'Equity security' is defined as a security of an issuer that carries a residual right to participate in the earnings of the issuer and, on liquidation or winding up of the issuer, in its assets – *see* NI 62-104, s. 1.1.

912. NI 62-104, s. 4.1. The purchase price cannot exceed the 'market price'. 'Market price' is defined as the simple average of the closing price for each business day on which there was a closing price over the previous twenty days – *see* NI 62-104, s. 1.11.

if the bid is made by way of a private agreement with five or fewer persons and the offer price does not exceed the market price by more than 15%.[913]

4. Closely Held Corporation Exemption

370. There is an exemption for the acquisition of shares of a relatively closely held corporation. The exemption applies where the number of shareholders of the class of shares sought is less than fifty, the offeree corporation has not made a distribution of its securities to the public, and there is no published market for the securities that are the subject of the bid.[914]

5. Limited Effect/*De Minimus*

371. A bid can also be exempt from the application of the takeover bid requirements of a given province where the bid has a relatively limited effect in the particular province and the shareholders are protected by similar takeover bid requirements of another jurisdiction. The exemption applies where less than 2% of the shares of the class are held by persons resident in the province, there are less than fifty holders of the shares sought by residents in the particular province, the security holders in the Canadian jurisdiction are entitled to participate in the bid on terms at least as favourable as the terms that apply to the general body of security holders of the same class of securities, and the bidder sends material relating to the bid to all shareholders of the class of shares sought who are resident in the Canadian jurisdiction (and files the material with the relevant securities commissions in Canada).[915]

6. Foreign Takeover Bid Exemption

372. There is also an exemption for foreign takeover bids where:

- beneficial security holders in Canada represent less than 10% of the outstanding securities of the class sought under the bid;
- the published market on which the greatest volume of trading in securities of that class occurred during the previous twelve months was not in Canada;
- security holders in the relevant Canadian jurisdictions are entitled to participate in the bid on terms at least as favourable as the terms that apply to the general body of security holders of the same class; and
- the material relating to the bid is filed in the relevant Canadian jurisdictions and sent to the security holders in Canada.[916]

913. NI 62-104, s. 4.2.
914. NI 62-104, s. 4.3.
915. NI 62-104, s. 4.5.
916. NI 62-104, s. 4.4.

7. Securities Commission Discretionary Exemption

373. Where a bid is made that falls within the definition of 'takeover bid' but does not fit any of the above-noted exceptions to the takeover bid requirements then an application can be made to the relevant securities commissions for an exemption from the takeover bid requirements. Securities commissions generally have the power to grant such exemptions where it would 'not be prejudicial to the public interest to do so'.[917]

D. Anti-avoidance Provisions

374. There are provisions that address potential techniques for avoiding the application of the takeover bid requirements. For instance, two or more persons might each acquire less than 20% of the shares but then act together in exercising the rights attached to those shares. To prevent this the bidder's shares are defined to include the shares of anyone with whom it is 'acting jointly or in concert'.[918] Thus in determining whether the bid will result in the bidder owning or controlling more than 20% of a class of shares of the offeree corporation the shares held, or to be acquired, by anyone with whom the bidder is acting jointly or in concert, must be added to the shares the bidder holds or will acquire under the bid. 'Affiliates' of the bidder are deemed to be acting jointly or in concert with the bidder and 'associates' of the bidder are presumed to be acting jointly or in concert with the bidder.[919] Also anyone with whom the bidder has an agreement, commitment, or understanding for the acquisition of shares of the same class is deemed to be acting jointly or in concert with the bidder and anyone with whom the bidder has an agreement, commitment, or understanding to jointly exercise voting rights, is presumed to be acting jointly or in concert with the bidder.[920] Otherwise it is said to be a 'question of fact' as to whether a person is acting jointly or in concert with another.[921]

375. The avoidance of the takeover bid requirements by purchasing options to acquire shares or by purchasing securities convertible into shares is precluded by deeming that the bidder, or any person acting jointly or in concert with the bidder, owns shares that it can acquire by exercising a conversion right, or some other right to acquire shares, within sixty days of a bid for shares of the offeree corporation.[922] Also, an 'offer to acquire' shares includes a direct or indirect offer to acquire shares

917. *See*, for example, ASA s. 179(2); BCSA s. 114(2); NSA s. 93(2); OSA s. 104(2); QSA s. 263 (not 'detrimental to the protection of investors').

918. NI 62-104, s. 1.1 'offeror's securities'.

919. NI 62-104, s. 1.9(1). 'Associate' is typically defined to include such persons as an issuer in which the person owns more than 10% of the outstanding voting securities, partners of the person, a trust in which the person serves as a trustee or has a substantial beneficial interest, and relatives (*See*, NI 62-104, s. 1.1 'associate'). 'Affiliate' is typically defined to include subsidiaries, parent companies, or companies which have a common parent (*See*, NI 62–104, s. 1.3).

920. NI 62-104, s. 1.9(1).

921. NI 62-104, s. 1.9(1).

922. NI 62-104, s. 1.7 and s. 1.8.

or to exercise control or direction over shares.[923] This prevents the bidder from avoiding the takeover bid requirements by, for instance, buying the shares of a holding corporation that holds the shares of the true intended offeree corporation.

376. There are provisions with respect to linked bids to ensure that the principle of offering identical consideration to all shareholders is not defeated by making private agreements with individual shareholders before or after the bid in reliance on the exemption with respect to private agreements. The consideration in the bid must be equal to or greater than the highest consideration paid in the previous ninety days for any shares of the class sought.[924] The bidder must also offer to purchase the percentage of shares that was the highest percentage purchased in any private transaction in the ninety days prior to the bid.[925] The offeror also cannot acquire shares of the class subject to the bid for twenty days after the expiry of the bid except by way of a transaction that is generally available to shareholders of the class subject to the bid and on terms identical to the terms of the takeover bid.[926]

E. Early Warning Disclosure

377. Securities laws also provide that anyone acquiring control of over 10% of a class of voting or equity securities of a corporation must issue and file a press release identifying the person and the extent of the person's control over the voting securities.[927] Subsequently, each time an acquisition results in the ownership or control over an additional 2% of a class of voting or equity securities of that corporation the person must issue a press release and file a report with the relevant securities commissions.[928]

F. Enforcement

378. The takeover bid requirements can be enforced through provincial securities commissions or the courts. Applications can be made to a securities commission for an order restraining the distribution of any record used in connection with a takeover bid, requiring an amendment to or variation of any record used in connection with a takeover bid, or directing any person to comply with the takeover bid requirements.[929] 'Interested persons' may also apply to court to rescind a transaction with the person, to require the disposition of securities acquired, to prohibit the exercise of voting rights, to require the trial of an issue, to make an order compensating an interested person, or to make any other order the court thinks fit in the circumstances.[930]

923. NI 62-104, s. 1.10.
924. NI 62-104, s. 2.4.
925. *Ibid.*
926. NI 62-104, s. 2.5.
927. NI 62-104, s. 5.2 and NI 62-103.
928. *Ibid.*
929. *See*, for example, ASA s. 179; BCSA s. 114(1); NSA s. 93; OSA s. 104(1); QSA s. 265; SSA s. 101.
930. ASA s. 180; BCSA s. 115; NSA s. 94; OSA s. 105; QSA s. 233.1; SSA s. 102.

G. *Post-takeover Force Out*

379. Several general statutes of incorporation in Canada provide that where a takeover bidder is successful in obtaining 90% or more of the class of shares to which the takeover bid relates (other than shares held by the bidder or its affiliates or associates at the date of the takeover bid) the bidder is entitled to acquire the shares held by the shareholders who did not tender if the bidder follows certain specified procedures.[931] These provisions are discussed above in paragraphs 248–249.

V. Constraints on Mergers and Takeovers

A. *Competition Act*

380. Mergers with competitors, suppliers, or customers are subject to regulation under the federal *Competition Act*.[932] 'Merger' is broadly defined in the act as a direct or indirect acquisition or establishment, by one or more persons, of control over or significant interest in the whole or part of the business of a competitor, supplier, customer, or other person. The acquisition or establishment of control or significant interest may occur through the purchase or lease of shares or assets, amalgamation or by combination, or otherwise.[933] One is considered to have a significant interest where one has the ability to influence materially the economic behaviour of the acquired person through such means as being able to elect directors to the board, block ordinary or special resolutions, or influence the purchasing or selling activity of the acquired business.

381. The Commissioner appointed under the *Competition Act* reviews individual mergers to assess whether they prevent or lessen, or are likely to prevent or lessen, competition substantially in the relevant market. In making the assessment several factors are considered such as the existence of barriers to entry, the availability of substitutes, foreign competition, the extent of effective competition remaining after the merger, and other relevant factors.[934] If the Commissioner is satisfied that a merger or proposed merger prevents or lessens, or is likely to present or lessen, competition then he or she may apply to the Competition Tribunal for a remedial order with respect to the merger.[935] The parties can avoid the imposition of a remedial order if they can establish:

- that gains in efficiency have accrued, or will accrue, from the merger;
- that these gains offset the effect on competition; and

931. In Ontario a shareholder may also force the corporation to purchase his or her shares when one person (or a group of persons acting jointly) acquires 90% or more of a class of shares – *see supra* paras 250–251.
932. R.S.C. 1985, c. C-34, as amended.
933. Section 91.
934. Section 93.
935. Section 92(1).

- that the gains will not be realized if an order is imposed by the Competition Tribunal.[936]

382. The Commissioner must be notified of mergers that exceed specified thresholds. If:

- the parties, together with their affiliates, have total assets in Canada or total gross annual revenues from sales in Canada, from Canada or into Canada, of over CAD 400 million; and
- the value of the assets in Canada, the shares to be acquired, or the gross revenues flowing from them, exceed CAD 80 million, then notification must be given.[937]

Before completing the merger the parties are required to wait for a period of between thirty days from the date of notification but if the Commissioner requires additional information within that thirty-day period, the period is extended by another thirty days.[938] After the delay the merger can proceed but the parties proceed at their own risk if the merger prevents or lessens, or is likely to prevent or lessen, competition. Failure to comply with the notification requirements can lead to an application by the Commissioner for an interim order from the Competition Tribunal and can lead to prosecution.[939] The parties to a merger can, however, apply to the Commissioner for an advance ruling to the effect that he would not have sufficient grounds to apply to the Competition Tribunal for an order in respect of the merger.[940]

B. Foreign Investment Reviews and Restrictions

1. The Investment Canada Act

383. Foreign investments in Canada are subject to review pursuant to the *Investment Canada Act*.[941] The Minister reviews foreign ('non-Canadian')[942] acquisitions where there is:[943]

---

936. Section 96.
937. Sections 109 and 110. The amounts given were effective January 2013. The amounts are adjusted yearly pursuant to s. 110(8).
938. Section 123.
939. Sections 100(1) and 65(2).
940. Section 102.
941. R.S.C. 1985, c. 28 (1st Supp.). For a more detailed discussion *see Foreign Investment in Canada: A Guide to the Law* (Scarborough, Ont.: Carswell, 1996 (looseleaf)).
942. A non-Canadian is a person who is neither a Canadian citizen nor a permanent resident and an entity that is controlled or beneficial owned by non-Canadians is also 'non-Canadian'. *See* the definitions of 'Canadian' and 'non-Canadian' in s. 3 of the *Investment Canada Act*.
943. Sections 14 and 28. 'Canadian business' is defined as a business carried on in Canada that has a place of business in Canada, one or more individuals employed, or self-employed in connection with the business and assets in Canada that are used in carrying on the business (*see* s. 3). The amount is adjusted for a 'WTO investor' (*see* s. 14.1). The 'Minister' normally responsible for the *Investment Canada Act* is the Minister of Industry.

- a proposed acquisition of the assets of a Canadian business which have a value of CAD 5 million or more; and
- a proposed acquisition of the voting shares of a corporation incorporated in Canada and carrying on a Canadian business, of voting interests of an entity that is carrying on a Canadian business (or that controls, directly or indirectly, another entity carrying on a Canadian business), or of voting interests of an entity that controls, directly or indirectly, an entity in Canada carrying on a Canadian business where the assets of the Canadian business and of all other entities in Canada the control of which is acquired have a value of CAD 5 million or more.

Much more lenient thresholds are provided for WTO investors or for investments by non-Canadians controlled by a WTO investor. The amount for WTO investors or investments by non-Canadians controlled by a WTO investor, as of 2017, is CAD 1 billion (*see* s. 14.1(1)(d) of the *Investment Canada Act*, as amended by S.C. 2017, c. 20, s. 194). The amount will be increased annually, beginning in 2019, by multiplying the rate for the prior year by the ratio of the current nominal gross domestic product divided by the previous year's nominal gross domestic product (*see* s. 14.1(1)(e) and s. 14.1(2) of the *Investment Canada Act* as amended by S.C. 2017, c. 20, s. 194). [944]

Other foreign acquisitions of Canadian businesses are subject to a notification requirement but are not generally subject to review.[945] Notification is required with respect to new business investments but these are not reviewable unless the investment is in an area that may affect Canada's cultural heritage or national identity.[946] Reviews by the Minister are to be done in forty-five days, with a possible extension to seventy-five days or such further period as may be agreed on by the applicant and the Minister.[947]

384. In reviewing the investment the Minister is to assess whether the investment will provide a net benefit to Canada.[948] In making this assessment the Minister is to take into account such factors as the impact of the investment on economic activity, efficiency and technology, Canadian participation, competition, compatibility with federal and provincial economic and industrial policies, compatibility with cultural policy, and the effect on Canada's international competitiveness.[949]

385. Several types of investment are exempt from the application of the *Investment Canada Act*. For instance, there is an exemption where the acquisition does not entail

---

944. A 'WTO investor' is defined in s. 14.1(6) of the *Investment Canada Act* as a member of the World Trade Organization established by Art. I of the WTO Agreement who is, for example, an individual, other than a Canadian, who is a national of a WTO Member or who has the right of permanent residence in relation to that WTO Member, a government of a WTO Member, whether federal, state or local, or an agency thereof, or an entity that is not a Canadian-controlled entity and that is a WTO investor-controlled entity. On the proclamation of the Canada-European Union Comprehensive Economic and Trade Agreement (CETA) the investment review threshold for European Union investors, and certain other free trade agreement partners pursuant to most favoured nation clauses (such as the United States, Mexico, Chile, Columbia, Panama, Peru, Honduras and South Korea), will be CAD 1.5 billion.

945. Section 11.

946. Section 15.

947. Sections 21 and 22.

948. Section 21(1).

949. Section 20.

the acquisition of control. Acquisitions by traders or dealers in securities in the ordinary course of their business are also exempt. Other exemptions include acquisitions in the ordinary course of business that provide venture capital, acquisitions resulting from the realization of security on loans or similar obligations, and acquisitions by devolution of estates.

2. Other Legislative Constraints

386. There are restrictions on foreign ownership of particular businesses. For instance, section 3 of the *Broadcasting Act* provides that 'the Canadian broadcasting system should be effectively owned and controlled by Canadians' so as 'to safeguard, enrich and strengthen the cultural, political, social and economic fabric of Canada'.[950] To effect this policy directions have been given to the Canadian Radio and Television Commission not to issue broadcasting licences to non-Canadians or non-Canadian corporations.

§6. Holding Corporations and Subsidiaries

I. Approach to the Regulation of Holding Corporations and Subsidiaries

387. Provisions dealing with holding corporations and subsidiaries are scattered throughout several statutes in the various jurisdictions in Canada. There are numerous provisions in general statutes of incorporation in Canada that deal with holding corporations and subsidiaries employing terms such as 'holding body corporate', 'subsidiary body corporate', and 'affiliate'. Provincial securities legislation also uses similar terms to address matters involving holding corporations and subsidiaries. The discussion that follows focuses briefly only on provisions that appear in general statutes of incorporation in Canada.

II. Definitions

388. Under the CBCA a corporation is a 'holding body corporate' if another corporation is its 'subsidiary'.[951] 'Subsidiary' is defined as a corporation that is 'controlled' by another corporation.[952] A corporation is controlled by another corporation if that other corporation has beneficial ownership of securities of the corporation carrying more than 50% of the votes that may be cast to elect directors of the corporation and the votes are sufficient to elect a majority of the directors of the corporation.[953] Also, a corporation is said to be 'affiliated' with another corporation if one is the

950. S.C. 1991, c. 11.
951. CBCA s. 2(4).
952. CBCA s. 2(5).
953. CBCA s. 2(3).

subsidiary of the other or both are subsidiaries of the same corporation or are controlled by the same person.[954]

III. Restrictions and Other Provisions

A. *Holding and Voting of Holding Corporation Shares*

389. A subsidiary is not permitted to hold shares in itself or its holding corporation and must not permit any of its subsidiaries to hold its shares.[955] If a subsidiary corporation holds shares of its holding corporation the holding corporation must cause its subsidiary corporation to dispose of those shares within five years from the date the subsidiary corporation became a subsidiary of the holding corporation.[956] There is an exception where the purpose of holding the shares of an affiliate is to qualify under prescribed laws of Canada or a province with respect to attaining or maintaining a specified level of Canadian ownership.[957]

390. A corporation holding shares in its holding body corporate shall not vote or permit those shares to be voted unless the corporation holds the shares in the capacity of a legal representative and has complied with requirements imposed on persons holding shares in a legal representative capacity.[958]

B. *Number of Canadian Resident Directors*

391. Corporations incorporated in Canada typically have to have a minimum number of Canadian directors.[959] The CBCA qualifies this minimum number requirement with respect to holding corporations. Normally one quarter of the directors of a corporation incorporated under the CBCA must be resident in Canada.[960] Where, however, the CBCA prescribes, or an Act of Parliament requires, with respect to a particular business sector, that there be a specified level of Canadian ownership or control then a majority of the directors must be resident Canadians.[961] Where there is a requirement for a majority of Canadian ownership in a particular business sector, there is an exception for a holding corporation that earns in Canada directly or through

954. CBCA s. 2(2).
955. CBCA s. 30(1). A corporation may hold shares in its holding corporation if it does so solely in the capacity of a legal representative without itself having a beneficial interest in the shares and may hold shares in its holding corporation by way of security for the purposes of a transaction entered into by it in the course of a business that includes the lending of money [CBCA s. 31].
956. CBCA s. 30(2).
957. CBCA s. 32. Related provisions dealing with shares owned for the purpose of meeting Canadian ownership requirements are ss 46, 49(10), and 174. *See supra* para. 69, notes 169 and 170 and the accompanying text.
958. CBCA ss 33, 153.
959. *See supra* paras 282 and 283.
960. CBCA s. 105(3). *See* para. 282.
961. CBCA s. 105(3.1).

its subsidiaries less than 5% of its total gross revenues in Canada. In that situation only one-third of the directors need be resident Canadians.[962]

C. *Financial Disclosure*

392. There are financial disclosure requirements for corporations.[963] Under the CBCA the financial statements must comply with the standards set out in the Handbook of the Canadian Institute of Chartered Accountants.[964] These standards generally require consolidated financial statements which include the statements of subsidiary corporations. Holding corporations are required to maintain a copy of the financial statements of subsidiaries available for inspection at its registered office.[965] A CBCA subsidiary corporation is not required to file financial statements with the Director if the financial statements of its holding corporation are in consolidated form, include the accounts of the subsidiary, and the consolidated financial statements of the holding corporation are included in the documents sent to the Director.[966]

393. The auditor of a holding corporation may have access to records, documents, books, accounts, and vouchers of any of the subsidiaries of the corporation as well as of the corporation itself.[967] In preparing the consolidated financial statements the auditor can rely on the report of auditors of subsidiary corporations.[968]

D. *Investigations*

394. A security holder (or the Director) may apply to a court for an order directing that an investigation be made of the corporation and the investigation can extend to any of the corporation's affiliates.[969]

E. *Insider Trading*

395. There are provisions dealing with insider trading in securities legislation in several provinces in Canada and in statutes of incorporation in several jurisdictions in Canada as well. There is also a federal Criminal Code prohibition of insider trading. These provisions impose a variety of sanctions with respect to trading in the securities of the corporation by insiders with knowledge of material information about the corporation. There are also obligations on insiders to report their trades in shares of the corporation of which they are an insider. The definition of insiders for the purpose

962. CBCA s. 105(4).
963. *See supra* §3.I.F, paras 265–266.
964. CBCA Reg. s. 71 and the definition of 'Canadian GAAP' in CBCA Regs. S. 70. Exception is made for a corporation the securities of which are registered under s. 12 of the *Securities Exchange Act of 1934* in the US. *See* CBCA Regs. s. 70 ('SEC Registrant') and CBCA Regs. s. 71.
965. CBCA s. 157.
966. CBCA s. 160(2).
967. CBCA s. 170.
968. CBCA s. 169.
969. CBCA s. 229.

of the reporting obligation is quite broad and includes holding corporations and subsidiaries as those terms are defined above. The definition of insiders for the purpose of the imposition of sanctions with respect to trading on undisclosed material information is even broader and includes holding corporations, subsidiaries, and affiliates as defined above.[970]

F. Short-Form Amalgamations

396. There are provisions for reduced approval requirements with respect to amalgamations between a holding corporation and a wholly owned subsidiary or between two or more wholly owned subsidiaries of the same holding corporation. These so-called short-form amalgamations are discussed above.[971]

G. Affiliates, Fiduciary Duties, and Derivative Actions

397. Directors and officers have a duty to act honestly and in good faith with a view to the best interests of the corporation.[972] Failure to meet this fiduciary obligation in dealings with affiliated corporations can lead to an action against the director or officer pursued by a shareholder (or other 'proper person') in a derivative action. Under the CBCA the derivative action can be brought not only by a beneficial owner of the shares of the corporation but it can also be brought by a shareholder of an affiliated corporation.[973] In a derivative action under the CBCA the court is given the power to make any order it thinks fit, including an order that any amount adjudged payable be paid, in whole or in part, directly to present or former security holders of the corporation or its subsidiary.[974]

H. Affiliates and the Oppression Remedy

398. Probably the most effective device for attacking the use of a web of affiliated corporations to the disadvantage of a shareholder or group of shareholders is through the oppression remedy.[975] Several jurisdictions in Canada have an oppression remedy that extends to the acts of the affiliates of a corporation. For instance, CBCA section 241 provides that a court may provide a remedy where:

(a) any act or omission of the corporation *or any of its affiliates* effects a result;
(b) the business or affairs of the corporation *or any of its affiliates* are or have been carried on or conducted in a manner; or
(c) the powers of the directors of the corporation *or any of its affiliates* are or have been exercised in a manner that is oppressive or unfairly prejudicial to, or unfairly disregards the interests of any security holder, creditor, director, or officer.

---

970. For a more detailed discussion of insider trading *see supra* §2.III.E, paras 155–165.
971. *See supra* §5.II.D, paras 352–353.
972. *See supra* paras 297 and 303.
973. CBCA s. 238.
974. CBCA s. 240(c). With respect to the derivative action generally *see supra* §3.I.B, paras 207–221.
975. The oppression remedy is discussed *supra* §3.I.C, paras 222–238.

§7. The Taxation of Corporations and Shareholders

I. Corporate Income Taxation

A. Introduction

399. Corporations are separate legal persons for income tax purposes. Corporations resident in Canada are subject to federal income tax on their worldwide income.[976] In addition each province (including the Yukon, Northwest Territories, and Nunavut) levies tax on corporate income allocable to a permanent establishment in the province.[977] The comments in this section refer to the federal law, but in general they apply equally to the provincial tax systems.[978] Non-resident corporations may also be subject to tax on income earned in Canada, subject to relief granted under international tax treaties.[979] Except where otherwise indicated, this section deals only with the taxation of Canadian resident corporations.

B. Classification of Corporations for Income Tax Purposes

1. Importance of the Classification

400. A corporation's income tax treatment depends in part on how it is classified under the *Income Tax Act* (ITA). The most basic distinction is between resident and non-resident corporations. Resident corporations are further divided into two classes – public corporations and private corporations. Within the larger categories several sub-classes are defined.

976. *Income Tax Act, S.C.* 1970–71–72, c. 63, as am. ('ITA'), ss 2(1), 248(1) 'person'. Unless otherwise noted, all statutory references are to the ITA.

977. Taxable income is allocated among provinces according to a formula under the federal ITA, based on gross revenues and labour compensation attributable to each permanent establishment of the corporation: Regulations, Part IV. Provincial corporate income taxes are imposed under the following statutes: *Alberta Personal Income Tax Act*, R.S.A. 2000, c. A-30; *Income Tax Act*, R.S.B.C. 1996, c. 215, as am.; *The Income Tax Act* (Manitoba), C.C.S.M. 1988, c. 110, as am.; *New Brunswick Income Tax Act*, S.N.B. 2000, c. N-6.001, as am.; *Income Tax Act*, S.N.L. 2000, c. I-1-1, as am.; *Income Tax Act*, R.S.N.W.T. 1988, c.I-1, as am.; *Income Tax Act*, R.S.N.S. 1989, c. 217, as am.; *Corporations Tax Act*, R.S.O. 1990, c. C.40, as am.; *Income Tax Act*, R.S.O. 1990, c. I.2; *Income Tax Act*, R.S.P.E.I. 1988, c. I-1, as am.; *Taxation Act*, R.S.Q. 1977, c. I-3, as am.; *The Income Tax Act*, R.S.S. 1978, c. I-2, as am.; *Income Tax Act*, R.S.Y. 2002, c. 118, as am.

978. The federal government collects corporate income tax on behalf of all provinces except Quebec and Alberta, which administer their own systems and therefore have greater freedom to deviate from the federal law. Even these provinces, however, harmonize with the federal rules to a great extent for the sake of administrative simplicity.

979. Section 2(3), Part XIII.

2. Resident and Non-resident Corporations

401. Corporate residence is determined by a combination of common law and statutory rules. Under common law principles a corporation will be resident in Canada if its central management and control is situated in Canada.[980] By statute a corporation generally is deemed to be resident if it was incorporated in Canada. If the incorporation took place before 27 April 1965[981] the corporation will be deemed resident only if it was also carrying on business or otherwise resident in Canada during a taxation year ending after 26 April 1965. A resident corporation will be a 'Canadian corporation' if it was incorporated in Canada or has been resident in Canada since 18 June 1971.[982] Such a corporation will be a 'taxable Canadian corporation' if it is not tax-exempt.[983] A corporation incorporated in Canada may qualify as a 'Non-Resident Owned investment corporation' (NRO) if all its shares and debt have been beneficially owned by non-residents and/or other NROs since it was incorporated, and if it meets certain criteria and restrictions concerning its income-earning activities.[984]

3. Public and Private Corporations

402. A 'public corporation' is a corporation which is resident in Canada and generally has at least one class of its shares listed on a prescribed Canadian stock exchange. Unlisted corporations may elect or be designated as public corporations if their shares are widely distributed.[985] A 'private corporation' is defined negatively as a Canadian resident corporation which is not a public corporation and is not controlled by one or more public corporations.[986] Private corporations cover a wide range, from small closely held companies to large corporations with many shareholders. A 'Canadian-controlled Private Corporation' (CCPC) is a subspecies of private corporation, defined as a Canadian corporation not controlled (directly or indirectly) by non-residents and/or public corporations.[987] Canadian courts have in most cases defined 'control' to mean de jure control for income tax purposes; that is, ownership of shares carrying more than 50% of the votes which may be cast to elect directors.[988] Expanded definitions of control have, however, been enacted which require additional factors to be taken into

---

980. *DeBeers Consolidated Mines Limited v. Howe*, [1906] A.C. 455 (H.L.); *Unit Construction Co. Ltd. v. Bullock*, [1959] 3 All E.R. 831 (H.L.); *Yamaska Steamship Co. Ltd. v. MNR*, 61 DTC 716 (T.A.B.).
981. Section 250(4).
982. Section 89(1).
983. Section 89(1).
984. Section 133(8).
985. Section 89(1), and *Income Tax Regulations*, C.R.C. c. 945, as am. ('Regulations'), ss 4800 and 4803.
986. Section 89(1).
987. Section 125(7).
988. *Buckerfields v. MNR*, 64 D.T.C. 5302 (Ex.Ct.); *MNR v. Dworkin Furs (Pembroke) Ltd.*, 67 D.T.C. 5035 (S.C.C.). The courts have sometimes considered de facto powers where voting shares are held equally by two shareholders, as to 50% each: *Oakfield Developments (Toronto) Ltd. v. MNR*, 71 DTC 5175 (S.C.C.); *The Queen v. Imperial General Properties Ltd.*, 85 D.T.C. 5500 (S.C.C.).

account for specific purposes. Thus, in determining CCPC status, control may be constituted by way of options or rights to acquire shares of the corporation held by any person, or, by powers of influence which, if exercised, would result in de facto control of the corporation.[989]

C. *Income Tax Rates*

1. Federal Rates

403. The basic federal rate is 38%,[990] subject to a 10% abatement for taxable income earned in a province.[991] The abatement is intended to account for provincial income tax liability but, as noted in paragraph 404 below, provincial tax rates may be significantly greater or less than 10%. The abated federal tax rate of 28% is further reduced by a general rate reduction.[992] The general rate reduction for in 2013 was 13% making the federal corporate tax rate 15%.[993] CCPCs are eligible for a small business credit (of 17%) which reduces the basic federal tax rate to 11% on the first CAD 500,000 of annual income from active businesses carried on in Canada.[994] Two or more CCPCs which are 'associated' must share the small business credit.[995] The federal rate may be further reduced by other credits, such as the investment tax credit[996] and the foreign tax credit in respect of taxes paid to another government on foreign-source income.[997] A special low tax rate will apply to a corporation which qualifies and elects to be treated as a 'non-resident owned investment corporation'.[998]

2. Provincial Rates

404. Basic provincial rates range from 10% in Alberta to 16% in Nova Scotia. All provinces give preferential treatment to small businesses, in the form of lower rates and/or temporary tax holidays.[999]

D. *Computing Income Tax Liability*

1. Overview

405. A corporation must compute its tax liability after each 'taxation year'.[1000] The ITA employs a source concept of income under which a corporation's profit from

989. Sections 251(5), 256(5.1), (6).
990. Section 123.
991. Section 124(1).
992. Section 123.4 and s. 125.1.
993. *See* s. 123.4.
994. Section 125(1).
995. Sections 125(3)–(5.1), 256.
996. Section 127.1.
997. Section 126.
998. Section 133.
999. Each province enacts its own rate schedule (*see* citations in s. A above).
1000. Sections 150, 151, 249.

each business or property and its income from any other source are determined separately. Profits from all sources are then aggregated with net taxable capital gains. This aggregate amount, less any current year non-capital losses and certain other deductions, is the corporation's income for the taxation year.[1001] Corporations use the accrual method of accounting to determine their income for tax purposes, except in limited circumstances where the ITA provides expressly for cash basis accounting.[1002] Income is adjusted by loss carryovers and other deductions to arrive at taxable income,[1003] to which the tax rates are applied. Any credits for which the corporation qualifies are applied to reduce its tax otherwise payable.

2. Income from Business

406. In computing income from a business, corporations generally may deduct reasonable current expenses incurred for the purpose of producing income.[1004] Tangible capital property (other than land) and certain intangible assets may be depreciated through annual deductions of 'Capital Cost Allowance' (CCA).[1005] Maximum rates of CCA are prescribed by regulation.[1006] Expenditures to purchase goodwill and other non-depreciable intangible property (to the extent of three-quarters thereof) may be amortized as 'cumulative eligible capital', at a rate not exceeding 7% per year.[1007] Excess business losses may be carried over and deducted from taxable income for any of the three preceding or twenty subsequent taxation years.[1008]

3. Income from Property: Introduction

407. Most forms of income from property received by a corporation, such as rent, interest, and royalties, are included in income and subject to tax at the top rate applicable to the corporation. Special rules apply to dividends (*see* paragraphs 409 and 410). The comments in paragraph 406 respecting computation of business income apply equally to income from property, except for the amortization of intangible capital assets which is available only to taxpayers carrying on business. For private corporations, a portion of the tax paid on income from property may be refunded upon payment of taxable dividends (*see* Section II: Integration of Corporate and Personal Income Taxes).

4. Foreign Accrual Property Income

408. A Canadian resident corporation which holds shares in a 'controlled foreign affiliate' may be required to include in its income a proportionate amount of the affiliate's 'Foreign Accrual Property Income' (FAPI) each year, whether or not such

1001. Section 3.
1002. *See*, for example, s. 28.
1003. Section 2(1), (2).
1004. Sections 9, 18(1)(a), 67.
1005. Sections 18(1)(b), 20(1)(a).
1006. Regulations, Part XI and Schedule II.
1007. Sections 14 and 20(1)(b).
1008. Section 111(1)(a), 111(8).

income has actually been paid or distributed by the affiliate.[1009] The attribution of FAPI is intended to limit the avoidance or deferral of Canadian tax on investment-type income earned through foreign entities. A 'foreign affiliate' is a non-resident corporation (or in some circumstances a trust) in which the taxpayer owns at least 1% of the issued shares of any class, either directly or through other corporations and the taxpayer and each person related to the taxpayer collectively own 10% of the shares.[1010] A 'controlled foreign affiliate' generally is one in which the taxpayer holds shares carrying more than 50% of the votes which may be cast to elect directors (shareholdings of non-arm's length persons or other Canadian residents may be counted for this purpose).[1011] FAPI includes most types of income from property, as well as income from certain service businesses, and net taxable capital gains from the disposition of properties not used principally for producing active business income.[1012] When FAPI is included in income, a concurrent deduction may be claimed for the amount thereof on which foreign income tax has been paid at a rate approximating that which would apply in Canada.[1013] Dividends paid by a controlled foreign affiliate may be received free of tax to the extent of any FAPI previously included in the shareholder's income.[1014]

5. Dividends from Canadian Resident Corporations

409. Taxable dividends from other Canadian resident corporations must be included in income, but normally may be fully offset by a concurrent deduction, provided that the payer is a taxable Canadian corporation or is controlled by the recipient.[1015] This inter-corporate dividend deduction in effect allows dividends to flow tax free between resident corporations. There are several important qualifications to this general rule. In particular, private corporations (as well as certain others) must pay a 33.3% refundable tax on portfolio dividends.[1016] The tax is fully refunded upon payment of sufficient taxable dividends by the corporation (*see* below, Section II: Integration of Corporate and Personal Income Taxes). The refundable tax aims to prevent individuals from deferring personal income tax on portfolio dividends by holding shares through a corporation. Special refundable or non-refundable taxes may also apply, or the inter-corporate dividend deduction may be denied, with respect to certain preferred shares held by financial institutions and public corporations.[1017] These anti-avoidance provisions are intended to remove the tax advantages of financing arrangements which substitute the issuance of preferred shares for ordinary loans at interest. Other anti-avoidance provisions may also apply to deny the inter-corporate

1009. Section 91(1).
1010. Sections 95(1), 94, 95(4).
1011. Section 95(1). *See* para. 402 regarding the meaning of 'control'.
1012. Section 95(1), 95(2), and Regulations, Part LIX.
1013. Sections 91(4), 95(1).
1014. Section 91(5).
1015. Sections 82(1), 112.
1016. ITA Part IV.
1017. Section 112(2.1) & (2.2), Parts IV.1 & VI.1.

dividend deduction.[1018] Capital dividends paid out of a private corporation's capital dividend account are exempt from tax (*see* below, paragraph 411).

6. Dividends from Non-resident Corporations

410. Dividends received from a non-resident corporation must be included in income.[1019] The recipient may, however, be entitled to a concurrent deduction of all or a portion of such dividends if they are paid by a foreign affiliate (defined above, paragraph 408).[1020] A deduction may be claimed to the full extent of any FAPI previously included in income in respect of a controlled foreign affiliate (*see* above, paragraph 408). If this deduction has been exhausted or does not apply, the amount which may be deducted depends on two factors:

(1) whether the dividend is derived from profits earned in a 'prescribed country'; and
(2) whether the dividend is paid out of 'exempt surplus', 'taxable surplus', or 'pre-acquisition surplus'.

The list of prescribed countries generally includes those with which Canada has a tax treaty.[1021]

7. Capital Gains

411. Capital gains have been subject to income tax in Canada since 1972, when the statute was amended to require that half of any capital gain realized be included in income as a 'taxable capital gain'. Allowable capital losses (presently half of capital losses) are applied to offset taxable capital gains, but generally may not be deducted against income from other sources. Net capital losses may be carried over and deducted from taxable income for the three preceding taxation years or any subsequent year, to the extent of the net taxable capital gains realized by the corporation in such years.[1022] A portion of net taxable capital gains is added to the 'refundable dividend tax on hand' of a private corporation, which is refunded to the corporation on payment of sufficient taxable dividends (*see* below, Section II: Integration of Corporate and Personal Income Taxes). Private corporations also maintain a notional 'capital dividend account' to which is added the non-taxable portion of net taxable capital gains. The corporation may distribute tax-exempt capital dividends to the extent of its capital dividend account.[1023]

1018. *See*, for example, ss 55(2)–(5) (dividends paid to reduce a capital gain on shares) and s. 112(2.3) (dividends paid pursuant to a dividend rental arrangement).
1019. Section 90(1).
1020. Section 113(1).
1021. Regulations, s. 5907(11).
1022. Section 111(l)(b), 111(8).
1023. Sections 83(2), 89(1) 'capital dividend account', 184.

II. Integration of Corporate and Personal Income Taxes

A. *Theory of Integration*

412. The integration provisions in the Canadian income tax system are based on the theory that an individual's total tax burden in respect of investment income should remain the same, whether the investments are held personally or through a private corporation. A rough integration of personal and corporate income taxes on investment income is achieved through two mechanisms:

(1) the refund of certain amounts to private corporations upon payment of taxable dividends; and
(2) the dividend tax credit for individuals.

B. *Refund of Corporate Income Tax*

413. Corporations are subject to tax on most forms of investment income and on their taxable capital gains. A portion of such amounts is, however, accumulated in a notional account known as the corporation's 'Refundable Dividend Tax On Hand' (RDTOH).[1024] The 33.3% tax payable by private corporations on portfolio dividends is also added to RDTOH (*see* above, paragraph 409). Upon payment of sufficient taxable dividends, the corporation becomes entitled to a refund of RDTOH.[1025]

C. *Dividend Tax Credit*

414. Like corporations, individual shareholders are required to include in income any taxable dividend they receive from a corporation. Where, however, the payer is a CCPC that is paying a dividend on income that benefited from the small business deduction, the individual must also include a gross-up amount equal to one quarter of the dividend received, to approximate the pre-tax income earned by the corporation.[1026] Provided the individual is resident in Canada, he/she is then entitled to a dividend tax credit that reduces his/her tax otherwise payable by an amount equal to thirteen-eighteenths of the gross-up amount included in income.[1027] The credit is intended to recognize tax already paid by the corporation, notionally on the individual shareholder's behalf. The credit assumes an effective corporate income tax rate of roughly 11% on small business income of up to CAD 500,000.

1024. Section 129(3).
1025. Section 129(1).
1026. Section 82(1)(a) and (b)(i).
1027. Section 121(1)(a).

Where the payer is a resident Canadian corporation, or a CCPC paying a dividend on income that did not benefit from the small business deduction,[1028] the individual must also include a gross-up amount equal to 38% of the dividend received, to approximate the pre-tax income earned by the corporation.[1029] Provided the individual is resident in Canada, he/she is then entitled to a dividend tax credit that reduces his/her tax otherwise payable by an amount equal to six-elevenths of the gross-up amount included in income.[1030] The credit assumes an effective corporate income tax rate of roughly 28% on income that does not benefit from the small business credit.

III. Taxation of Corporate Reorganizations

415. A transfer or other change in the ownership of shares or other property normally constitutes a disposition, potentially giving rise to recaptured depreciation or a terminal loss in the case of depreciable property, and/or a capital gain or loss.[1031] Where such property is transferred to a related corporation or other non-arm's length person, the transferor generally is deemed to receive consideration equal to the property's fair market value, thereby realizing any accrued capital gain or loss for tax purposes.[1032]

416. A number of exceptions exist, however, under which corporate reorganizations may be effected on a tax-deferred or 'rollover' basis. Detailed and often complex requirements must be met in each case in order for the rollover treatment to apply. In some cases taxpayers are required to file elections to obtain a rollover. In basic terms, the types of transactions covered include:

- a transfer of certain property to a taxable Canadian corporation for consideration which includes shares of the capital stock of the transferee corporation;[1033]
- a transfer of shares to a Canadian corporation in exchange for new shares of the Canadian corporation;[1034]
- an amalgamation or merger of two or more taxable Canadian corporations, in which all shareholders of the predecessor corporations receive shares of the merged corporation;[1035] and
- a winding-up of one taxable Canadian corporation (a 'subsidiary') by another taxable Canadian corporation (a 'parent') which owns at least 90% of the issued

1028. The small business credit is available only on the first CAD 500,000 of active business income. Thus, where a CCPC has more than CAD 500,000 of active business income, the amount in excess of CAD 500,000 will not benefit from the small business credit (and thus the tax on that amount will be at a higher rate than on the first CAD 500,000). On the small business credit *see* para. 403.

1029. Section 82(1)(a.1) and (b)(ii).

1030. Section 121(1)(b).

1031. Sections 13(21)(c), 13(1), 20(16), 54 & 40(1).

1032. Sections 69(1), 251.

1033. Section 85.

1034. Section 86.

1035. Section 87.

shares of each class of the subsidiary, where all the remaining shares of the subsidiary are owned by persons who deal at arm's length with the parent.[1036]

IV. Other Taxes

A. Sales Taxes

417. As of 1 January 1991 the federal Manufacturer's Sales Tax was repealed and replaced by the 7% (now 5%) Goods and Services Tax (GST), the first multi-stage value-added tax enacted in Canada. Most provinces continue to impose their own retail sales taxes or goods and services taxes. Both levels of government also impose a variety of direct and indirect sales taxes on specific goods such as tobacco, alcohol, and fuel.

B. Selected Other Taxes

418. Other taxes for which corporations may be liable in Canada include payroll taxes, federal customs duties, provincial land transfer taxes, and municipal property and business taxes.

1036. Section 88.

Chapter 2. The Closely Held Corporation

§1. Historical Background

419. When Canadian legislatures began enacting general incorporation legislation in the nineteenth century, they did not draw any distinctions between companies with closely held shares and businesses with publicly traded equity.[1037] This began to change in 1910. In that year, the province of British Columbia introduced the private company concept, which had initially been adopted in England in 1907. By the 1940s, most Canadian jurisdictions had followed suit.

Companies were treated as private companies if they met three criteria:

(1) having documents of incorporation which stipulated that the number of shareholders was limited to fifty;
(2) having shares which were subject to transfer restrictions; and
(3) not having shares which had been distributed to the public.

The legislative advantages associated with private company status varied from jurisdiction to jurisdiction. Most of the benefits, however, involved relief from filing and financial disclosure requirements.

At the same time that legislators were developing the private company concept, smaller businesses were incorporating with greater frequency. Before the turn of the century, incorporated companies in Canada usually were businesses seeking to raise large amounts of capital. After the turn of the century, however, smaller manufacturing enterprises began to incorporate at an increasing rate, and after the Second World War incorporation became popular for small businesses in all sectors of the economy.

Despite the rapid emergence of closely held corporations in the first two-thirds of the twentieth century, such businesses received scant attention in Canadian legal circles. Academic writing on the topic was sparse. The courts did little to develop any form of separate jurisprudence for private companies.[1038] Also, legislators made few alterations to the provisions governing private companies.

1037. *See* W.K. Fraser, *Handbook on Canadian Company Law*, 4th ed., (Toronto: Carswell, 1945) at 25–41, 51–56; F.W. Wegenast, *The Law of Canadian Companies* (Toronto: Burroughs, 1931) at 189–190, 707–708; F. Iacobucci & D.L. Johnston, '*The Private or Closely-Held Corporation*' in J.S. Ziegel, ed. *Studies in Canadian Company Law*, vol. 2 (Toronto: Butterworths, 1973) 68 at 71–75, 77–78 and T. Hadden et al., *Canadian Business Organizations Law* (Toronto: Butterworths, 1984) at 23, 34, 65, 66, 129, 184–186.

1038. An exception was applications for winding up. *See* D. Huberman, '*Methods of Resolving Intra-Corporate Disputes*' (1968) 3 *U.B.C. L. Rev.* 1 at 1–3.

§2. Statutory Reform

420. Most Canadian jurisdictions enacted new corporate legislation between 1970 and the end of the 1980s. As part of this process, legislative treatment of closely held corporations changed significantly. One important change was the elimination of the private company concept. Those responsible for drafting the new legislation justified this step on the basis that some businesses were taking improper advantage of private company status and on the grounds that more subtle methods could be used to deal with the particular needs of smaller companies.[1039]

421. As part of the reform process, government officials considered the possibility of creating a separate statute for smaller corporations. They decided, however, that distinct legislative treatment was not needed. They said that properly drafted general incorporation legislation could meet the requirements of close corporations, which meant that separate legislation would cause needless statutory complexity. The relevant officials also pointed out that defining which companies should be governed by the legislation would be very difficult.[1040]

422. Because of the abolition of the private company concept and the absence of separate legislation, provisions in present Canadian corporate statutes usually apply to all corporations governed by the relevant Act. This is the situation, for example, under the CBCA, which the federal Parliament enacted in the mid-1970s.[1041] The same pattern exists in the six provinces which have borrowed heavily from the CBCA in formulating their corporate legislation.[1042]

The CBCA and the legislation modelled after it do not neglect, however, the needs of closely held corporations. The concerns of smaller businesses are addressed in two ways. First, the statutes contain provisions which are particularly useful for closely held businesses despite applying to all corporations. Second, the legislation sets out a small number of provisions which specifically offer special treatment for closely held corporations.

1039. Ontario, Legislative Assembly, *Interim Report of the Select Committee on Company Law* (Toronto: Queen's Printer, 1967) (Chair: A.F. Lawrence; referred to as the 'Lawrence Report') at 14–17; R.W.V. Dickerson et al., *Proposals for a New Business Corporations Act for Canada*, 2 vols (Ottawa: Supply and Services, 1971) at 10–11 (hereinafter 'Dickerson Report'); New Brunswick, 'Company Law Project Law Reform Division,' R. Bird ed. *Report on Company Law* (Fredericton: Department of Justice, 1974) at 36–37 (hereinafter 'Bird Report') and Institute of Law Reform and Research, *Proposals for a New Business Corporations Law for Alberta* (Edmonton: Institute of Law Research and Reform, University of Alberta, 1980) at 15–16 (hereinafter 'Alberta Report').

1040. *See* Dickerson Report, *supra* , n. 1039, at 55 and Alberta Report, *supra* n. 1039, at 15–16. For a further discussion of the issues involved, *see* B.R. Cheffins, '*US Close Corporations Legislation: A Model Canada Should Not Follow*' (1989) 35 McGill L.J. 160.

1041. R.S.C. 1985, c. C-44.

1042. The provinces which have borrowed the federal model are Ontario, Alberta, Saskatchewan, Manitoba, New Brunswick, and Newfoundland. The federal model has also been borrowed in Nunavut, Northwest Territories, and Yukon Territories.

423. The following paragraphs examine how closely held businesses are treated under the CBCA and the legislation modelled after it.[1043] Three topics are discussed:

(1) corporate formalities;
(2) planning, and
(3) statutory remedies.

424. The CBCA and the legislation modelled after it generally deal with closely held corporations in the same manner. Consequently, for the purposes of convenience, this discussion will focus on the CBCA.

§3. Legislative Provisions

I. Corporate Formalities

A. Reducing Formalities

425. Reducing formalities and increasing clarity and simplicity was a general objective of those who framed the CBCA and the legislation modelled after that Act.[1044] Though the drafters did not see closely held corporations as the sole beneficiaries of this process, they recognized that such corporations would benefit from simpler legislation.[1045]

B. Simplified Incorporation Process

426. One area where the minimal formality which the CBCA provides for can potentially assist smaller businesses is incorporation. Traditionally, under federal companies' legislation, incorporation was granted as an act of administrative discretion. Under the CBCA, however, the discretionary element no longer exists. Consequently, if the statutory prerequisites for incorporation are fulfilled, incorporation is to occur as a matter of right.[1046] Furthermore, the statutory prerequisites are not onerous, as only three documents (the corporation's articles of incorporation, a list of the corporations' first directors, and a notice setting out the location of the corporation's registered office) have to be filed. The internal regulations of the corporation, which are referred to as by-laws, do not have to be submitted.[1047]

427. Incorporation is further simplified because Canadian corporate legislation does not require corporations to have any form of minimum paid-up capital. This

1043. On the provisions in Prince Edward Island, Quebec and New Brunswick, *see* H. Sutherland, et al., *Fraser's Handbook on Canadian Company Law* (Toronto: Carswell, 1985) at 139–164, 224–228, 234–245, 289–303.

1044. Dickerson Report, *supra* n. 1039, at 2–4, 56 and Alberta Report, *supra* n. 1039, at 5.

1045. Dickerson Report, *supra* n. 1039, at 56–58.

1046. CBCA s. 8 and Dickerson Report, *supra* n. 1039, at 4, 22–24.

1047. Sections 5–7, 19 and 106.

situation did not arise as a result of the statutory reforms in the 1970s and 1980s. Instead, Canadian statutes have traditionally not imposed such requirements.[1048]

C. Simplified Director and Shareholder Meetings

428. The CBCA also helps to reduce formalities for corporations after incorporation. For example, the act contains a number of provisions which allow corporations to streamline the conduct of director and shareholder business. The CBCA does so by authorizing directors to pass resolutions without a meeting if all consent in writing and by allowing shareholders to do the same.[1049] While all corporations can use these provisions, smaller corporations will usually be able to do so more readily. This is because as a practical matter the unanimity requirements can be met more easily in closely held companies than in larger businesses.

D. Exemption for Proxy Solicitation and Disclosure

429. In addition to reducing formalities by way of provisions which apply to all corporations, the CBCA makes some specific allowances for smaller businesses. For example, in situations where corporate managers agree to act as proxies for shareholders at shareholder meetings, a series of disclosure requirements ordinarily must be complied with. These provisions generally do not apply, however, when a corporation is not a distributing corporation and has fifty or fewer shareholders.[1050]

E. Exemptions for Financial Disclosure

430. Another area where the CBCA makes allowances for smaller businesses is the preparation and filing of financial information. The act requires corporations to appoint an auditor and to produce and file annual financial statements. If a corporation does not have publicly traded shares, however, its shareholders can, by written unanimous resolution, waive the obligation to appoint an auditor.[1051] Also, corporations of this type are not required to file financial statements.[1052]

1048. Prior to statutory reform, only New Brunswick imposed a minimum capital requirement. This was removed when the province adopted a CBCA style statute. *See* the Bird Report, *supra* n. 1039, at 60–61.

1049. CBCA ss 117, 142. *See* Dickerson Report, *supra* n. 1039, at 78, 94, 96.

1050. CBCA s. 149. If management actually solicits proxies it also must comply with the proxy provisions. This is not the case under all statutes modelled after the CBCA. *See Ontario Business Corporations Act*, 1982, S.O. 1982, c. 4, ss 111, 113.

1051. CBCA s. 163. A corporation that is not a 'distributing corporation' also does not have to have an audit committee. *See* CBCA s. 171(1). Shares are deemed to be distributed to the public if the corporation has filed or should have filed documentation under applicable securities regulation – *see* the definition of 'distributing corporation' in s. 2(1), ss 2(6)–(8) and CBCA Regs. s. 2.

1052. CBCA ss 160.

II. Planning

431. Participants in closely held companies can clarify the nature of their business relationship and can reduce the possibility of future disputes by engaging in advance planning. Canadian corporate legislation makes no specific allowances for planning in closely held companies. This is not particularly troublesome, though. Most well-drafted schemes should be fully enforceable. Part of the reason is that Canadian judges tend to be tolerant of corporate planning devices.[1053] Also, legislative provisions clarify a number of doubtful areas. For example, while companies were not allowed to purchase their own shares at common law, this procedure is specifically authorized by the CBCA and the statutes modelled after it.[1054]

432. Another area where Canadian legislation attempts to foster corporate planning is shareholders' agreements. Technically, shareholders' agreements can be used in any corporation, but they are employed most frequently in closely held corporations. For the most part, courts will enforce such arrangements. At common law, however, agreements which transfer managerial authority from the directors to the shareholders are of doubtful validity.[1055] Consequently, the CBCA and the statutes modelled after it stipulate that provisions in shareholder agreements which reallocate managerial authority are valid.[1056] The special statutory protection only applies, however, to written agreements affirmed by all of the shareholders.

III. Statutory Remedies

A. Generally

433. Despite the latitude provided by Canadian corporate legislation, planning cannot solve all the problems that may arise between participants in closely held corporations. Part of the reason is that in many small businesses analysis and treatment of legal issues is only perfunctory. Furthermore, even with corporations where substantial planning occurs, disputes can arise which could not be predicted when planning was taking place. This is particularly likely when a company is closely held. Interpersonal relationships often play a key role in such businesses and these relationships can break down in ways which the participants have difficulty contemplating in advance.

When relations within closely held corporations become strained, minority shareholders can be in a difficult situation. If they work for the company, they may find their jobs are in jeopardy, given that the majority likely will want to fire them and will probably have sufficient control over the board of directors to orchestrate dismissal. Also, disgruntled minority shareholders will find it difficult to sell their shares. This is because there is usually no market for minority shares in a closely held corporation.

1053. On judicial tolerance of corporate planning *See*, for example, *The Queen v. McClurg*, [1990] 3 S.C.R. 1020 (S.C.C.), per Dickson C.J.C.

1054. Section 34, overruling *Trevor v. Whitworth* (1887), 12 A.C. 409 (H.L.).

1055. *See*, for example, *Motherwell v. Schoof* (1949), 4 D.L.R. 812 (Alta. S.C.).

1056. CBCA s. 146. The most comprehensively worded provision of this type is s. 146 of the ABCA.

B. The Oppression Remedy

434. One of the most important changes made as part of the statutory reforms of the 1970s and 1980s was the introduction of a number of new statutory remedies for shareholders. None of the remedies apply solely to closely held corporations. Still, the provisions appreciably enhance minority protection in such businesses.

The most important of the new statutory remedies is the oppression remedy. The provisions in the CBCA which create this remedy stipulate that shareholders can apply to court for relief on the grounds of oppression, unfair prejudice, or unfair disregard of existing interests. A judge can grant any of a wide range of remedies upon a successful application.[1057]

435. Canadian courts have, for the most part, interpreted the oppression remedy liberally, and have granted remedies in a wide range of cases. Not all of the applications have involved close corporations. Nevertheless, the majority of cases have involved such businesses, and some judges have suggested that the remedy is primarily aimed at those companies which are closely held.[1058]

C. The Appraisal Remedy

436. Another remedy introduced as part of the statutory reforms of the 1970s and 1980s was appraisal rights. Appraisal rights give shareholders who dissent, when faced with prescribed fundamental changes, the right to demand that the corporation purchase their shares.[1059] If an applicant follows the mandatory statutory procedure, the corporation is required to buy the shares for a fair value. If the parties cannot agree on a fair value, an application can be made to court to have a judge set the price.[1060]

437. The reported cases indicate that the appraisal remedy is used more frequently in public corporations than it is in closely held businesses.[1061] This is somewhat surprising, given that a dissatisfied shareholder in a closely held company will have difficulty selling his shares whereas his counterpart in a public corporation should be able to rely on the market. The reason for the pattern may be the tight time limits and complex procedure associated with appraisal rights. Dissatisfied shareholders in public corporations perhaps obtain appropriate legal advice quickly enough to rely on the appraisal remedy whereas shareholders in closely held firms might do so too late.[1062]

1057. CBCA s. 241. For a general discussion of the oppression remedy *see supra* §3.I.C, paras 222–238.

1058. *See* B.R. Cheffins, '*The Oppression Remedy in Corporate Law: The Canadian Experience*' (1988), 10 U. Pa. J. Int. Bus. L. 305 at 317–330.

1059. *See,* for example, CBCA ss 176, 190.

1060. Appraisal rights are discussed *supra* §3.I.E, paras 244–264.

1061. B.R. Cheffins & J.M. Dine, '*Shareholder Remedies: Lessons from Canada*' (1992) 13 *Co. Lawyer* 89 at 93.

1062. On the complexities associated with the procedure under the CBCA and the statutes modelled after it, *see* Hadden, *supra* n. 1037, at 255–260.

D. The Derivative Action

438. A third remedy introduced as part of the reforms in the 1970s and 1980s was the statutory derivative action. At common law, applicants who wanted to litigate on behalf of the company faced significant procedural obstacles. Under the statutory derivative action, however, shareholders can apply to court for permission to conduct such litigation.[1063] This change, however, has had relatively little impact. The primary reason is that dissatisfied shareholders have tended to rely on the oppression remedy rather than the statutory derivative action.[1064]

§4. The Taxation of the Closely Held Corporation

439. The closely held corporation generally will be classified as a private corporation (or a CCPC for income tax purposes), or as a non-resident corporation. The income tax treatment of such corporations is discussed above, at paragraphs 402 and 403. Individual Canadian resident shareholders of closely held corporations may be exempt from tax on up to CAD 750,000 of capital gains realized on the disposition of their shares, provided the corporation is a 'small business corporation' at the time of disposition and several other conditions for obtaining the exemption are satisfied.[1065] In general terms, a small business corporation is a CCPC if all or substantially all of the assets of the corporation were used principally in an active business carried on primarily in Canada.[1066]

1063. CBCA ss 238–240.

1064. On the relationship between the two remedies, *see* J.G. MacIntosh, '*The Oppression Remedy: Personal or Derivative*' (1991) 70 Can. Bar Rev. 29.

1065. ITA s. 110.6.

1066. ITA s. 248(1).

Part II. Partnerships

Chapter 1. Types of Canadian Partnerships and Their Nature

§1. Jurisdiction over Partnerships

440. Jurisdiction over partnerships is allocated to the provinces as part of their jurisdiction over property and civil rights within the provinces. All provinces, therefore, have their own legislation on the topic.[1067] There is, however, a good deal of commonalty among the nine statutes in the common law provinces.[1068] All these acts are based upon the English statute of 1890.[1069] Quebec follows a different system which is closer to the European.

§2. Types of Partnerships

441. In the common law provinces, two kinds of partnerships exist: the general and the limited.[1070] Some provinces also provide for limited liability partnerships that are different from limited partnerships.

1067. The provincial partnership acts are Alberta, R.S.A. 2000, c. P-3; British Columbia, R.S.B.C. 1996, c. 348; Manitoba, C.C.S.M., c. P30; New Brunswick, R.S.N.B. 1973, c. P-4; Newfoundland, R.S.N. 1990, c. P-3; Nova Scotia, R.S.N.S. 1989, c. 334; Ontario, R.S.O. 1990, c. P.5; Prince Edward Island, R.S.P.E.I. 1988, c. P-1; Quebec, Code Civil 1991, Arts 2186–2266; Saskatchewan, R.S.S. 1978, c. P-3. For convenience, these statutes will be cited by the abbreviation of the province and the letters 'P.A.' to designate Partnership Act only.

1068. Where the statutes are substantially similar, reference will be made only to one or two examples. However, differences among them will be noted.

1069. For a discussion of this statute and its history, *see Lindley & Banks On Partnership*, 16th ed., (London, 1990) Ch. 1.

1070. Several provinces have provisions for limited partnerships within their Partnership acts cited above. These are: Alta., B.C., Man., Sask. The other five common law jurisdictions have separate statutes for limited partnerships. These are: N.B., *Limited Partnerships Act*, S.N.B. 1984, c. L-9.1; Nfld., *Limited Partnerships Act*, R.S.N. 1990, c. L-17; N.S., *Limited Partnerships Act*, R.S.N.S. 1989, c. 259; Ont., *Limited Partnerships Act*, R.S.O. 1990, c. L.16; P.E.I., *Limited Partnerships Act*, R.S.PE.I. 1988, c. L-13. Henceforth the various Limited Partnership Acts will be cited by the abbreviation of the province followed by the initials 'LPA.'

As in the US, limited liability partnerships in Canada were primarily a response to an increased liability exposure of professionals who were not permitted, pursuant to regulations governing their profession, to carry on their businesses through corporations. Texas was the first state in the US to adopt limited liability partnership legislation in 1991. In Canada the province of Ontario was the first province to enact limited liability partnership legislation doing so in 1998. All provincial and territorial jurisdictions in Canada except for the province of Prince Edward Island and the territory of Nunavut have enacted limited liability partnership legislation.[1071]

Some limited liability partnership legislation provide 'partial shield' liability protection while other limited liability partnership legislation provides 'full shield' liability protection. Alberta has partial shield legislation that only allows limited liability partnerships to be used by regulated professions.[1072] It provides that partners in a limited liability partnership are not liable for the malpractice of fellow partners or employees unless they were directly supervising the activity.[1073] Also, partners are not liable to indemnify their fellow partners who have been found liable for malpractice.[1074] The partners otherwise remain personally liable for other debts of the firm. Ontario had originally enacted partial shield legislation but in 2006 adopted full shield liability protection by providing that a partner in a limited liability partnership:[1075]

> is not liable, by means of indemnification, contribution or otherwise, for, (a) the debts, liabilities or obligations of the partnership or any partner arising from negligent or wrongful acts or omissions that another partner or an employee, agent or representative of the partnership commits in the course of the partnership business while the partnership is a limited liability partnership; or (b) any other debts or obligations of the partnership that are incurred while the partnership is a limited liability partnership.

An Ontario limited liability partnership can only be used for the purpose of practising a profession governed by a statute of the province and only if that statute specifically permits the use of a limit liability partnership.[1076] British Columbia has limited liability partnership legislation that is not restricted to use for the purpose of carrying on a professional business and allows for the adoption of either partial shield or full shield liability protection.[1077]

In Quebec, the Civil Code provides for partnerships 'en nom collectif'[1078] (general partnership), 'en commandite'[1079] (limited partnership), 'en participation'[1080](undeclared

1071. *See*, for example, the APA s. 12 and ss 81–104; BCPA ss 94–129; MPA ss 67–88; NBPA ss 46–54; NSPA ss 48–71; OPA ss 44.1–44.4; SPA ss 78–110.

1072. *See* the Alberta *Partnership Act*, R.S.A. 2000, c. P-3, s. 81.

1073. *Ibid.*, s. 12.

1074. *Ibid.*

1075. *See* the Ontario *Partnerships Act*, R.S.O. 1990, c. P.5, s. 10(2).

1076. *Ibid.*, s. 44.2.

1077. *See* the British Columbia *Partnership Act*, R.S.B.C. 1996, c. 348, Part 6, ss 94–129 (particularly s. 104 with respect to full shield or partial shield liability protection).

1078. Civil Code, 2198–2235.

1079. *Ibid.*, 2236–2249.

1080. *Ibid.*, 2250–2266.

partnership), or under the Code des Professions, a société en nom collectif à responsibilité limitée (limited liability partnership).[1081] Perhaps the chief difference among all these kinds of partnerships resides in the liability the partners incur toward third parties.

§3. Definition of Partnership

442. Partnership is defined in all nine common law statutes as the 'relation which subsists among persons carrying on business in common with a view to profit'.[1082] While a corporation, as a 'person', can be a partner, these acts generally provide that a corporation is not itself a partnership even if a business is carried on through it with a view of profit to be shared among shareholders.[1083] The Quebec Civil Code also defines partnership. It states that '[a] contract of partnership is a contract by which the parties, in a spirit of cooperation, agree to carry on an activity, including the operation of an enterprise, to contribute thereto by combining property, knowledge or activities and to share any resulting pecuniary profits'.[1084] Both definitions require a cooperative effort and a sharing of the profits.[1085]

§4. Legal Nature of Partnership

443. Most Canadian partnerships do not have a legally recognized personality separate from the individuals in the partnership. The one exception is that under the Quebec Civil Code, a partnership may also be a joint-stock company and in that case, it is a legal person.[1086] In any event, rules of civil procedure generally permit partnerships to sue and to be sued in the firm name.[1087]

1081. *See* the *Code des Professions*, R.S.Q., c. C-26, Ch. VI.3. This allows regulated professions to carry on business through a limited liability partnership.

1082. *See*, for example, NPA s. 2; OPA s. 2; SPA s. 3. Factors considered in whether a relationship is one of partnership were discussed by the Supreme Court of Canada in *Backman v. Canada* (2001), 196 D.L.R. (4th) 193 (S.C.C.).

1083. *See*, for example, SPA s. 3(2); MPA s. 3.

1084. Article 2186.

1085. Under the Quebec Civil Code, Art. 2186, a similar organization not formed to make pecuniary profits is an association.

1086. Civil Code, Art. 2188.

1087. In Quebec, *see ibid.*, Art. 2225; *see also*, for example, the B.C. Supreme Court Rules, Rule 20.

Chapter 2. The Creation of the Partnership

§1. Contractual Nature of Partnership

444. Although the legislation in the common law provinces does not mention 'contract', in contrast to the Quebec Civil Code,[1088] the relationship of partners in these provinces also clearly depends on a contract, express or implied.[1089]

§2. Rules for Determining the Existence of Partnership

445. These statutes also contain a series of rules by which the existence of a partnership may be determined.[1090] The rules, however, are not determinative, and indeed not particularly helpful. They provide that neither joint ownership of property nor the sharing of gross returns is sufficient in itself to constitute a partnership. By contrast, sharing profits is prima facie evidence of a partnership, although once again it is not in itself enough. The statutes list several situations, which, although providing for a sharing of profits, do not alone create a partnership. These include the payment of a liquidated sum out of profits; remuneration of employees varying with profits; repayment of certain loans in which the rate of interest varies with profits;[1091] and payment of annuities based on the profits to certain classes of persons.[1092]

§3. Agency Nature of Partnership

446. The true test of partnership in the common law provinces, however, has been held to be whether the persons involved intend to carry on a business as agents of each other.[1093] As will be seen, the relationship between the law of partnership and the law of agency is crucial in the common law jurisdictions.

1088. Article 2186.

1089. *Sproule v. McConnell*, [1925] 1 W.W.R. 609 (Sask. C.A.).

1090. *See,* for example, APA s. 4; BCPA s. 4.

1091. To fall within this exception, the contract must be in writing and be signed by all parties. *See* BCPA s. 4(c)(iv) for the typical example. A penalty is, however, attached. Such creditor is postponed to the claims of other creditors for valuable consideration in the event of the borrower becoming insolvent. *See,* for example, OPA s. 4.

1092. For instance, to a surviving spouse or child of a deceased partner (which in Ontario specifically includes a person living with a partner of the opposite sex in a conjugal relationship outside marriage immediately before the partner's death) or a person receiving payment for sale of the business' goodwill.

1093. *Cox v. Hickman* (1860), 8 H.L. Cas. 268.

§4. The Creation of Partnership and Registration of Partnerships

447. To create a general partnership requires no particular formality. All jurisdictions, however, with the exception of Newfoundland, provide for registration of at least certain types of general partnerships.[1094] Which partnerships must register varies among the jurisdictions. Some provide for registration of all partnerships;[1095] others only for those carrying on particular kinds of businesses.[1096]

§5. The Consequences of Failing to Register

448. The consequences of failing to register vary somewhat. In some provinces, a partnership that should be registered but is not may not be able to bring action in the courts.[1097] In other provinces, the only real penalty is a fine.[1098] Once the partnership is registered, the statements in its declaration cannot be controverted.[1099] Moreover, as long as a person remains listed in the declaration as a partner, a presumption exists that she remains a partner.[1100] That does not limit the liability of one who, although not listed as a partner, is one in fact.

§6. The Creation of Limited Partnerships

449. Limited partnerships must be created by filing a certificate. Failure to file will mean that the limitation of liability available to limited partners is not applicable.[1101] If the supposed 'limited partners' (referred to as 'special partners' in the Quebec Civil

1094. Alberta, P.E.I. and British Columbia include registration provisions in their Partnership Acts. The legislation in the other jurisdictions is: Man., *Business Names Registration Act*, R.S.M. 1987, c. B110; N.B., *Partnerships and Business Names Registration Act*, R.S.N.B. 1973, c. P-5; N.S., *Partnerships and Business Names Registration Act*, R.S.N.S. 1989, c. 335; Ont., *Business Names Act*, R.S.O. 1990, c. B.17; Quebec, *Companies and Partnerships Declaration Act*, R.S.Q. 1977, c. D-1; Sask., *Business Names Registration Act*, R.S.S. 1978, c. B-11.

1095. Sask., Ont. (unless partnership name composed of all partners' names), P.E.I. and Man. provide for universal registration.

1096. Alta.: 'trading, manufacturing, contracting or mining purposes'; B.C. and N.B.: 'trading, mining or manufacturing purposes'; N.S. all except partnerships for 'farming, fishing' or 'persons who solely as tenants in common operate grist or saw mills'; Quebec: 'trading, manufacturing or mechanical purposes or for purpose of construction of roads, dams, bridges or other works or for purposes of colonization or of settlement or of land traffic'.

1097. APA, s. 113; N.B. *Partnerships and Business Names Registration Act*, s. 16; N.S., Ont.

1098. B.C., Man., Sask., Quebec, P.E.I.

1099. *See,* for example, APA s. 114; BCPA s. 84.

1100. *See,* for example, BCPA s. 84(b).

1101. *See,* for example, MPA s. 55. Most jurisdictions, however, provide some protection for the person who mistakenly believes herself to be a limited partner. Typically, she will escape liability as a partner if once the mistake is known, she renounces her interest in the business. *See,* for example, BCPA s. 75.

Code)[1102] are in fact members of a partnership, therefore, they will be liable as other partners. In Quebec, the Civil Code provides that 'failing that [proper registration], it is deemed to be an undeclared partnership, subject to the rights of third persons in good faith'.[1103] This applies to both limited and general partnerships.

§7. Who May Form a Partnership?

450. Partnerships may be formed by legal persons of full capacity, whether individuals or bodies corporate. Commonly, in fact, corporations do form partnerships, particularly for single ventures. These are often referred to as 'joint ventures' – a term which has no clear legal meaning. A joint venture may in fact be a true partnership formed for one enterprise or may be an arrangement short of partnership in which each party is carrying on its own business, although linked by some contractual arrangement.[1104] Usually limited partnerships are formed with a corporation as the general partner (thus obtaining the benefits of limited liability for the promoters of the venture) and individuals as the limited partners.

§8. Written Partnership Contracts

451. Because of the inherently contractual nature of partnerships in all Canadian provinces, many of the arrangements between partners will be expressed in a written contract. Naturally, these contracts generally cannot limit the legal liability of partners to third parties. This liability will be considered in Chapter 6.

1102. Code Civil, Art. 2236.

1103. *Ibid.*, Art. 2189.

1104. Canadian courts have often treated joint ventures as displaying very much the same characteristics as partnerships, but simply formed for one venture rather than a less defined period. *See C.M.H.C. v. Omega Investments* (1981), 34 N.B.R. (2nd) 291 (C.A.) for a discussion of the characteristics of joint ventures. As to a type of joint venture which does not exhibit these common qualities, *see* Lindley & Banks, *supra* n. 1069, p. 61.

Chapter 3. Partnership Property

452. As already noted, the Civil Code explicitly recognizes contribution by partners of property, knowledge, or activities as an inherent part of its definition of a partnership.[1105] Furthermore, a partner is made a debtor to the partnership for that which he has agreed to contribute.[1106] Where the contribution is of knowledge or services, the partner is obliged to continue supplying these as long as she remains a partner.[1107] If a partner competes with the partnership or engages in an activity that deprives the partnership of the benefit of his promised contribution, the partnership is entitled to any profits so gained.[1108]

453. Although the same explicit requirement is not a part of the legislation in the common law jurisdictions, it is clearly anticipated that partners will usually make contributions to the partnership. Because the firm has no distinct legal personality, however, a partner cannot be considered the firm's debtor if he fails to make his promised contribution.[1109] Once property is contributed to the firm, it must be held and used for the purposes of the partnership only.[1110] A presumption also exists that property bought with partnership funds is partnership property.[1111] Property of the partnership is treated as personal property.[1112] Most provinces provide in their Partnership Act that firm property cannot be seized in legal proceedings except after a judgment against the firm.[1113] If a creditor has a separate judgment against one of the partners personally, she can only obtain a charging order over that partner's interest in the property.[1114]

454. Requirements in the partnership contract that partners contribute knowledge or service are safeguarded by a section in the statutes of the common law provinces providing that a partner must account to the firm for profits earned with partnership property.[1115] Also, if a partner carries on a competing business without the consent of other partners, she must pay to the firm all profits made by her in that business.[1116]

1105. Civil Code, Art. 2186.
1106. *Ibid.*, Art. 2198.
1107. *Ibid.*, Art. 2200.
1108. *Ibid.*, Art. 2204.
1109. *See* the discussion in Lindley and Banks, *supra* n. 1069, at p. 27. Limited partners are, however, generally made liable to the firm for unpaid contributions. *See,* for example, BCPA s. 63.
1110. *See,* for example, PEIPA s. 23; NSPA, s. 23(1).
1111. *See,* for example, NPA s. 22; OPA s. 22.
1112. The NPA does not contain this provision.
1113. Manitoba, Ontario and P.E.I. do not have such a provision.
1114. *See,* for example, SPA s. 25; MPA s. 26. Ontario does not have this section in its act, although the possibility of a charging order is clearly contemplated by it (*see* OPA s. 33(2)).
1115. *See,* for example, APA s. 33(1); BCPA s. 32(1).
1116. *See,* for example, APA s. 34; BCPA s. 33.

Chapter 4. Management of the Partnership

§1. The Management Powers of Partners

455. All Canadian provinces provide that, in the absence of agreement to the contrary, all partners of a general partnership have the right to participate in management.[1117] They also have by their acts in the normal course of partnership business, the power to bind the firm and other partners in it.[1118] As well, a partner expending money for the partnership is entitled to reimbursement for it.[1119]

§2. The Exercise of Management Powers

456. Generally, decisions as to everyday running of the partnership are to be made by majority decision.[1120] Decisions to change the nature of the partnership business or expel a partner must, however, in the common law provinces, be made unanimously unless a provision of the partnership agreement otherwise provides.[1121] In Quebec, decisions changing the nature of the partnership contract must, subject to contrary agreement, be approved unanimously.[1122]

457. In practice, even in the common law provinces, one or more partners are commonly given management powers. Under the Quebec Civil Code, this organization is explicitly recognized. It provides that the partners may appoint one or more administrators and, as long as they act without fraud, they are entitled to manage the partnership without interference from the other partners. Without cause, this power cannot be revoked during the partnership's duration if the power was conferred in the agreement of partnership. Otherwise, the power to manage is recognized as revocable.[1123]

§3. Management Powers in Limited Partnerships

458. The situation is different if the partnership is a limited partnership. In all ten provinces, a chief feature of the limitation of limited (or special) partners' liabilities

1117. In the common law provinces, *See*, for example, NBPA s. 25(e); PEIPA s. 27(e). In Quebec, *see* the Civil Code, Art. 2215.

1118. In the common law provinces, *See*, for example, NSPA s. 8; NPA s. 6. In Quebec, *see* the Civil Code, Art. 2219.

1119. In the common law provinces, *See*, for example, OPA s. 24, Rule 2; SPA s. 26, Rule 2. In Quebec, *see* the Civil Code, Art. 2205.

1120. In the common law provinces, *See*, for example, MPA s. 27(h); APA s. 28(h). In Quebec, *see* the Civil Code, Art. 2216.

1121. *See*, for example, BCPA s. 27(h) and s. 28; NBPA s. 25(h) and s. 26.

1122. Civil Code, Art. 2216.

1123. Civil Code, Art. 2213. The administrator need not be a partner.

toward third parties is the exclusion of such partners from management roles. If the limited partner does participate in the prohibited fashion, she loses her limited liability and becomes liable as a general partner.[1124] In Quebec, this liability may extend only to those obligations directly resulting from the prohibited acts. Broader liability extending to all the debts of the partnership may, however, be incurred depending upon 'the importance or number of such acts'.[1125]

459. In the common law provinces, the limitation is generally expressed as prohibiting taking part 'in the control of the business'[1126] or 'in the management of the business'.[1127] In Quebec, the special partners 'may not give other than an advisory opinion with regard to the management of the partnership'. Specifically, they are prohibited from negotiating any matter on behalf of the partnership, acting in the capacity of an agent, or having their names used in any partnership activity.[1128]

460. The power of management in limited partnerships, therefore, resides primarily with the general partners. The legislation gives these general partners the same rights, powers, and liabilities as partners in a general partnership. These rights are modified somewhat to require proper accounting to and provide some safeguards for the limited partners.[1129] Naturally, since limited partners are investors in the enterprise, they usually want some control over the operation of the business, often more extensive control than the protections found in legislation. The extent to which such powers can be conferred without exposing the limited partners to the risks of greater liability is uncertain and a matter of considerable debate.[1130]

1124. *See,* for example, NBLPA s. 17(1); NLPA s. 16.

1125. Civil Code, Art. 2244.

1126. All provinces except B.C. adopt this wording. *See,* for example, OLPA s. 13; PEILPA s. 12. For cases discussing the application of these restrictions on the participation of limited partners in the management of the limited partnership business *See,* for example, *Haughton Graphic Ltd. v. Zivot* (1986), 33 B.L.R. 125 (Ont. H.C.); and *Nordile Holdings Ltd. v. Breckenridge* (1992), 66 B.C.L.R. (2nd) 183 (B.C.C.A.).

1127. BCPA s. 64.

1128. Civil Code, Art. 2244.

1129. In the common law provinces, *See,* for example, SPA s. 56; OLPA s. 8. Limitations on their rights include such matters as a prohibition against contravening the certificate by which the partnership was formed, admitting new general partners or new limited partners unless the certificate permits it or consenting to a judgment against the partnership without written consent of or ratification by the limited partners. In Quebec, *see* the Civil Code, Art. 2238.

1130. For further discussion of this issue in the Canadian context, *see* E. Apps, '*Limited Partnerships and the 'Control' Prohibition: Assessing the Liability of Limited Partners*' (1991) 70 Can. Bar Rev. 611.

Chapter 5. Relationship among the Partners

§1. The Sharing of Profits

461. The relationship among partners with respect to partnership property and management of the firm has already been discussed. A further area of importance is the sharing of profits and losses in the firm. As already noted in paragraph 442, the definitions of partnership in all Canadian provinces expressly require a sharing of profit. The Quebec Civil Code further makes void a provision of a partnership agreement that prohibits a partner participating in profits.[1131] In the common law jurisdictions, such a provision would mean that no partnership existed as between that person and the other contracting parties. The presumption is that profits will be shared equally, although that may be varied and, of course, frequently is.[1132]

§2. The Sharing of Losses

462. While partners may happily agree to the division of anticipated profits, they may not be so clear about losses. Again, all jurisdictions require that partners share in the losses of the firm. The presumption also is that they be shared equally.[1133] If, however, no provision is made for sharing losses, but a provision in the partnership agreement allocates profits in other then equal shares, then losses will be presumed to be shared the same way.[1134] Under the Quebec Civil Code, this equality of treatment also extends to the partner's share in assets of the partnership.[1135]

§3. The Mutual Rights and Duties of the Partners

463. All jurisdictions permit the variation of mutual rights and duties among the partners to be made by agreement. A chief additional source of common law duties between partners in the common law jurisdictions is the relationship of agency that exists among them.[1136] By virtue of that relationship, they owe to each other fiduciary

1131. Code Civil, Art. 2203.

1132. *See,* for example, MPA s. 27(a); APA s. 28(a).

1133. In the common law provinces, *See,* for example, BCPA, s. 27(a). In Quebec, *see* the Civil Code, Art. 2202.

1134. This is not expressly stated in the statutes of the common law provinces, although the section providing for settlement of accounts on dissolution implies that it would be so. *See,* for example, BCPA s. 47(a); NBPA s. 45(a). The result has been approved in the case law. *See Re Albion Life Assurance Society* (1880), 16 Ch.D. 83; *Fitzgerald v. McGill* (1905), 5 O.W.N. 769 (H.C.). In Quebec, *see* the Civil Code, Art. 2202.

1135. Civil Code, Art. 2202.

1136. *See,* for example, PEIPA s. 7; NPA s. 6.

duties of loyalty, good faith, and the avoidance of conflicts of interest, even apart from duties imposed by the statute.[1137] The Quebec Civil Code imposes many similar duties specifically, as already noted. Further, under the Civil Code, a general partner in a limited partnership owes the duties to a special partner owed by 'an administrator charged with full administration of the property of others towards the beneficiary of the administration'.[1138] The duties of partners to one another in an undeclared partnership under the Quebec Civil Code are, unless the contrary is agreed, the same as those in a general partnership.[1139]

1137. *See,* for example, *Rochwerg v. Truster* (2002), 58 O.R. (3rd) 687; and *McKnight v. Hutchinson* (2002), 28 B.L.R. (3rd) 269 (B.C.S.C.).

1138. Civil Code, Art. 2238.

1139. *Ibid.*, Art. 2251.

Chapter 6. Partners and Third Parties

464. General partners are usually liable to third parties for the debts of the partnership without limitation.[1140] No agreement to the contrary among the partners is effective against an innocent third party.[1141] Further, even if a person is not a partner, but acts as one, she may incur this liability as an apparent partner to those who rely on the representation.[1142]

465. Limited or special partners will normally be liable only up to the amount they have agreed to contribute to partnership capital.[1143] As to the situations in which this limitation may be lost, *see* paragraphs 458–460 above. The right of a limited or special partner to claim back his contribution from the partnership is postponed until other creditors of the partnership have been satisfied.[1144]

466. In an undeclared partnership under the Quebec Civil Code, a partner retains *vis-à-vis* third parties, ownership of the property that constitutes her contribution to the partnership.[1145] She will usually contract in her own name and alone be liable to third parties.[1146] If, however, a third party knows that the person is acting as a partner, then each partner becomes liable.[1147] Their liability is in equal shares, despite inequality in their shares in the partnership.[1148] The idea of an undeclared partnership is foreign to the common law jurisdictions. In those jurisdictions, it is a question of fact whether or not a partnership existed; if the question is answered affirmatively, then all partners share liability as general partners (assuming a limited partnership has not been created) whether or not a third party knew of them at the time of contracting.

1140. In the common law provinces, *See,* for example, OPA s. 10; SPA s. 11. In Quebec, *see* the Civil Code, Art. 2221.

1141. In Quebec, *see* the Civil Code, Art. 2203. In the common law provinces, the liability of partners is not subject to agreement although, as among themselves, they may agree to vary the rights of contribution which each has.

1142. In Quebec, *see* the Civil Code, Art. 2222. In the common law jurisdictions, *See,* for example, SPA s. 16; MPA s. 17.

1143. In the common law jurisdictions, *see* MPA s. 53; BCPA s. 57. In Quebec, *see* the Civil Code, Art. 2246.

1144. In Quebec, *see* the Civil Code, Art. 2248. In the common law provinces *See,* for example, MPA s. 60(2) and (3).

1145. Civil Code, Art. 2252.

1146. *Ibid.*, Art. 2253.

1147. *Ibid.*

1148. *Ibid.*, Art. 2254.

Chapter 7. Withdrawal, Expulsion, and Retirement of Partners

§1. Withdrawal Right Depends on Contract in Common Law Jurisdictions

467. In the common law provinces, a partner's right to withdraw or retire depends upon his/her contract of partnership. If she has no contractual right and cannot negotiate one, then, while the partnership continues, she must remain a partner unless she has the right to have the firm dissolved.[1149] The circumstances in which this right arises will be discussed in Chapter 8.

§2. Withdrawal under the Quebec Civil Code

468. The Quebec Civil Code is more generous with rights of partners in general partnerships to withdraw. If a general partnership is not for a fixed term, a partner may withdraw upon notice, provided she acts in good faith and does not withdraw at 'an inopportune moment'.[1150] In a fixed term partnership, a majority of partners may agree to allow any partner to withdraw.[1151] Of course, as in the common law jurisdictions, additional rights to withdraw may be placed in the contract.[1152] Further, if one of the partners does not perform his obligations or disrupts partnership activities, a court may allow a partner to withdraw or may expel the guilty partner.[1153]

§3. Return of Contribution of Limited Partners

469. Limited partners may under some circumstances require the return of their contribution. Under the Civil Code, a special partner may not withdraw his contribution unless he obtains the consent of the majority and the remaining property is sufficient to pay the partnership's liabilities.[1154] In the common law provinces, a limited partner may demand return of her contribution before dissolution with unanimous consent of the partners or if the time for its return specified in the certificate constituting the partnership has arrived or, if no such time is fixed, upon six months' notice in writing.

1149. *See* Lord Lindley's rules on retirement, Lindley & Banks, *supra* n. 1069, at p. 620. If, however, the partnership is for no fixed time then, subject to agreement, the partnership may be dissolved by notice of any partner. *See infra* , Ch. 8.

1150. Civil Code, Art. 2228.

1151. *Ibid.*

1152. *Ibid.*, Arts 2226, 2228.

1153. *Ibid.*, Art. 2229.

1154. Civil Code, Art. 2241.

This is subject to the proviso that after return of the contribution, the partnership must still have enough assets to pay its liabilities and that the certificate of the partnership must be appropriately amended.[1155]

§4. Expulsion of a Partner

470. In the common law provinces, partners cannot be expelled by majority vote unless the contract provides for it.[1156] Indeed absent such provision, the only method for removing a delinquent partner is to have the firm dissolved. The Quebec Civil Code permits expulsion by majority vote of a partner in a general partnership who is acting improperly. As noted in paragraph 468, this expulsion can also be ordered by a court.[1157]

1155. *See,* for example, NLPA s. 14(1) and (2); BCPA s. 62(1) and (2).
1156. *See,* for example, NBPA s. 26; PEIPA s. 28.
1157. Civil Code, Art. 2229.

Chapter 8. Dissolution of Partnerships

§1. Automatic Dissolution in Common Law Jurisdictions

471. In the common law jurisdictions, a partnership is automatically dissolved if the carrying on of its business becomes illegal.[1158] Subject to the parties' agreement, it is also dissolved where it was entered into for a fixed term which is over or a single venture which is completed or by the notice of any partner where the partnership has no such limiting characteristic.[1159] Also subject to agreement, the death or bankruptcy of any partner dissolves the partnership.[1160]

§2. Dissolution under the Quebec Civil Code

472. Under the Quebec Civil Code, general partnerships are dissolved in the manner provided for in the contract, by the consent of all or if the object of the partnership has been accomplished or cannot now be accomplished.[1161] Partners may also agree to continue partnerships for a fixed term beyond that term.[1162] The death or bankruptcy of a general partner does not dissolve the partnership in the absence of agreement but simply means that partner is treated as withdrawn from the partnership.[1163] This is in contrast to the situation pertaining for undeclared partnerships in which death or bankruptcy of a partner or a partner's being placed under protective supervision terminates the contract.[1164] Further, a general partnership which is reduced to one partner need not be dissolved unless another partner fails to join within 120 days.[1165] Undeclared partnerships that are not for a fixed term may also be terminated by mere notice from any partner. Any undeclared partnership may also be terminated for a legitimate cause.[1166]

473. An undeclared partnership under the Civil Code is also terminated by seizure of a partner's share of the partnership.[1167] In the common law jurisdictions, the

1158. *See,* for example, NPA s. 34; OPA s. 34.
1159. *See,* for example, SPA s. 34; MPA s. 35.
1160. *See,* for example, APA s. 37(1); NBPA s. 34(1). B.C. expressly deals with the situation in which there are only two partners. In that case, death or bankruptcy dissolves the firm, irrespective of any agreement to the contrary. B.C. also alone provides for the dissolution of a general partnership upon the dissolution of one of the partners. *See* BCPA s. 36. Not all provinces require actual bankruptcy to trigger dissolution. In Nfld. (s. 33), Ont. (s. 33), Man. (s. 36), P.E.I. (s. 36) and N.S. (s. 36) the insolvency of a partner also dissolves the partnership.
1161. Civil Code, Art. 2230.
1162. *Ibid.*, Art. 2231.
1163. *Ibid.*, Art. 2226.
1164. *Ibid.*, Art. 2258.
1165. *Ibid.*, Art. 2232.
1166. *Ibid.*, Arts 2260, 2261.
1167. Civil Code, Art. 2258.

equivalent event is a charging order against a partner's share for separate debt.[1168] If such an order is issued, the partners have an option to dissolve the firm.[1169]

§3. Court Dissolution

474. All Canadian jurisdictions provide for court dissolution of partnerships.[1170] Under the Quebec Civil Code, the court may dissolve a partnership 'for a legitimate cause'.[1171] A more extensive list of grounds for court dissolution is provided in the statutes of the common law jurisdictions. These events include a partner becoming mentally or otherwise incapable,[1172] behaving in a way that is prejudicial to the business or in persistent breach of the partnership agreement or the partners' being able to carry on the business only at a loss. An order of dissolution on these grounds is at the discretion of the court. As well, the statutes of these provinces provide that a court may wind up the partnership where 'it is just and equitable'. This ground is a 'catch all' provision allowing an order when the court considers it impracticable to continue the business as, for example, if its object has become impossible to attain.[1173]

§4. Dissolution of Limited Partnerships

475. Limited partnerships are dissolved on the same grounds as general partnerships. Some additional provisions, however, exist. In Quebec, where the general partners can no longer act, the limited partnership will be dissolved unless they are replaced within 120 days.[1174] In the other jurisdictions, limited partnerships are dissolved upon the death, retirement, or mental incompetence of any general partner. This is subject to a right in the constituting certificate of the limited partnership to carry on in such case or to the agreement of all partners.[1175] Further, if a limited partner is entitled to the return of her contribution and it is not returned or cannot be returned because the partnership has insufficient assets to pay other liabilities, she may require the dissolution of the partnership.[1176]

1168. The statutes provide that a judgment is not issued against the firm for separate debt, but that a partner's share may be charged. *See,* for example, NSPA s. 26; BCPA s. 26.

1169. *See,* for example, OPA s. 33(2); MPA s. 36(2).

1170. *See,* for example, NPA s. 35; OPA s. 35.

1171. Civil Code, Art. 2230.

1172. *See,* for example, MPA s. 38(a). Under Art. 2226 of the Civil Code, a general partner ceases to be a partner if he is placed under protective supervision. Under Art. 2258, this event automatically dissolves an undeclared partnership.

1173. That is a ground for automatic dissolution under the Quebec Civil Code, Art. 2230.

1174. Civil Code, Art. 2245.

1175. *See,* for example, NLPA s. 19. A number of jurisdictions also include dissolution of a general corporate partner in this list. They are: BCPA s. 67; NBLPA s. 25; NSLPA s. 20; OLPA s. 21; and PEILPA s. 20. This recognizes the fact that general partners are very often corporate bodies.

1176. *See,* for example, SPA s. 62(4).

Chapter 9. Taxation of Partnerships

476. Partners are subject to taxation as any other person under taxing powers of both federal and provincial governments. Because a partnership has no separate legal personality, income of the partnership is treated for tax purposes as income of the individual partners and is taxed at either corporate or personal rates, depending upon the juridical nature of the partner. For this reason, partnership may be a particularly attractive form of business organization where losses are initially expected in the partnership or other tax advantages are available to it. The partners may then set these losses off directly against their other income. This explains why partnerships are frequently used as the business structure for industries that receive special tax advantages that may produce losses for tax purposes in early years.[1177]

1177. *See* P.E. Mcquillan, J. Thomas & C. Cochrane, *Understanding the Taxation of Partnerships*, 2nd ed., (Don Mills, Ont.: CCH Canadian, 1987).

Selected Bibliography

Aerts, K. *Taken en aansprakelijkheden van commissarissen en bedrijfsrevisoren.* Brussel: Larcier, 2002.

Alberta Report. *Proposals for a New Business Corporations Law for Alberta.* Edmonton: Institute of Law Reform and Research, University of Alberta, 1980.

Ash, V.H. *Extra-provincial Corporate Registrations in Canada.* Markham, Ont.: LexisNexis Canada, 2008.

Bird, R. '*New Brunswick, Company Law Project Reform Division*'. In *Report on Company Law*, edited by R. Bird. Fredricton: Department of Justice, 1974.

Bourgeois, D.J. *Charities and Not-for-Profit Administration and Governance Handbook.* 2nd edn. Canada: LexisNexis, 2009.

Bourgeois, D.J. *The Law of Charitable and Non-profit Organizations.* 3rd edn. Canada: LexisNexis, 2002.

CCH Canadian Limited. *Canada Corporations Law Reporter*, looseleaf, 3 vols. Don Mills, Ont.: CCH Canadian, 1976.

CCH Canadian Limited. *Ontario Corporations Law Guide*, looseleaf, 2 vols. Don Mills, Ont.: CCH Canadian, 1982.

Crete, R. *The Proxy System in Canadian Corporations: A Critical Analysis.* Montreal: Wilson & LaFleur, 1986.

Davies, W. & S. Beck. *Canadian Corporate Law Precedents.* Toronto: Carswell, 1989.

Dickerson, R.V.W., et al. *Proposals for a New Business Corporation's Law for Canada*, 2 vols. Ottawa: Queen's Printer, 1971.

Findlay, P.G. (ed.). *Securities Law and Practice.* Toronto: Carswell, 2003 (looseleaf).

Gillen, M.R. *Securities Regulation in Canada.* 3rd edn. Toronto: Carswell, 2007.

Gray, W.D. *Ontario Corporation Manual*, looseleaf, 4 vols. Toronto: Carswell, 2012.

Hadden, T., R.E. Forbes & R.L. Simmonds. *Canadian Business Organizations Law.* Toronto: Butterworths, 1984.

Hodgson Report. *Legislative Assembly Select Committee on Company Law: Report on Mergers, Amalgamations and Certain Related Matters.* Toronto: Queen's Printer, 1973.

Hughes, E.R. & R.B. Love. *Alberta Corporation Manual*, looseleaf, 3 vols. Toronto: Richard De Boo, 1959 (looseleaf).

Ish, D. *Co-operatives in Principle and Practice.* Saskatoon: Centre for the Study of Co-operatives, University of Saskatchewan, 1992.

Ish, D. *The Law of Canadian Co-operatives*. Toronto: Burroughs, 1981.

Lawrence Report. *Legislative Assembly Select Committee on Company Law: Interim Report*. Toronto: Queen's Printer, 1967.

Martineau, Y. (ed.). *Quebec Corporation Manual*, looseleaf, 3 vols. Toronto: Carswell, 1994.

Mcguinness, K.P. *Canadian Business Corporations Law*. 2nd edn. Markham, Ont.: LexisNexis Canada, 2007.

Morin, D.B. & W. Chippendale (eds). *Acquisitions and Mergers in Canada*. Toronto: Methuen, 1970.

Nathan, H.R. *Nathan's Company Meetings Including Rules of Order*. Toronto: CCH Canadian, 2007.

Nicholls, C.G. *Corporate Law*. Toronto: Emond Montgomery, 2005.

Peterson, D.H. & M.J. Cumming. *Shareholder Remedies in Canada*. 2nd edn, Canada: LexisNexis, 2009.

Puri, P., et al. *Cases, Materials and Notes on Partnerships and Canadian Business Corporations*. 5th edn. Toronto: Carswell, 2011.

Quin, J. *Canada Business Corporations Manual*. 2nd edn. Toronto: Carswell, 2011 (looseleaf).

Sarna, L. (ed.). *Corporate Structure, Finance and Operations: Essays on the Law and Business Practice*, 7 vols. Toronto: Carswell, 1982.

Special Lectures of the Law Society of Upper Canada. *Company Law*. Toronto: DeBoo, 1950.

Special Lectures of the Law Society of Upper Canada. *Corporate and Securities Law*. Toronto: DeBoo, 1972.

Special Lectures of the Law Society of Upper Canada. *Corporate Law in the 1980s*. Toronto: DeBoo, 1982.

Special Lectures of the Law Society of Upper Canada. *Developments in Company Law*. Toronto: DeBoo, 1968.

Special Lectures of the Law Society of Upper Canada. *Securities Law in the Modern Financial Marketplace*. Toronto: DeBoo, 1989.

Stewart, J.L. & M.L. Palmer. *Company Law in Canada*. 5th edn. Toronto: Carswell, 1962.

Sutherland, H., D.B. Horsley & J.M. Edmiston. *Fraser's Handbook on Company Law*. 7th edn. Toronto: Carswell, 1985.

Van Duzer, J.A. *The Law of Partnerships and Corporations*. 3rd edn. Toronto: Irwin Law, 2009.

Wainberg, J.M. & M.I. Wainberg. *Duties and Responsibilities of Directors in Canada*. 6th edn. Don Mills, Ont.: CCH Canadian, 1987.

Wegenast, E.W. *The Law of Canadian Companies*. Toronto: Burroughs, 1931.

Selected Bibliography

Welling, B.L. *Corporate Law in Canada: The Governing Principles*. 3rd edn. Mudgeerba, Qld., Australia: Scribblers Publishing, 2006.

Yalden, R., et al. *Business Organizations: Principles, Policy and Practice*. Toronto: Emond Montgomery, 2007.

Ziegel, J.S. (ed.). *Studies in Canadian Company Law*, vol. 1. Toronto: Butterworths, 1967.

Ziegel, J.S. (ed.). *Studies in Canadian Company Law*, vol. 2. Toronto: Butterworths, 1973.

Selected Bibliography

Index

The numbers here refer to paragraph numbers.

Index

Index

Index

Index

Index

Made in the USA
Monee, IL
13 September 2026

62974281R00136